Quick Guide to Local Birds

This guide is organized by  ... s are shown together. The Species Account p ... e following manner:

WATERFOWL (Whistling-Ducks, Geese, Ducks)

GAMEBIRDS (Turkey, Quail) – LOONS – GREBES – PELICANS – CORMORANTS – WADING BIRDS (Bitterns, Herons, Egrets, Ibis, Spoonbill)

VULTURES – DIURNAL RAPTORS (Eagles, Hawks, Falcons)

RAILS – COOT – CRANE – SHOREBIRDS (Plovers, Stilt, Avocet, Jacana, Sandpipers, Dowitchers, Snipe, Phalaropes) – GULLS – TERNS

PIGEONS – DOVES – CUCKOO – ANI – OWLS – NIGHTHAWKS – NIGHTJARS

SWIFTS – HUMMINGBIRDS – TROGONS – KINGFISHERS – WOODPECKERS

FLYCATCHERS (Tyrannulet, Pewees, Flycatchers, Phoebes, Kingbirds) – BECARDS

SHRIKES – VIREOS – CORVIDS (Jays, Nutcracker, Crow, Ravens) – LARK – SWALLOWS

CHICKADEES – TITMICE – VERDIN – BUSHTIT – NUTHATCHES – CREEPER – WRENS – DIPPER – KINGLETS – GNATCATCHERS – THRUSHES

CATBIRD – MOCKINGBIRDS – THRASHERS – PIPITS – WAXWING – PHAINOPEPLA

WARBLERS – TANAGERS

NATIVE SPARROWS AND BUNTINGS (Towhees, Sparrows, Juncos, Longspurs, Grosbeaks, Buntings)

BLACKBIRDS (Blackbirds, Meadowlarks, Grackles, Cowbirds, Orioles) – FINCHES (Finches, Goldfinches, Siskin)

STARLING – HOUSE SPARROW

BIRDS OF SOUTHEASTERN ARIZONA

By

Richard Cachor Taylor

R.W. Morse Company
Olympia, Washington

For Lynne Taylor

Published by R.W. Morse Company, Olympia, Washington

Library of Congress Control Number: 2010925906

EAN 9780964081079
First Edition 2010
Fifth Printing 2016

$19.95 Softcover
© 2010 R.W. Morse Company

Printed: South Korea, BookPrinters Network (Broker)

Author: Richard Cachor Taylor

Executive Editor: Christina Duchesne Morse

Editor: Barbara Bickel

Design: Christina Merwin and Nicholas Hausman

Maps and Elevation Graph Designs: Eric G. Taylor

Bird Drawings: Eric Kraig

Cover Photograph Elegant Trogon: Jim Burns

Contents

Sample Elevation Charts

In Southeastern Arizona birds occupy fairly sharply defined bands of habitat that can usually be described by elevations. Eight different elevation charts show at a glance each species's seasonal or yearly occurrence, as well as the altitudes it occupies. Birds which occur throughout the year but which are not presently known to breed are shown with a lavender color bar.

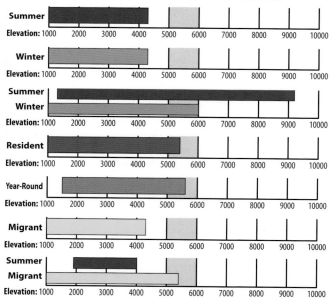

A selection of towns and popular birding locales are included on one graph on each page to provide a geographic context for the elevations.

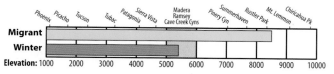

Common Local Birds

These are some of the most common birds in Southeastern Arizona. For more information about each bird, go to its Species Account.

Northern Shoveler
p. 32

Pied-billed Grebe
p. 52

Gambel's Quail
p. 46

Great Blue Heron
p. 64

American Coot
p. 106

American Kestrel
p.100

Red-tailed Hawk
p. 94

Turkey Vulture
p. 74

Cooper's Hawk
p. 84

Killdeer
p. 114

Rock Pigeon
p. 150

Elf Owl
p. 170

Great Horned Owl
p. 166

Greater Roadrunner
p. 158

Anna's Hummingbird
p. 188

Black-chinned Hummingbird
p. 186

Mourning Dove
p. 152

White-winged Dove
p. 152

Gila Woodpecker
p. 202

Vermilion Flycatcher p. 224

Western Kingbird p. 234

Common Raven p. 256

Barn Swallow p. 266

Northern Mockingbird p. 308

Cactus Wren p. 278

Curve-billed Thrasher p. 312

Black-tailed Gnatcatcher p. 292

Phainopepla 318

Verdin p. 272

Black-throated
Sparrow
p. 362

Yellow-rumped Warbler
p. 328

White-crowned
Sparrow
p. 376

Hooded
Oriole
p. 408

Northern
Cardinal
p. 386

Lesser
Goldfinch
p. 418

House
Finch
p. 412

Great-tailed
Grackle
p. 404

Red-
winged
Blackbird
p. 400

European
Starling
p. 420

House
Sparrow
p. 420

x

Introduction

Southeastern Arizona is where the high Rocky Mountains from the north meet the tortured canyonlands of the Sierra Madre from the south, and where the subtropical Sonoran Desert of northwest Mexico merges with the higher elevation, much colder Chihuahuan Desert of Mexico's vast interior. Elements of both the Great Basin and the Great Plains also find their way into the cornucopia of habitat types that characterize Southeastern Arizona. Over 400 species of birds–almost half of all the birds of the United States and Canada combined–occur in an area that occupies less than one percent of the land area of North America.

This amazing concentration of birds has not gone unnoticed. Southeastern Arizona is consistently recognized as one of America's foremost birding destinations. This is not just because of the sheer diversity of birds that use this region annually; equally important, many of these birds do not regularly occur anywhere else north of Mexico. Such beautiful birds as Berylline Hummingbird, Elegant Trogon, Arizona Woodpecker, Sulphur-bellied Flycatcher, Rufous-backed Robin, Rufous-capped Warbler, and Flame-colored Tanager–among many others–are otherwise not regularly available in all the U.S.

Birds of the Southeastern Arizona is meant to be a guide for all birdwatchers who wish to identify and enjoy the birds in this unique corner of the world. All regularly occurring species are treated, as well as virtually all of the Mexican specialties, regardless of their abundance. Species Accounts address not only the key field marks required for identification, but also how to eliminate other birds that appear similar. Each bird's seasonal status, habitats, and behavior, as well as primary songs or calls are described. Most accounts conclude with a note about the species, usually specific to its occurrence within Southeastern Arizona. An "Elevation Graph" shows at a glance the season and altitudes where selected species can be found. All of this information is juxtaposed with photographs of the bird on the facing page. While these photographs were selected to show patterns, colors, and structural characters, they are often of coffee-table-book quality. The photos are meant to inspire; the text is designed to provide all of the information needed to identify all of the birds in the area.

Birds of Southeastern Arizona focuses on the birds that live in, or migrate through, Pima, Santa Cruz, and Cochise Counties, as well as southern Maricopa, Pinal, Graham, and Greenlee Counties, an area of approximately 25,000 square miles. This book will also identify almost all of the regularly occurring birds within the state of Arizona, all the way from Organ Pipe Cactus National Monument to Grand Canyon National Park. Many of these same species range from Southern California to West Texas, and *Birds of Southeastern Arizona* should help provide a solid foundation for understanding the avian dynamics of the American Southwest. Naturally the abundance, seasonality, and even the behavior of birds will change with changes in the environment. Those very differences can help illuminate the environmental factors that shape the life of a bird, as well as the irreducible requirements for its future conservation.

CONSERVATION

A diverse and thriving avifauna is perhaps the best indication of a healthy environment. Southeastern Arizona has seen rapid development surround its larger cities. With urban sprawl comes the clearing of native vegetation and the loss of habitat vital to the survival of not only birds, but also to the entire community of wildlife. Because most birds are active during the day when most mammals are hidden, they are the most observable form of wildlife. Their presence or absence and their relative abundance will tell us just how well we are succeeding in the preservation of our natural heritage. A knowledge of birds may help turn progress down pathways that benefit not only our human communities, but also the native birds and wildlife with which we share these desert valleys.

Identifying Birds

Initially, learning to identify birds may seem difficult. Many birds are very small, move quickly, remain hidden in dense cover, and many resemble other birds. First, look at the general shape, size, and color of the bird. Check the Common Local Birds (pages vii - x) and see if it is there. If not, scan through the Species Account pages. Read the description–especially the boldfaced text–to see how it matches your bird. Compare similar species, voice, and habitat. Check the elevation and the seasons of its occurrence. Keep comparing until you have a match.

The colors and patterns of a bird's feathering ("plumage") and bare parts (bill, legs, feet, eyes) provide some of the best clues to identify a bird. Be aware, however, that plumages may vary within the same species between the sexes, between adults and younger birds, by season, and by geographical location. Learn the parts of a bird; consult the diagrams on pages 4 and 5. Often birds can be identified by head pattern alone.

Good examples of common birds where the male and the female have distinctly different plumages are Gambel's Quail, Anna's Hummingbird, Vermilion Flycatcher, Northern Cardinal, and Hooded Oriole. Usually males display more brilliant colors, as in these examples, while females have muted colors that serve as camouflage while they sit immobile on a nest. Other species such as Black-bellied Whistling-Duck, Elf Owl, Violet-crowned Hummingbird, Bridled Titmouse, and Western Meadowlark show no obvious plumage distinctions between the sexes. In a few species, such as the phalaropes, where the males are responsible for incubation, females are more brightly colored than males.

Most birds seen in our area in spring and summer display what is known as their breeding–or "alternate"–plumage. Birds present in winter are usually in their non-breeding–or "basic"–plumage. To attract mates at the onset of spring, males of most species molt out of their worn and drab basic plumage into fresher and more colorful

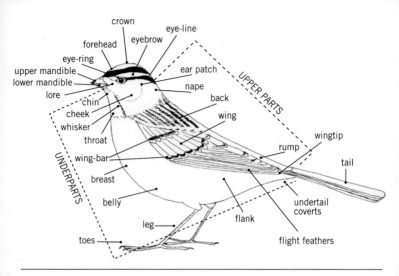

Parts of a Bird. It is helpful to know the names of the different parts of a bird. These sketches of a White-crowned Sparrow and a Mallard in flight show the terms most frequently used to describe bird topography in this guide.

alternate plumage. Note, however, that some birds, many flycatchers, for example, molt their worn feathers after breeding, just before migration. These birds are at their brightest in the fall. Usually breeding plumage appears more colorful or highly patterned than non-breeding plumage.

Most birds also display different plumages as they mature. Some birds, such as California Gull, require up to four years to attain adult plumage. Other birds, such as Cactus Wrens, however, essentially look like adults from the moment they leave the nest.

The term "juvenile plumage" refers to the first true plumage worn by a young bird–a juvenile–after it molts its downy feathers. Some species maintain this plumage for only a few weeks after fledging,

4

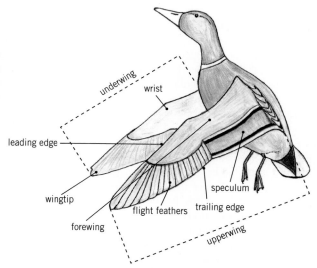

underwing

wrist

leading edge

wingtip

forewing

flight feathers

speculum

trailing edge

upperwing

while others may hold it into winter. "First-year plumage" refers to the plumage held during the first 12 months of a bird's life. "Immature" refers to all plumages before the bird gains its adult plumage. For many species, such as hummingbirds, immature males resemble adult females.

Plumage colors and patterning may also vary considerably within birds of the same species across geographical populations. For instance, the nearly black race of Red-tailed Hawk that occasionally winters in Southeastern Arizona, the "Harlan's Hawk," is quite different from the extremely pale "Fuertes's" subspecies that breeds in our region.

Differences within a species can be great even within the same local population. Some adult Red-tailed Hawks in our area may show a "belly band" of heavy black streaks; others almost lack a belly band altogether. Nesting pairs of Red-tails in Southeastern Arizona may represent both extremes. In cases like this, this book will highlight the structural elements and plumage patterns necessary to identify either adult as a Red-tailed Hawk.

Finally, do not expect every bird you see to look exactly like the photographs in this guide. Like people, birds express individual variation. To appreciate just how different birds of the same species can be, study the ones that come regularly to a feeding station. Male House Finches, for example, show a range of coloration that runs the gamut from deep red to dull orange. You may find that, with practice, you can learn to recognize individual birds by the subtle differences in their markings.

In this book the birds are presented in family groupings, as shown in the Quick Guide to Local Birds (inside the front cover). Learning the characteristics of the different bird families will make bird identification easier. Birds in the same family tend to show similarities in appearance and behavior. A bird's structure, including head shape, general body shape, and the length of its wings, tail, legs, and bill, provide important clues to both the family to which it belongs and, often, its species.

It should be noted that birds in this book do not always appear in the most recent taxonomic sequence. Egrets, for example, are members of the heron family that appear similar by virtue of their entirely white plumage, but which are not necessarily closely related. To facilitate identification, the white egrets appear together on a single page where they can easily be compared.

Although *Birds of Southeastern Arizona* focuses on visual field marks, the identification of a bird is often clinched by its voice. Experienced birders can recognize most of this region's species by ear. In this book an effort is made to transcribe bird calls and songs into English sounds, hoping it may make it possible to positively identify heard birds at night, in poor light, or in dense cover. With practice, the unique quality or pattern of a vocalization may enable an observer to identify birds without even a glimpse of the songster. A minority of the birds in SE Arizona, often transient species or only here as winter visitors, are largely silent. This information is noted for those species.

Bird Habitats of Southeastern Arizona

With the exception of such generalists as Common Raven, birds typically require specialized habitats. These are areas where topography combines with temperature and rainfall to create a distinctive plant community. Because average temperatures decrease four degrees Fahrenheit per thousand feet as the air grows thinner, and rainfall increases approximately four inches per thousand feet of elevation gain, the giant saguaro cactus that grace the Sonoran Desert below 4,000' are symbolic of a habitat that bears no resemblance to the fir and aspen forests that mantle our mountaintops above elevations of 8,000'. The Cactus Wrens found in Tucson and in the foothills of the Santa Catalina Mountains occur in conjunction with the thorny plants of the desert. Mountain Chickadees are found almost a vertical mile higher in the boreal forests of the upper Santa Catalinas. Cactus Wrens and Mountain Chickadees require completely different habitats. Under normal circumstances, these two species would never encounter one another in the wild. For the birder, knowledge of a species' habitat preferences is the key to finding that bird. Throughout ***Birds of Southeastern Arizona*** reference is made to the following 10 habitats.

STREAMS AND RIVERS; PONDS AND LAKES: 1,000-4,500'

Surface water is scarce in Southeastern Arizona, yet many families of birds are utterly dependent on water for food or shelter, regardless of whether they are simply migrating through or actually nesting in our region. Among the list of water-dependent bird families are ducks and geese, herons and egrets, cormorants and pelicans, avocets and stilts, rails and coots, plovers and sandpipers, and gulls and terns. The importance of artificial impoundments–regardless of size–cannot be overstated. From murky stock tanks with less than a surface acre of water to sewage treatment ponds and full-sized recreation lakes, any body of water in Arizona is a magnet for birds. In our area the Gila River in the northeast corner, along with portions of Sonoita and Aravaipa Creeks,

Habitats of Southeastern Arizona

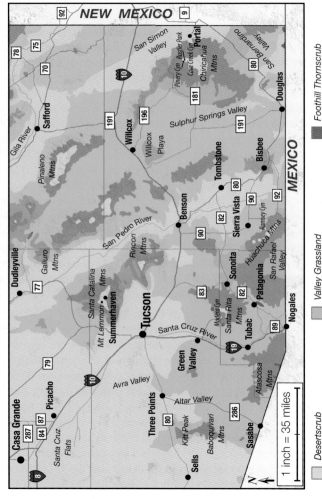

Desertscrub

Valley Grassland

Foothill Thornscrub

Mountain Interior Chaparral

Mountain Pine-Oak Woodland

Mountain Coniferous Forest

1 inch = 35 miles

N

8

and the Santa Cruz and the San Pedro Rivers always have perennial water. There are many small creeks in the mountains, but few flow above ground once they reach the arid valleys. Some of the many man-made ponds and lakes include Sweetwater Wetlands, Lakeside Park, and Agua Caliente Park in Tucson; Avra Valley Sewage Ponds and Aguirre Lake (seasonal) at Buenos Aires National Wildlife Refuge west of Tucson; Picacho Reservoir (occasionally dry) and Arizona City Lake north of Tucson; Peña Blanca Lake, Palo Duro Pond, Kino Springs, and Patagonia Lake south of Tucson near Nogales; Parker Canyon Lake (at an elevation of 5,300' the highest large lake in our area); Kingfisher Pond and Sierra Vista Wastewater Ponds at Sierra Vista; Lake Cochise at Willcox; Whitewater Draw Wildlife Area north of Douglas; Willow Tank near Portal; and Cluff Ranch Ponds and Roper Lake near Safford. Almost all of these areas lie below 4,500'.

DESERTSCRUB: 1,000-4,500'

Much of Southeastern Arizona, especially north and west of Tucson, is below an elevation of 4,500'. The Santa Cruz Flats, in fact, average only 1,500', and areas near Phoenix are only 1,000' in elevation–or lower. Where they have not been altered by man, these low-lying areas are covered with Sonoran desertscrub. Elevations are generally above 3,000' in the valleys east of Tucson, but fingers of the Chihuahuan Desert from west Texas and the Interior Valley of Mexico reach high up into the foothills of the border ranges. Plants such as prickly pear cactus, ocotillo, creosote bush, and mesquite are shared by both deserts, and–not surprisingly–so are many species of birds. Some of these include Gambel's Quail, Cactus Wren, Curve-billed Thrasher, and Verdin. Very few birds, such as Gilded Flicker in the Sonoran Desert and Scaled Quail in the Chihuahuan Desert, are largely confined to one desert or the other.

VALLEY GRASSLAND; AGRICULTURAL FIELDS: 1,500-4,500'

Historically, Southeastern Arizona supported some of North America's richest grasslands. Overgrazing, agriculture, water

9

withdrawal, fire suppression, and the elimination of millions of Black-tailed Prairie Dogs have all contributed to reducing the size of these grasslands. Sadly, the last certain record of a wild Aplomado Falcon in Southeastern Arizona in 1942 coincides with the extirpation of prairie dogs. Nonetheless, many species are still dependent on grasslands or–in lieu of native savanna–large fields for their existence during at least part of the calendar year. Among these are Ferruginous Hawk, Sandhill Crane, Mountain Plover, Horned Lark, McCown's and Chestnut-collared Longspurs, and Eastern Meadowlark. Some of the best grasslands and agricultural zones in Southeastern Arizona are located in the Santa Cruz Flats between Tucson and Phoenix, near Sonoita southeast of Tucson, in the beautiful basin of grass called the San Rafael Valley east of Patagonia, and in the broad Sulphur Springs Valley between Willcox and Douglas.

VALLEY GROVES, PECAN FARMS, AND DESERT OASES: 1,500-4,500'

Where water lies near or on the surface in the Santa Cruz, San Pedro, and Gila River Valleys, green ribbons of Fremont cottonwood and willow mark the flow. Tucson itself and other valley towns and cities with urban plantings support groves of big trees otherwise surrounded by an arid landscape. These are classic desert oases. In other areas, mankind has replaced the native trees with enormous pecan orchards that may extend for miles. While lacking any understory, pecan farms seem to afford birds many of the same benefits as cottonwood groves. These concentrations of food, water, and shelter not only harbor a community of riparian obligate-nesting birds, such as Gray Hawks, Yellow-billed Cuckoos, Tropical Kingbirds, and Summer Tanagers, they also provide a safe flyway for hundreds of species of migratory birds. Over 300 different species of birds have been recorded using the San Pedro River National Conservation Area east of Sierra Vista. Tucson is reputed to have one of the highest concentrations of Cooper's Hawks in the entire United States. The Arizona-Sonora Desert Museum, a desert oasis boasting only a dozen cottonwoods on the grounds, still supports a breeding enclave of Hooded Orioles and a bird list of over 200 species.

FOOTHILL GROVES: 2,500-5,000'

Often at slightly higher elevations than valley groves, often with sycamores mixed with the gallery forest, foothill groves attract a unique subset of the birds found in valley groves. Included among these are some of Southeastern Arizona's most sought-after species. Common Black-Hawks, Violet-crowned Hummingbirds, Thick-billed Kingbirds, Rose-throated Becards, and Rufous-capped Warblers are all most apt to be found in foothill canyons or between the canyon walls that flank Sonoita Creek at Patagonia, along nearby Harshaw Creek, in Aravaipa Canyon, along Arivaca Creek, or in Sycamore Canyon in the Atascosa Mountains. In some of the higher border ranges, foothill groves reach up into the outlets of mountain canyons. Examples of these mountain foothill groves include lower Madera and Florida Canyons in the Santa Rita Mountains, French Joe Canyon in the Whetstone Mountains, and Cave Creek Canyon in the Portal area of the Chiricahua Mountains.

FOOTHILL THORNSCRUB: 3,500-5,000'

Above 3,500' and below 5,000' the walls of foothill canyons near the border are often blanketed with an impenetrable layer of spiny shrubbery. A suite of Mexican tropical species follows these tendrils of thornscrub across the Arizona border into legendary birding areas such as Sycamore Canyon and California Gulch in the Atascosa Mountains; Sonoita Creek—especially between the town of Patagonia and Patagonia Lake; lower Madera Canyon, lower Florida Canyon, and lower Montosa Canyon in the Santa Rita Mountains; and the San Bernardino Ranch and Guadalupe Canyon east of Douglas in the extreme southeast corner of the state. Inhabitants of thornscrub slopes include Buff-collared Nightjar, Black-capped Gnatcatcher, Varied Bunting, and Five-striped Sparrow.

MOUNTAIN INTERIOR CHAPARRAL AND PINYON-JUNIPER WOODLAND: 5,000-7,000′

Cold winter nights in the mountains eliminate many of the spiny plants that characterize the subtropical thornscrub of the lower foothills. Dense stands of mountain mahogany on rocky limestone and thickets of manzanita on volcanic soils form an interior chaparral at elevations between 5,000 and 7,000′. Usually pinyon pine and junipers punctuate the chaparral, and in some favorable locations, pinyon-juniper may mantle whole slopes. These habitats are especially attractive to species derived from the Great Basin. Some of the breeding birds include Gray Vireo, Western Scrub-Jay, Juniper Titmouse, Virginia's Warbler, and Black-chinned Sparrow. Unpredictably irruptive flocks of Pinyon Jays may occupy these habitats during invasion winters. Areas with mountain interior chaparral or pinyon-juniper woodland include Molino Basin in the Santa Catalina Mountains; Scheelite Canyon and Coronado National Memorial in the Huachuca Mountains; and Chiricahua National Monument, lower Rucker Canyon, and Silver Creek near Portal in the Chiricahua Mountains.

MOUNTAIN PINE-OAK WOODLAND: 5,000-7,000′

Mexico's single largest habitat is Sierra Madrean pine-oak woodland. The border ranges of Southeastern Arizona, usually between elevations of 5,000-7,000′, as low as 3,600′ in Sycamore Canyon in the Atascosa Mountains, mark the northernmost limits of this admixture of spring deciduous oaks and fire-tolerant pines. Here we may find Montezuma Quail, Whiskered Screech-Owls, Arizona Woodpeckers, Mexican Jays, Bridled Titmouse, Painted Redstart, and Hepatic Tanagers–species that typify some of Arizona's most famous mid-elevation birding locales. This list includes Madera Canyon in the Santa Rita Mountains; Garden, Ramsey, and Miller Canyons in the Huachucas; and Cave Creek and South Fork Cave Creek in the Chiricahua Mountains.

MOUNTAIN CANYON GROVES: 5,000-6,500′

Large, white-barked Arizona sycamore belies the presence of

permanent water, either in an above-ground stream or just below the surface. Between elevations of 5,000 and 6,500' the larger mountain canyonbeds in Southeastern Arizona support an ivory latticework of these elegant riparian trees, and they in turn provide homes for such "Mexican" birds as Elegant Trogon and Sulphur-bellied Flycatcher. Aside from these two riparian near-obligates, almost all of the birds mentioned above for pine-oak woodland reach their greatest population density in mountain canyon groves. Trees, shrubs, and vines flourish in the deeper, better-watered soils along the canyon floor, and food, shelter, and water are all more available to birds here than on the adjacent slopes. Upper Sycamore Canyon in the Atascosa Mountains; Madera Canyon in the Santa Rita Mountains; Ramsey, Miller, and Garden Canyons in the Huachuca Mountains; and South Fork and Cave Creek Canyons in the Chiricahua Mountains all exemplify this highly productive habitat.

Mountain Coniferous Forest: 7,000-10,000'

"Sky Islands," the larger mountains of Southeastern Arizona that rise above 7,000' in elevation, support forests of Ponderosa pine, Douglas fir, Gambel's oak, and quaking aspen that evoke the Rocky Mountains. The two highest mountain ranges in Southeastern Arizona, the Pinaleños and the Chiricahuas, with elevations approaching or exceeding 10,000', also sustain pure stands of Engelmann spruce and large mountain meadows. Naturally, the highland bird communities that occupy these mountain islands are more reminiscent of Colorado than of Sonora, Mexico. Some of the birds to watch for are Northern Saw-whet Owl, Hairy Woodpecker, Steller's Jay, and Pygmy Nuthatch. Other species such as Greater Pewee, Olive Warbler, and Yellow-eyed Junco, however, are essentially confined in the U.S. to Southeastern Arizona, and underscore this region's proximity to the Sierra Madres. Paved or well-graded roads reach above 7,000' in the Santa Catalina, Huachuca, Chiricahua, and Pinaleño Mountains.

Helpful Resources

BIRD BOOKS AND AUDIO:

Brown, David E. 1985. *Arizona Wetlands and Waterfowl.* University of Arizona Press.

Brown, David E. 1989. *Arizona Game Birds.* University of Arizona Press and the Arizona Game and Fish Department.

Burns, Jim. 2008. *Arizona Birds from Backyard to the Backwoods.* University of Arizona Press.

Corman, Troy E., and Cathryn Wise-Gervais, editors. 2005. *Arizona Breeding Bird Atlas.* University of New Mexico Press.

Glinski, Richard L., editor. 1998. *The Raptors of Arizona.* University of Arizona Press.

Keller, Geoffrey A. 2001. *Bird Songs of Southeastern Arizona and Sonora, Mexico* (2 CD set). Cornell Laboratory of Ornithology.

Monson, Gale, and Allan R. Phillips. 1981. *Annotated Checklist of the Birds of Arizona.* University of Arizona Press.

Phillips, Alan, Joe Marshall, and Gale Monson. 1964. *The Birds of Arizona.* University of Arizona Press.

Rosenberg, Gary H., and Dave Stejskal. 2002. *Field Checklist of the Birds of Arizona.* Arizona Bird Committee.

Taylor, Richard Cachor. 2010. *Location Checklist to the Birds of the Chiricahua Mountains.* Borderland Productions.

Taylor, Richard Cachor. 1995. *Location Checklist to the Birds of the Huachuca Mountains and the Upper San Pedro River.* Borderland Productions.

Taylor, Richard Cachor. 1994. *Trogons of the Arizona Borderlands.* Treasure Chest Books.

BIRD-FINDING GUIDES:

Stevenson, Mark, editor. 2007. *Tucson Audubon Society's Finding Birds in Southeastern Arizona.* Tucson Audubon Society.

Taylor, Richard Cachor. 2005. *A Birder's Guide to Southeastern Arizona.* American Birding Association.

There are two excellent bird-finding guides for Southeastern

Arizona, one published by the American Birding Association, and the other by the Tucson Audubon Society. Both provide detailed driving directions and maps for all of the primary birding sites in this region, bar-graphs showing relative abundance for each species every week of the year, and solid introductory materials that include–but are not limited to–topics such as the weather, what to wear, and where to stay, with lists of campgrounds, motels, and other facilities. The ABA guide is designed primarily for out-of-area birders, and the TAS guide is written primarily for residents. Both are indispensible companion books for finding the birds described in this field guide.

JOURNALS:

North American Birds (quarterly reports of bird sightings and related articles and summaries; published by the American Birding Association)

Western Birds (the quarterly journal of the Western Field Ornithologists; research papers, bird records committee reports, distribution and identification analyses, with many contributions from amateurs)

ORGANIZATIONS:

Arizona Field Ornithologists (AZFO)
　　Web site: www.azfo.org

The Southeastern Arizona Bird Observatory (SABO)
　　Web site: www.sabo.org; email: sabo@sabo.org

Tucson Audubon Society (TAS)
　　The Vermilion Flycatcher (bi-monthly bulletin).
　　Web site: www.tucsonaudubon.org

Huachuca Audubon Society (HAS)
　　The Trogon News (bi-monthly bulletin).
　　Web site: www.huachuca-audubon.org

RARE BIRD REPORTS:

Arizona/New Mexico Listserve Archives:
　　listserv.arizona.edu/archives/birdwg05.html

TAS Rare Bird Alert (to hear a taped report or to report a rare bird sighting): 520-629-0510.

Species Accounts

This book presents a comprehensive overview of all regularly-occurring birds of Southeastern Arizona. An effort has also been made to include all of the tropical, Sierra Madrean, and Southwestern U.S. specialties that attract birdwatchers from throughout the world.

Information on each species is presented in a standardized format; see the sample page (opposite) for an explanation. Birds are grouped by families, color-coded, and thumb-indexed. The Quick Guide to Local Birds (inside the front cover) will help you locate bird families.

Standardized terms are used to describe the relative abundance of each species and the likelihood of finding it in a particular season. These definitions were developed by the American Birding Association.

- **Common:** Found in moderate to large numbers, and easily seen in appropriate habitat at the right time of year. This category includes some birds like Mourning Dove that may be locally abundant.
- **Fairly Common:** Found in small to moderate numbers, and usually easy to find in appropriate habitat at the right time of year.
- **Uncommon:** Found in small numbers, and usually–but not always –seen with some effort in appropriate habitat in the correct season.
- **Rare:** Occurs annually in very small numbers. Not to be expected on any given day, but may be found with extended effort over the course of the appropriate season(s).
- **Casual:** Occurs less than annually, but there tends to be a seasonal pattern of occurrence in appropriate habitat; 4 or more records in the past 10 years.
- **Accidental** Represents an exceptional occurrence that might not be repeated for years; 3 or fewer records in the past 10 years.

In this book the terms "casual" or "accidental" are sometimes used to describe the status of birds that have occurred in a season when they are unexpected.

Birds shown in the photographs opposite the Species Accounts are adults unless the captions indicate otherwise.

COMMON NAME OF THE SPECIES, *Its Scientific Name*

Description: Length (and wingspan for larger birds) is given in inches, followed by key field marks. Key field marks pertain to diagnostic structural details and plumage patterns that separate similar species. These often begin with bill and head shapes. Color and pattern are especially useful for distinguishing sexes and ages within a species of bird, and these are described when the differences are obvious in the field. When a juvenile resembles an adult, often the female, this plumage is not mentioned in the text. Bold-faced words indicate crucial identification features.

Similar Species: Identifies similar-appearing species and describes how to differentiate them.

Voice: Limited to the main calls or songs that are apt to be heard in Southeastern Arizona. These may be vital for species identification— species of some families, owls and flycatchers, for example, are often best told by their vocalizations. Note that non-breeding species may be almost totally silent in our area.

Status & Habitat: Provides information on the relative abundance, seasonality, and preferred habitats where this bird may be found in Southeastern Arizona. See facing page for definitions of abundance terms. Major habitats are discussed on pages 7-13, as well as specific birding areas within these habitats.

Behavior: Highlights one or more behavioral characteristic of the species.

Noteworthy: Provides other interesting facts about the species, often specific to Arizona or Southeastern Arizona in particular.

Elevation Chart: Represents the seasonal or yearly elevation range occupied by the species. The chart shows the extreme altitudes where a given bird regularly occurs; ordinarily birds will be most common in the mid-range of the elevations shown. A selection of cities, towns and popular birding locales are included on the elevation charts to provide a geographic context for the relative elevations occupied by each species. See page vi for sample elevation charts.

Black-bellied
Whistling-Duck

Fulvous
Whistling-Duck

Description: 21". Richly-colored, **long-necked, long-legged duck**. ADULT: Fluorescent **orange-red bill**; gray face; long, bright **pink legs**. JUVENILE: Gray bill; gray legs; subdued colors overall. FLIGHT: Black belly; **broad white stripe on upperwing**.

Similar Species: Fulvous Whistling-Duck (photo upper right, accidental in SE Arizona) has tawny face and slaty bill, gray legs, and broken white bar on flanks; in flight shows black upperwings and "U"-shaped white band at the base of the tail. Only four SE Arizona records of Fulvous Whistling-Duck in past 50 years, but more common in Phoenix area."

Voice: Common flight call is high, thin, rapidly repeated series of *pee-hee-hee* whistles.

Status: Irregularly fairly common but local in summer (Apr-Nov); uncommon in winter (Dec-Mar); numbers fluctuate from year to year. **Habitat:** Desert oases; flooded fields, and valley ponds abutting cottonwood groves. Rio Rico, Kino Springs, and Patagonia Lake are usually good locations. Some years this duck also visits treeless sewage ponds and stock tanks.

Behavior: Feeds by grazing grasses and foraging in shallow water. Nests in tree hollows.

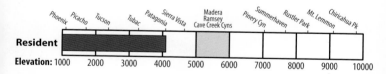

Noteworthy: In Mexico the name of Black-bellied Whistling-Duck is *Pijiji* (pronounced as transcribed above) for the sound of its whistles.

Snow Goose Juvenile

Snow Goose

Ross's Goose

Ross's Goose Juvenile

SNOW GOOSE, *Chen caerulescens*

Description: 28". **Medium-sized** white goose with **sloping forehead**; pink bill shows **black "grin patch"** along edges where the mandibles meet. BLUE MORPH: Variably slate-gray on neck, breast, and back. JUVENILE: Dull pinkish-gray bill; gray wash on neck, back, and wings. **Similar Species:** Smaller Ross's Goose (below) lacks "grin patch." White domestic geese do not have black wingtips. **Voice:** Call is raucous, fairly high yelping *wowk* or *wow*. **Status:** Uncommon in winter (mid Oct-mid Mar). **Habitat:** Valley ponds and lakes without vegetated banks. **Behavior:** Grazes on grasses, consumes grain and shallow pond vegetation. Associates with other goose species, especially Ross's Goose. **Noteworthy:** Blue morphs constitute about 1% of Snow Geese in SE Arizona.

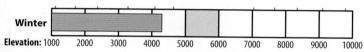

Winter

Elevation: 1000   2000   3000   4000   5000   6000   7000   8000   9000   10000

ROSS'S GOOSE, *Chen rossi*

Description: 23". **Small** version of Snow Goose with **steep forehead; stubby, triangular bill**. JUVENILE: Like pale gray adult. **Similar Species:** Larger Snow Goose (above) has black "grin patch" where the mandibles meet, and a proportionally longer bill that merges with sloping forehead. **Voice:** Like Snow Goose but more shrill. **Status:** Rare in winter (late Oct-mid Mar). **Habitat:** Valley ponds and lakes without vegetated banks. **Behavior:** Eats grasses, grain, and marsh vegetation. **Noteworthy:** Often found in flocks of Snow Geese. "Blue" plumage morph has only been documented once or twice in Arizona. Populations of Ross's Geese in the U.S. have increased from approximately 2,500 in the early 1950s to over a million today.

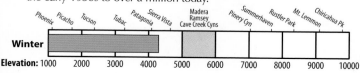

Winter

Elevation: 1000   2000   3000   4000   5000   6000   7000   8000   9000   10000

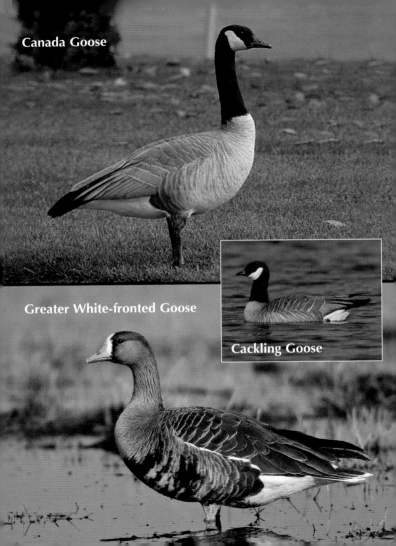

Canada Goose

Greater White-fronted Goose

Cackling Goose

CANADA GOOSE, *Branta canadensis*

Description: 43". Large brown goose with **black neck, white "chin strap,"** and **flat crown. Similar Species:** Much smaller Cackling Goose (below) has smaller, stubbier bill, rounder crown, and shorter neck. **Voice:** Loud, resonant *ha-ronk*. **Status:** Uncommon in winter (mid Oct-mid Mar). **Habitat:** Valley lakes and ponds. **Behavior:** Forages for plants and invertebrates in lakes, large ponds, and on golf courses. **Noteworthy:** The large pale "Great Basin," *B. c. moffitti*, subspecies is Arizona's typical wintering Canada Goose.

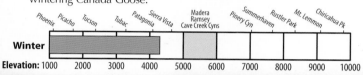

CACKLING GOOSE, *Branta hutchinsii*

Description: 27". Small goose with **small, stubby bill, rounded crown**, and relatively **short neck. Status:** Casual in winter (Dec-Feb). **Habitat:** Valley lakes and ponds.

GREATER WHITE-FRONTED GOOSE, *Anser albifrons*

Description: 28". Gray-brown goose with a **pinkish bill**; bright **orange legs**. ADULT: **White foreface**; irregular black blotches across the belly. JUVENILE: Lacks white on the face and black belly blotches. **Similar Species:** Similar-looking domestic Graylag Geese lack black belly blotches and usually look pot-bellied. Sleek juvenile White-fronteds stay with adults first winter. **Voice:** Common flight call is high, yelping *kah-la-luck*. **Status:** Rare in winter (late Sep-Mar). **Habitat:** Valley ponds and lakes without trees. **Behavior:** Feeds by grazing grasses and foraging in shallow water. Over-wintering birds often associate with other geese species. **Noteworthy:** Breeding in Alaska and Canada and wintering to Mexico, Greater White-fronted Goose has the longest migration route of any North American goose species.

Wood Duck
Male

Wood Duck
Female

Gadwall
Male

Gadwall
Female

WOOD DUCK, *Aix sponsa*

Description: 18.5". Large **drooping hindcrest**. MALE: **Colorful** and elaborate head pattern; **red bill base and eye-ring**. FEMALE: Tapering **white patch envelopes eye**. FLIGHT: **Long, rectangular tail**. **Similar Species:** Female Hooded Merganser (p. 43) lacks white around eye. Feral male Mandarin Duck has red bill and tawny face; female has long, thin white stripe behind eye. **Voice:** High whistles, squeaks. Female's call a penetrating squeal *ooEEK*. **Status:** Rare in summer (May-Sep); uncommon in winter (Oct-Apr). **Habitat:** Wooded valley ponds, rivers, and streams. **Behavior:** Rests under overhanging trees and roots. Feeds on invertebrates, seeds, and fruits in shallow water; does not dive. **Noteworthy:** In lieu of scarce natural tree cavities, Wood Ducks readily use nest boxes.

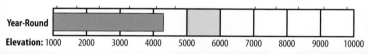

Year-Round

Elevation: 1000   2000   3000   4000   5000   6000   7000   8000   9000   10000

GADWALL, *Anas strepera*

Description: 20". Medium-sized, plain duck with **squarish head**, orange legs, white belly. MALE: Gray with contrasting **buff head and neck**, dark gray bill, **black rear end**. FEMALE: Contrasting paler head and neck and **orange sides to bill**; **white wing patch** often visible at rest. FLIGHT: **Square white wing patch**. **Similar Species:** Female Mallard lacks boxy head shape and has blue wing patch–not white. **Voice:** Female gives high-pitched, nasal *quack*; male quavering *rrep rrep*. **Status:** Fairly common in winter (Sep-May), rare in summer (Jun-Aug). **Habitat:** Valley ponds and lakes. **Behavior:** Forages for vegetation in shallow water by tipping up. Often in pairs. **Noteworthy:** Has bred at ponds near Nogales.

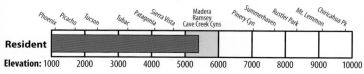

Resident

Elevation: 1000   2000   3000   4000   5000   6000   7000   8000   9000   10000

25

American Wigeon
Male

American Wigeon
Female

Eurasian Wigeon
Male

AMERICAN WIGEON, *Anas americana*

Description: 18″. **Gray-headed duck** with short, black-tipped, bluish-gray bill. MALE: Bright green "racing stripe" behind eye; narrow white crown stripe; pinkish breast and flanks. FEMALE: Mottled grayish head; rusty brown breast and flanks. FLIGHT: Mostly white wing linings and pointed tail. **Similar Species:** Male Eurasian Wigeon (below) has red–not gray–head lacking green stripe; brownish-headed female Eurasian lacks neck-breast contrast of female American Wigeon and black outline at base of bill. In flight Eurasian shows mostly gray–not white–wing linings. **Voice:** Whistled *wi-WE-whew*. **Status:** Common in winter (Sep-Apr); casual in summer (May-Aug). **Habitat:** Valley ponds, especially adjacent to fields of grass, golf courses, or urban parks. **Behavior:** Grazes in grassy areas. Flocks frequently number in the hundreds. **Noteworthy:** In Arizona American x Eurasian Wigeon hybrids are nearly as rare as pure Eurasian Wigeons.

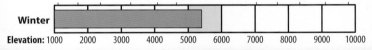

Winter									

Elevation: 1000   2000   3000   4000   5000   6000   7000   8000   9000   10000

EURASIAN WIGEON, *Anas penelope*

Description: 18″. MALE: **Bright rufous head** with yellowish crown stripe; gray back and flanks. FEMALE: Unicolored head, neck, and breast are brown or cinnamon-brown. FLIGHT: Mostly **gray wing linings**. **Similar Species:** American Wigeon (above) has grayish head and neck that contrasts with breast, and white—not gray—wing linings. **Voice:** Single descending whistle is *wEEEEEEr*. **Status:** Rare in winter (Nov-mid Apr). **Habitat:** Valley ponds adjacent to fields of grass. **Behavior:** Usually more shy than American Wigeons in the same flock. **Noteworthy:** In our area unknown away from American Wigeon flocks.

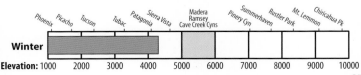

Phoenix   Picacho   Tucson   Tubac   Patagonia   Sierra Vista   Madera Ramsey Cave Creek Cyns   Pinery Cyn   Summerhaven   Rustler Park   Mt. Lemmon   Chiricahua Pk

Winter

Elevation: 1000   2000   3000   4000   5000   6000   7000   8000   9000   10000

Mallard
Male

Mallard
Female

"Mexican Duck"

MALLARD, *Anas platyrhynchos*

Description: 23". Large duck with blue wing patch bordered by white; orange legs. MALE: Green head, **bright yellow bill, white neck ring**, reddish breast, curly black central tail feathers. FEMALE: Dark line through eye; orange bill with blotchy black saddle, rarely all black bill. FLIGHT: White underwings. **Similar Species:** Long, spatulate bill of Northern Shoveler (p. 33) apparent. Female Gadwall (p. 25) shows boxy head shape and white wing patch. **Voice:** Female *quacks*. **Status:** Common in winter (mid Aug-mid May); rare in midsummer (mid May-mid Aug). **Habitat:** Lakes, ponds, rivers, and streams. Flocks occasionally descend on alfalfa fields. **Behavior:** Forages for vegetation by tipping up; grazes on land. **Noteworthy:** Most males in Arizona migrate too early to breed with hen "Mexican Ducks."

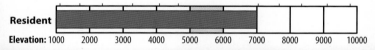

Resident									
Elevation: 1000	2000	3000	4000	5000	6000	7000	8000	9000	10000

"MEXICAN DUCK", *Anas platyrhynchos diazi*

Description: 23". Like **dark** hen Mallard **with contrasting paler head and neck**. MALE: **Bill unmarked olive-yellow**. FEMALE: **Brown outer tail feathers**. FLIGHT: Very white underwings. **Similar Species:** Male Mallard (above) has yellow bill. Female Mallard has white–not brown–outer tail feathers. **Voice:** Like Mallard. **Status:** Fairly common resident. **Habitat:** Valley lakes, permanent ponds, and rivers. **Behavior:** Usually in pairs year-round. Nests after most "Northern" race Mallards migrate. **Noteworthy:** Recent DNA studies show genetically pure "Mexican Ducks" are more closely related to American Black Duck of Eastern U.S. than to Mallard. Hybrids, however, are common; male hybrids often show curly black tail feathers.

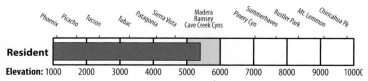

	Phoenix	Picacho	Tucson	Tubac	Patagonia	Sierra Vista	Madera Ramsey Cave Creek Cyns	Pinery Cyn	Summerhaven	Rustler Park	Mt. Lemmon	Chiricahua Pk
Resident												
Elevation: 1000	2000	3000	4000	5000	6000	7000	8000	9000	10000			

Green-winged Teal
Male

Green-winged Teal
Female

Blue-winged Teal
Male

Blue-winged Teal
Female

Cinnamon Teal
Male

Cinnamon Teal
Female

GREEN-WINGED TEAL, *Anas crecca*

Description: 14″. **Short black bill; bright green speculum**. MALE: Chestnut head with **broad green ear patch; vertical white "shoulder" stripe**. FEMALE: Off-white undertail coverts. **Similar Species:** Female Blue-winged (below) and Cinnamon Teals (below) have larger bills and blue-gray forewings, lack whitish undertail. **Status:** Common in winter (mid Aug-mid May); rare in midsummer (mid May-mid Aug). **Habitat:** Valley ponds and lakes. **Behavior:** All three teals dabble in shallows. **Noteworthy:** Smallest dabbling duck, weighing about 10 ounces.

BLUE-WINGED TEAL, *Anas discors*

Description: 15″. Medium-long black bill; dull orange legs. MALE: Bluish-gray head with **bold white foreface crescent**. FEMALE: Diffuse, pale foreface. FLIGHT: Pale blue forewing and green speculum. **Similar Species:** Cinnamon Teal (below) has long bill and male usually has red eye. **Status:** Uncommon migrant (Feb-May and Aug-Nov); rare in midsummer (Jun-Jul) and midwinter (Dec-Jan). **Habitat:** Valley ponds and lakes. **Noteworthy:** Some fall juvenile Blue-winged and Cinnamon Teals are probably not safely distinguished.

CINNAMON TEAL, *Anas cyanoptera*

Description: 16″. **Long black bill** slightly spatulate; yellow legs. MALE: **Rich cinnamon-red** with red eyes. FEMALE: Uniform plain brown head. FLIGHT: Pale blue forewing and green speculum. **Similar Species:** Female Northern Shoveler (p. 33) has huge bill. **Status:** Fairly common in winter (Aug-May); uncommon in summer (Jun-Jul). **Habitat:** Valley ponds and lakes. **Noteworthy:** This is the only nesting teal species in SE Arizona.

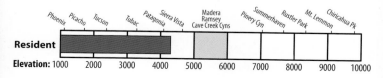

31

Northern Shoveler
Male

Northern Shoveler
Female

Northern Pintail
Male

Northern Pintail
Female

NORTHERN SHOVELER, *Anas clypeata*

Description: 19". Medium-sized dabbler with **long, spatulate bill**. MALE: Green head with **yellow eyes**, white breast, and cinnamon sides. FEMALE: Nondescript with enormous bill. FLIGHT: Pale-blue forewing. Loud wing beats upon take-off. **Similar Species:** Many other female ducks similar, but none have huge bill. Spring males have reverse Mallard (p. 29) underpart pattern with white chest and rusty flanks. **Voice:** Females *quack*, males give soft *thup-tup*. **Status:** Common in winter (Sep-Apr); rare in midsummer (May-Aug). **Habitat:** Valley lakes and ponds. **Behavior:** Specialized bill enables Shovelers to filter feed on plankton. Groups often circle with their heads underwater, straining food stirred up from below. **Noteworthy:** In winter Northern Shoveler is the most abundant duck in Arizona.

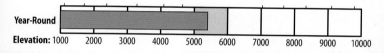

Year-Round									
Elevation: 1000	2000	3000	4000	5000	6000	7000	8000	9000	10000

NORTHERN PINTAIL, *Anas acuta*

Description: Male 26", female 20". Slender, long-necked dabbling duck with gray bill and **long, pointed tail**. MALE: Brown head with **white neck stripes**. FEMALE: Very round head. FLIGHT: Distinctive long neck and tail. **Similar Species:** Other midsized dabbling ducks have shorter, stockier necks and lack the long, pointed tail. **Voice:** Female uses hoarse quacks. Male gives wheezy whistle and musical *droop droop*. **Status:** Fairly common in winter (mid Aug-Apr); casual in midsummer (May-mid Aug). **Habitat:** Valley lakes and ponds. **Behavior:** Feeds by tipping up, with long tail pointed skyward and head and neck underwater. **Noteworthy:** Northern Pintails have been timed flying over 50 mph in Arizona.

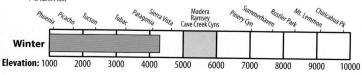

Phoenix	Picacho	Tucson	Tubac	Patagonia	Sierra Vista	Madera Ramsey Cave Creek Cyns	Pinery Cyn	Summerhaven	Rustler Park	Mt. Lemmon	Chiricahua Pk

Winter									
Elevation: 1000	2000	3000	4000	5000	6000	7000	8000	9000	10000

Ring-necked Duck Male

Ring-necked Duck Female

Lesser Scaup Male

Lesser Scaup Female

Greater Scaup Male

Greater Scaup Female

RING-NECKED DUCK, *Aythya collaris*

Description: 17". **Gray bill with crisp white ring** and black tip; peaked hindcrown. MALE: Black with **white "shoulder" wedge**, head glossed purple. FEMALE: White eye-ring and diffuse, whitish foreface. FLIGHT: Mostly gray underwings. **Similar Species:** Scaups (below) lack white ring on bill. Female scaups lack eye-ring. **Status:** Common in winter (Oct-Apr); casual in midsummer (May-Sep). **Habitat:** Valley lakes and ponds. **Behavior:** Like scaups, forages for aquatic plants and invertebrates; joins flocks of scaups and other ducks. **Noteworthy:** Inconspicuous violaceous neck ring on male gives species its name.

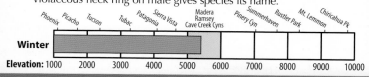

	Phoenix	Picacho	Tucson	Tubac	Patagonia	Sierra Vista	Madera Ramsey Cave Creek Cyns	Pinery Cyn	Summerhaven	Rustler Park	Mt. Lemmon	Chiricahua Pk
Winter												
Elevation:	1000	2000	3000	4000	5000	6000	7000	8000	9000	10000

LESSER SCAUP, *Aythya affinis*

Description: 16.5". **Peaked hindcrown** and bluish-gray bill. MALE: Head usually glossed purple, may look green; blackish on both ends, whitish in middle. FEMALE: Brownish with crisp white foreface. FLIGHT: **Short white upperwing stripe** halfway to wingtip. **Similar Species:** Greater Scaup (below) has rounded head, larger bill, long white upperwing stripes. **Status:** Fairly common in winter (Oct-Apr); rare in midsummer (May-Sep). **Habitat:** Valley lakes and ponds.

GREATER SCAUP, *Aythya marila*

Description: 18". **Rounded head** and bluish-gray bill. MALE: Head usually glossed green, may look purple; blackish on both ends, whitish in middle. FEMALE: Brownish with crisp white foreface; often shows diagnostic whitish ear patch. FLIGHT: **Long white upperwing stripe** almost to wingtip. **Status:** Rare in winter (Nov-Apr); accidental in midsummer (May-Oct). **Habitat:** Valley lakes and ponds. **Noteworthy:** Usually found with Lesser Scaups in Arizona.

Canvasback Male

Canvasback Female

Redhead Male

Redhead Female

CANVASBACK, *Aythya valisineria*

Description: 21". Long body; **sloping forehead** slides into **long, black bill**. MALE: Chestnut head, black breast, white body. FEMALE: Tan head, neck, and chest contrast with pale gray body. **Similar Species:** Redhead (below) has rounded head with shorter, white-banded bill. **Voice:** Usually silent. **Status:** Uncommon in winter (mid Oct-mid Apr); casual in summer (mid Apr-mid Oct). **Habitat:** Valley lakes and ponds. **Behavior:** Dives for aquatic plants and invertebrates and strains seeds from bottom mud. Joins large mixed flocks with Redheads and other wintering diving ducks. **Noteworthy:** Highly susceptible to poisoning from lead shot because of feeding ecology.

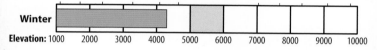

Winter									

Elevation: 1000   2000   3000   4000   5000   6000   7000   8000   9000   10000

REDHEAD, *Aythya americana*

Description: 19". Compact body; **rounded head**; medium-long **tricolored bill** with white band near black tip. MALE: Rich red head with pale blue bill; smoke-gray body. FEMALE: Dull brown overall; slate-gray bill. **Similar Species:** Female Greater and Lesser Scaups (p. 35) have distinct white forefaces. Female Ring-necked Duck (p. 35) has peaked hindcrown and dark upperparts. Long-bodied Canvasback (above) has much longer bill. **Voice:** Usually silent. **Status:** Uncommon in winter (Nov-Mar) becoming rare in midsummer (Apr-Oct). **Habitat:** Valley lakes and ponds. **Behavior:** Dives for aquatic plants and invertebrates and strains seeds from bottom mud. Joins large mixed flocks with Canvasbacks and other wintering diving ducks. **Noteworthy:** Has nested at Picacho Reservoir.

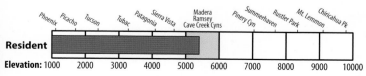

Phoenix   Picacho   Tucson   Tubac   Patagonia   Sierra Vista   Madera Ramsey Cave Creek Cyns   Piney Cyn   Summerhaven   Rustler Park   Mt. Lemmon   Chiricahua Pk

Resident

Elevation: 1000   2000   3000   4000   5000   6000   7000   8000   9000   10000

Bufflehead
Male

Bufflehead
Female

Common Goldeneye
Male

Common Goldeneye
Female

BUFFLEHEAD, *Bucephala albeola*

Description: 13". **Small duck** with a small, gray bill. MALE: **Balloon-headed** with white cowl. FEMALE: Rectangular head with an **oval white cheek patch**; gray upperparts with a small white speculum. **Similar Species:** Common Goldeneye (below) has bright golden eyes. From a distance, male Goldeneye shows round white face spot and white "piano key" markings on wing. Female Goldeneye lacks the oval cheek patch of female Bufflehead. Winter female Ruddy Duck (p. 43) shows pale lower half of entire face with a diffuse line across the cheek. **Voice:** Usually silent in our area. **Status:** Uncommon in winter (mid Oct-Apr); casual in summer (May-mid Oct). **Habitat:** Valley lakes and ponds, usually with surrounding trees and shrubbery. **Behavior:** Dives for aquatic invertebrates and small fish in small, loose flocks. **Noteworthy:** Buffleheads rarely leave the water to walk on the ground.

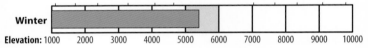

Winter									

Elevation: 1000   2000   3000   4000   5000   6000   7000   8000   9000   10000

COMMON GOLDENEYE, *Bucephala clangula*

Description: 18". Chunky, medium-sized diving duck with **bright yellow eyes**. MALE: Bulbous green head peaked in center of crown; **round white face patch**. FEMALE: Chocolate-brown head with golden eye and gray body; in winter **bill yellow-tipped**. **Similar Species:** Bufflehead (above) lacks golden eyes. **Voice:** Usually silent in our area. **Status:** Rare in winter (Nov-Mar); casual in spring (Apr). **Habitat:** Valley lakes and ponds, usually with surrounding trees and shrubbery. **Behavior:** Dives for aquatic invertebrates. **Noteworthy:** Goldeneyes often associate with Buffleheads in Arizona.

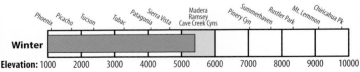

Phoenix   Picacho   Tucson   Tubac   Patagonia   Sierra Vista   Madera Ramsey Cave Creek Cyns   Pinery Cyn   Summerhaven   Rustler Park   Mt. Lemmon   Chiricahua Pk

Winter									

Elevation: 1000   2000   3000   4000   5000   6000   7000   8000   9000   10000

**Common Merganser
Male**

**Common Merganser
Female**

**Red-breasted Merganser
Male**

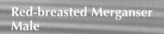

**Red-breasted Merganser
Female**

COMMON MERGANSER, *Mergus merganser*

Description: 25″. Diving duck with **deep-based**, long, slender, red bill. MALE: Green head with short hindcrest; **snow-white breast and flanks**. FEMALE: Rusty head with **crisp white chin spot;** rusty neck contrasts sharply with gray breast. **Similar Species:** Male Red-breasted Merganser (below) has shaggy crest and white collar; female lacks white chin spot. **Voice:** Usually silent. **Status:** Fairly common but local in winter (Nov-Mar). **Habitat:** Large lakes, especially Patagonia Lake, Parker Canyon Lake, and Lake Cochise. **Behavior:** Dives for fish, which it catches and holds with "saw-toothed" bill. Usually seen in flocks. **Noteworthy:** Merganser "teeth," usually invisible under field conditions, are projections on the horny sheath of the bill.

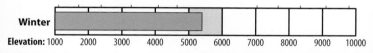

Winter									
Elevation: 1000 2000 3000 4000 5000 6000 7000 8000 9000 10000

RED-BREASTED MERGANSER, *Mergus serrator*

Description: 23″. Diving duck with **narrow-based**, long, reddish-orange bill. BREEDING MALE: Dark green head with **shaggy crest**, conspicuous **white neck ring**, mottled reddish breast, and **gray flanks**. NON-BREEDING MALE: Resembles female but shows more white in wing. FEMALE: **Tawny brown head** with thin, shaggy crest; tawny neck blends into gray body. **Similar Species:** Male Common Merganser (above) lacks shaggy crest and white collar; female has bright rusty head with white chin spot. **Voice:** Usually silent. **Status:** Rare in winter (Nov-Feb). **Habitat:** Larger ponds and lakes. **Behavior:** Dives for fish, which it catches and holds with "saw-toothed" bill. **Noteworthy:** Typically only singles—or rarely pairs—of Red-breasted Merganser occur in SE Arizona.

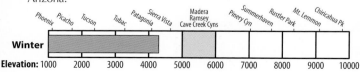

Phoenix   Picacho   Tucson   Tubac   Patagonia   Sierra Vista   Madera Ramsey Cave Creek Cyns   Pinery Cyn   Summerhaven   Rustler Park   Mt. Lemmon   Chiricahua Pk

Winter									
Elevation: 1000 2000 3000 4000 5000 6000 7000 8000 9000 10000

Hooded Merganser Male

Hooded Merganser Female

Ruddy Duck Male

Non-breeding Male

Ruddy Duck Female

HOODED MERGANSER, *Lophodytes cucullatus*

Description: 18″. Small, puffy-headed diving duck with **fan-shaped crest** and short narrow bill. MALE: White crest outlined in black; folded-back crest reduced to thick white stripe; black bill. FEMALE: Tawny-brown crest and bill mostly yellow. JUVENILE MALE: Like female with black bill. **Similar Species:** Male Bufflehead (p. 39) has white sides. Other mergansers much larger with red bills. **Voice:** Usually silent. **Status:** Uncommon in winter (Nov-Feb); casual in migration (Oct and Mar-Apr). **Habitat:** Small, clear water ponds. **Behavior:** Dives for small fish and aquatic invertebrates. **Noteworthy:** Clear nictitating membrane acts like goggles and allows Hooded to hunt underwater.

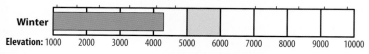

Winter									
Elevation: 1000	2000	3000	4000	5000	6000	7000	8000	9000	10000

RUDDY DUCK, *Oxyura jamaicensis*

Description: 15″. Small duck with **pale cheeks**; long, **stiff tail, often pointed upward**. BREEDING MALE: Rich chestnut-red back and sky-blue bill. NON-BREEDING MALE: Gray with dark crown and large white cheek patch. FEMALE: Shows dark line across pale cheek. **Similar Species:** Female Bufflehead (p. 39) lacks white lower face. **Voice:** Male displays with accelerating series of low, popping notes ending in low croak, *fup fup fup fup fuf-fuf-fuf-frrrrrp.* **Status:** Common in winter (Oct-mid Apr); uncommon in summer (mid Apr-Sep). **Habitat:** Valley lakes and ponds; prefers ponds and lakes with cattails in summer. **Behavior:** Dives for aquatic plants, as well as small fish and invertebrates. Dives when approached. **Noteworthy:** Unlike many other ducks, Ruddies are brightest in summer and dullest in winter.

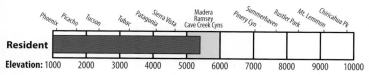

	Phoenix	Picacho	Tucson	Tubac	Patagonia	Sierra Vista	Madera Ramsey Cave Creek Cyns	Pinery Cyn	Summerhaven	Rustler Park	Mt. Lemmon	Chiricahua Pk
Resident												
Elevation: 1000	2000		3000	4000		5000	6000	7000		8000	9000	10000

Male

Female

WILD TURKEY, *Meleagris gallopavo*

Description: Male: 46″, female: 37″. **Large** gamebird with **naked head and neck**. "Mexican" race tail feathers tipped whitish. MALE: Head pale blue with grotesque red neck wattles; long, black "beard" projects from breast; legs are pink and stout with "fighting" spurs on hind-tarsus. FEMALE: Smaller; head is pink-red and wattles are small. In Arizona about 20% have short "beard" on breast; some females have short spurs on hind-tarsus.

Similar Species: Domestic turkey is usually larger, plumper, often partially or all white.

Voice: Displaying male gives familiar descending *gobble*, females give *tuk* notes and series of *yike* calls.

Status: Locally fairly common resident. **Habitat:** Large mountain canyons and open coniferous forest and meadows at higher elevations. Rare and sporadic observations in gallery forest along the San Pedro River and Sonoita Creek probably represent natural incursions from Mexico.

Behavior: Forages on ground (often by scratching) for seeds, nuts, fruits, insects. Seldom flies, except to roost in trees at night. In breeding display, male puffs out feathers, spreads tail, swells facial wattles, droops wings, and gobbles. Nomadic and gregarious after breeding season, turkeys often gather in flocks.

Noteworthy: "Mexican" Wild Turkey (also known as "Gould's") has been reintroduced into the Santa Catalina, Santa Rita, Huachuca, and Chiricahua Mountains. In Arizona fall gobblers weigh up to 26 pounds and average about 18 pounds; hens weigh about 12 pounds.

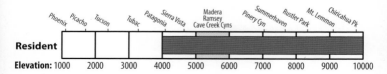

Scaled Quail

Gambel's Quail
Male

Gambel's Quail
Female

Scaled Quail, *Callipepla squamata*

Description: 10″. Plump, blue-gray quail with **tawny crest; appears scaly on neck and chest**. MALE: White-tipped crest.   FEMALE: Buffy crest. **Similar Species:** Gambel's Quail (below) has dapper black topknot– not tawny crest–chestnut flanks, and unscaled underparts. **Voice:** Sharp *querk!* or *pic-ture pic-ture*. **Status:** Common resident. **Habitat:** Valley grassland and open Chihuahuan Desert scrub, primarily east of the Santa Cruz River. Prefers flat and gently rolling terrain. **Behavior:** Forages for seeds, plants, and insects. Forms large flocks in non-breeding season. **Noteworthy:** Although shorter overall, on average Scaled Quail outweighs Gambel's Quail by about one ounce.

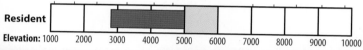

Resident									
Elevation: 1000	2000	3000	4000	5000	6000	7000	8000	9000	10000

Gambel's Quail, *Callipepla gambelii*

Description: 11″. Plump blue-gray quail with dapper **black topknot**; chestnut flanks pin-striped white. MALE: Chestnut cap, long topknot, black face, and black belly. FEMALE: Lacks chestnut cap, black face, and black belly. **Similar Species:** Scaled Quail (above) has shorter, tawny crest and scaly neck and breast. Rare Gambel's x Scaled Quail hybrids usually retain Gambel's topknot but show scaly neck and breast. **Voice:** Quavering *wah-h* and loud *chi-CA-go-ga-go*. **Status:** Common resident. **Habitat:** Both Sonoran and Chihuahuan Desertscrub, as well as residential areas within these habitats. Usually occupies areas with more brush than Scaled Quail. **Behavior:** Forages for seeds, plants, and insects. Flocks in non-breeding season. **Noteworthy:** Winter precipitation is most important factor determining abundance the following year. Gambel's Quail readily use backyard seed feeders.

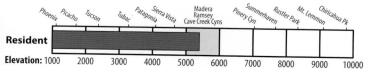

	Phoenix	Picacho	Tucson	Tubac	Patagonia	Sierra Vista	Madera Ramsey Cave Creek Cyns		Pinery Cyn	Summerhaven	Rustler Park	Mt. Lemmon	Chiricahua Pk
Resident													
Elevation: 1000		2000	3000	4000	5000	6000		7000		8000	9000		10000

Montezuma Quail
Male

Montezuma Quail
Female

"Masked" Bobwhite
Female

"Masked" Northern Bobwhite
Male

MONTEZUMA QUAIL, *Cyrtonyx montezumae*

Description: 9". Plump, short-tailed, strikingly patterned quail with blob-like **"pony-tail" crest** on hindhead. MALE: **"Clown" face**. FEMALE: Muted facial pattern of male. **Similar Species:** Gambel's Quail (p. 47) has a dark topknot and Scaled Quail (p. 47) has a distinct crest. Masked Bobwhite (below)–confined to Buenos Aires NWR–lacks the "pony-tail" crest of Montezuma Quail. **Voice:** Ventriloquial, airy *vee-urrr* call, like distant falling bomb. **Status:** Fairly common resident. **Habitat:** Foothill and mountain grassy oak woodlands, pine-oak woodland, and open coniferous forests. **Behavior:** Forages for seeds, plants, and insects. Freezes when disturbed, and does not run or explode into flight unless danger is within 10-15'. **Noteworthy:** Populations of Montezuma Quail are directly correlated to precipitation the previous summer.

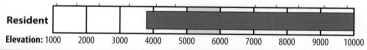

Resident								
Elevation: 1000	2000	3000	4000	5000	6000	7000	8000	9000	10000

"MASKED" NORTHERN BOBWHITE, *Colinus virginianus ridgwayi*

Description: 9.75". **Quail lacking crest**. MALE: Black foreface and throat with cinnamon underparts. FEMALE: Buffy eyestripe and throat; lacks chestnut belly. **Similar Species:** Scaled and Gambel's Quail (p. 47) predominantly blue-gray and crested. Intricately patterned Montezuma Quail (above) has "pony-tail" on hindhead. **Voice:** Explosive *bob-whoit!* **Status:** Eliminated by overgrazing from Arizona by 1897, reintroduction attempts began in 1974 on the Buenos Aires NWR 50 miles southwest of Tucson. **Habitat:** Wide grassy swales in the Altar Valley. **Behavior:** Forages for seeds, plants, and insects. Forms flocks in non-breeding season. **Noteworthy:** Breeding season is timed to take advantage of the summer monsoons, and cocks begin calling after rains commence in July.

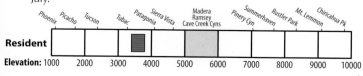

Pacific Loon
Non-breeding

Common Loon
Juvenile

PACIFIC LOON, *Gavia pacifica*

Description: 25". **Medium-sized** loon with rounded crown and straight **tapering bill**. NON-BREEDING: Dark brown upperparts and crown; **dark sides of neck contrast sharply with white throat**. Most show thin, dark "chinstrap." **Similar Species:** Larger Common Loon (below) has heavy, chisel-shaped bill; lacks crisp black-white contrast on sides of neck; and—in close view—lacks the Pacific's black chinstrap. **Voice:** Usually silent in our area. **Status:** Rare in winter (late Oct-Feb). **Habitat:** Large valley ponds and lakes, including city parks, golf courses, and sewage treatment ponds, such as Lakeside Park in Tucson, at Benson Sewage Ponds, and Lake Cochise in Willcox. **Behavior:** Dives for fish. **Noteworthy:** In SE Arizona, Pacific Loons may overwinter, but usually only visit a week or two.

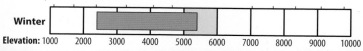

Winter									
Elevation: 1000	2000	3000	4000	5000	6000	7000	8000	9000	10000

COMMON LOON, *Gavia immer*

Description: 32". **Large loon** with a blocky head shape and **heavy, chisel-tipped bill**. NON-BREEDING: Gray-brown above; **partial white collar** with diffuse edges; thick white arcs around eyes. **Similar Species:** Smaller Pacific Loon (above) has sharp black-white contrast between hindneck and throat; smaller, thinner, more tapering bill; and—in close view—usually a dark chinstrap. **Voice:** Distinctive yodels seldom heard in our area. **Status:** Rare in winter (mid Oct-Mar). **Habitat:** Large valley and canyon ponds and lakes, such as Pena Blanca, Patagonia, and Parker Canyon Lakes. **Behavior:** Makes long dives for fish. **Noteworthy:** Usually only one or two Common Loons overwinter in SE Arizona.

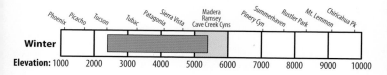

Winter									
Elevation: 1000	2000	3000	4000	5000	6000	7000	8000	9000	10000

Least Grebe

Pied-billed Grebe
Breeding

Pied-billed Grebe
Non-breeding

LEAST GREBE, *Tachybaptus dominicus*

Description: 9.5". **Tiny** diving bird with short **thin neck**, short black bill, and **golden-yellow eyes**. **Similar Species:** Larger Pied-billed Grebe (below) has dark eyes and thicker—often banded—bill. Larger Eared and Horned Grebes (p. 55) have red eyes, longer necks, and thinner bills. **Voice:** Rattling, drawn-out nasal scold. **Status:** Rare year-round, with singles or pairs present at the same site from several weeks to several years. **Habitat:** Lakes and ponds, especially with cattails and reeds. Apparently bred at Pena Blanca Lake in 2010 for first time in Arizona since 1962. **Behavior:** Dives for and also chases aquatic insects and small fish. **Noteworthy:** Often rides high in the water like a "toy duck."

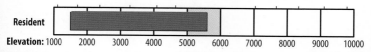

Resident
Elevation: 1000 2000 3000 4000 5000 6000 7000 8000 9000 10000

PIED-BILLED GREBE, *Podilymbus podiceps*

Description: 13". Short **thick neck** and short **thick bill**. BREEDING: Silvery bill with **black ring**; black throat. NON-BREEDING: Unmarked horn-colored bill. JUVENILE: Striped face. **Similar Species:** Eared and Horned Grebes (p. 55) have longer, slimmer necks and thin bills; smaller Least Grebe (above) has golden-yellow eyes. **Voice:** Vocal in summer. Male's song is loud *kuh kuh kuh kow kow kow kow-ah kow-ah and huzza-huzza-huzza*. **Status:** Uncommon in summer (Jun-Sep); fairly common migrant and winter visitor (Oct-May). **Habitat:** Lakes and ponds, especially with cattails and reeds. **Behavior:** Dives for fish and aquatic invertebrates. Nest is well-concealed floating platform attached to emergent vegetation. **Noteworthy:** When disturbed Pied-billed Grebes slowly submerge and then swim away underwater.

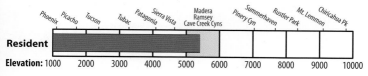

Phoenix Picacho Tucson Tubac Patagonia Sierra Vista Madera Ramsey Cave Creek Cyns Pinery Cyn Summerhaven Rustler Park Mt. Lemmon Chiricahua Pk

Resident
Elevation: 1000 2000 3000 4000 5000 6000 7000 8000 9000 10000

Horned Grebe
Breeding

Horned Grebe
Non-breeding

Eared Grebe
Breeding

Eared Grebe
Non-breeding

HORNED GREBE, *Podiceps auritus*

Description: 14". Small, big-headed diver with relatively **flat crown, straight bill with ivory tip**. BREEDING: **Thick yellow "horns"** behind red eyes and **rufous neck**. NON-BREEDING: Bicolored head with white lower half; **white throat and foreneck**. **Similar Species:** Non-breeding Eared Grebe (below) has dusky foreneck, peaked crown, grayish cheek outlined with paler rear crescent, and subtly upcurved bill. **Voice:** Usually silent in our area. **Status:** Rare migrant (Mar-mid Apr and mid Oct-Nov); casual in winter (Dec-Feb). **Habitat:** Large ponds and lakes. **Behavior:** Dives for small fish and aquatic invertebrates. **Noteworthy:** In Arizona only rarely seen in full breeding plumage and only in spring.

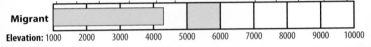

Migrant

Elevation: 1000   2000   3000   4000   5000   6000   7000   8000   9000   10000

EARED GREBE, *Podiceps nigricollis*

Description: 13". Dainty diver with **peaked crown**, slightly-**upcurved thin bill**; usually rides high in the water. BREEDING: **Wispy golden fan** behind red eyes and **black neck**. NON-BREEDING: Peaked crown; gray cheek outlined with whitish rear crescent; neck variably washed with gray. May have dull yellow eyes in winter. **Similar Species:** Horned Grebe (above) has a flatter crown, white lower face, clean white foreneck, and straight, pale-tipped bill. **Voice:** High, whistled, repeated *ooEEK*. **Status:** Rare and irregular summer resident (Jun-Aug); fairly common in winter (Sep-May). **Habitat:** Large ponds and lakes. **Behavior:** Dives for small fish and aquatic invertebrates. Occasionally found in flocks of 20 or more birds during migration. **Noteworthy:** Lone pairs formerly bred at Lake Cochise near Willcox.

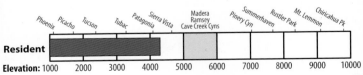

Phoenix   Picacho   Tucson   Tubac   Patagonia   Sierra Vista   Madera Ramsey Cave Creek Cyns   Pinery Cyn   Summerhaven   Rustler Park   Mt. Lemmon   Chiricahua Pk

Resident

Elevation: 1000   2000   3000   4000   5000   6000   7000   8000   9000   10000

Western Grebe
Breeding

Western Grebe
Non-breeding

Clark's Grebe
Breeding

Clark's Grebe
Non-breeding

WESTERN GREBE, *Aechmophorus occidentalis*

Description: 25". Large grebe with long slender neck; **dull yellow-olive bill**; bright red eyes. SUMMER: **Black crown envelopes eyes**. WINTER: Patch surrounding eye fades to gray. **Similar Species:** Clark's Grebe (below) has bright orange bill; during summer shows white above eye. **Voice:** Loud, grating *kree-kreeek*. **Status:** Uncommon in winter (mid Sep-May); casual in summer (Jun-mid Sep). **Habitat:** Large ponds and lakes. Possible throughout region but Patagonia Lake has the most records. **Behavior:** Dives for fish in lakes and ponds. **Noteworthy:** Famous for elaborate courtship dance where pairs race across water in unison.

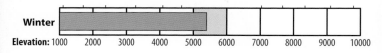

Winter									
Elevation: 1000	2000	3000	4000	5000	6000	7000	8000	9000	10000

CLARK'S GREBE, *Aechmophorus clarkii*

Description: 25". Large grebe with long slender neck; **distinctly orange bill**; bright red eyes. SUMMER: **Eyes completely surrounded by white**. WINTER: Black crown with pale lores. **Similar Species:** Western Grebe (above) has dull yellow-olive bill. During summer black cap envelopes eye; in winter grayish eyebrow connects eye to crown. In direct comparison, the dark on hindneck of Clark's is more restricted with more extensive white on wings and flanks. **Voice:** Single drawn-out *kreeeek*. **Status:** Rare in winter (mid Sep-May); casual in summer (Jun-mid Sep). **Habitat:** Large ponds and lakes. Possible throughout region but Patagonia Lake has the most records. **Behavior:** Dives for fish in lakes and ponds. Usually found with Western Grebes. **Noteworthy:** Clark's was formerly considered a plumage morph of Western Grebe.

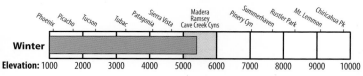

Phoenix	Picacho	Tucson	Tubac	Patagonia	Sierra Vista	Madera Ramsey Cave Creek Cyns	Pinery Cyn	Summerhaven	Rustler Park	Mt. Lemmon	Chiricahua Pk
Winter											
Elevation: 1000	2000	3000	4000	5000	6000	7000	8000	9000	10000		

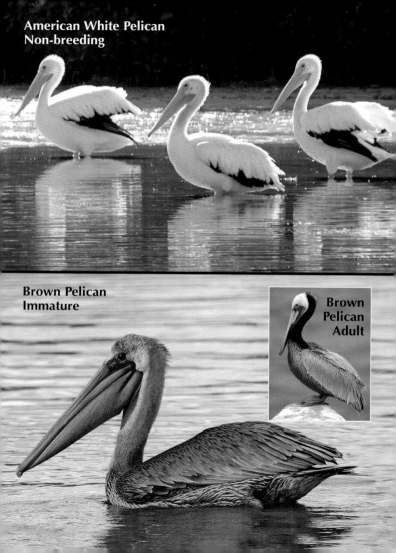

**American White Pelican
Non-breeding**

**Brown Pelican
Immature**

**Brown
Pelican
Adult**

AMERICAN WHITE PELICAN, *Pelecanus erythrorhynchos*

Description: 60", wingspan 108". **Enormous white water bird** with huge, scoop-shaped **yellowish-orange bill**. FLIGHT: White forewing and black hindwing. **Similar Species:** Brown Pelican immature (below) is entirely brown and substantially smaller than American White Pelican. Soaring Brown Pelican shows entirely dark wings. **Voice:** Generally silent. **Status:** Rare transient year-round. **Habitat:** Large ponds and lakes. **Behavior:** Forages for fish in shallows. Eats between 20-40% of its weight in fish each day. **Noteworthy:** American White Pelicans often feed cooperatively by encircling fish, then simultaneously dipping their heads.

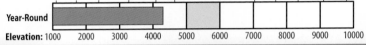

Year-Round

Elevation: 1000   2000   3000   4000   5000   6000   7000   8000   9000   10000

BROWN PELICAN, *Pelecanus occidentalis*

Description: 48", wingspan 84". **Large gray or brown water bird** with big, scoop-shaped **greenish-gray bill**. ADULT: Whitish head and silvery-gray body. IMMATURE: Brown overall. FLIGHT: Entirely dark wings. **Similar Species:** American White Pelican (above) is entirely white and substantially larger than Brown Pelican. Soaring White Pelican has all-white forewing and all-black hindwing. Magnificent Frigatebird, casual in SE Arizona and always soaring, is approximately the same size as Brown Pelican, but exhibits a "mosquito" silhouette with long thin bill, wings, and tail. **Voice:** Generally silent. **Status:** Rare transient year-round, especially in late summer (Jul-Aug). **Habitat:** Large ponds and lakes. **Behavior:** Plunge-dives for fish in shallows. **Noteworthy:** Most Arizona records pertain to immatures. Some summers 100 or more juvenile Brown Pelicans are found in southern Arizona, apparently pushed into our area by ferocious storms in the Gulf of California.

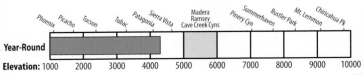

Year-Round

Elevation: 1000   2000   3000   4000   5000   6000   7000   8000   9000   10000

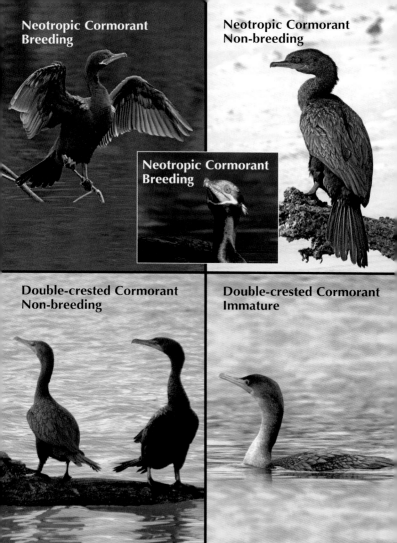

Neotropic Cormorant
Breeding

Neotropic Cormorant
Non-breeding

Neotropic Cormorant
Breeding

Double-crested Cormorant
Non-breeding

Double-crested Cormorant
Immature

NEOTROPIC CORMORANT, *Phalacrocorax brasilianus*

Description: 26″. **Pointed, triangular-shaped bare yellowish skin on throat**, dark lores, relatively thin neck, relatively **long tail**. ADULT: Black overall. Breeding birds have white outlining throat pouch. IMMATURE: Unicolored brown. FLIGHT: Head-and-neck appear same length as long tail. **Similar Species:** Double-crested Cormorant (below) is larger with rounded gular patch, thick neck, and short tail. Immature has pale underparts; orange lores. **Voice:** Generally silent. **Status:** Uncommon year-round transient. **Habitat:** Large ponds and lakes; usually year-round at Patagonia Lake State Park. **Behavior:** Pursues fish underwater. Often seen out of water with wings spread to dry. **Noteworthy:** This species only officially entered the ranks of Arizona avifauna in 1961.

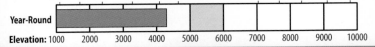

Year-Round

Elevation: 1000 2000 3000 4000 5000 6000 7000 8000 9000 10000

DOUBLE-CRESTED CORMORANT, *Phalacrocorax auritus*

Description: 33″. **Rounded, bare orange patch of skin on throat,** orange lores, relatively thick neck, relatively **short tail**. ADULT: Black overall. Breeding birds have wispy white plumes behind eyes. IMMATURE: Varies from brown to almost whitish on neck and breast. FLIGHT: Head-and-neck appear longer than short tail. **Similar Species:** Neotropic Cormorant (above) is smaller with triangular throat patch, thin neck, and tail about as long as head-and-neck. Immatures have uniform brown throat and breast; dark lores. **Voice:** Generally silent. **Status:** Uncommon year-round transient. **Habitat:** Large ponds and lakes; year-round at Patagonia Lake State Park. **Behavior:** Pursues fish underwater; at surface they ride low in water with bill angled upward. **Noteworthy:** In SE Arizona immatures of both cormorant species greatly outnumber adults.

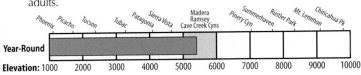

Phoenix Picacho Tucson Tubac Patagonia Sierra Vista Madera Ramsey Cave Creek Cyns Pinery Cyn Summerhaven Rustler Park Mt. Lemmon Chiricahua Pk

Year-Round

Elevation: 1000 2000 3000 4000 5000 6000 7000 8000 9000 10000

American Bittern

Least Bittern

LEAST BITTERN, *Ixobrychus exilis*

Description: 13". Miniature heron with **burnished-buff shoulders**. FLIGHT: Conspicuous bright buff shoulders. **Similar Species:** Larger Green Heron (p. 71) lacks buff shoulders and cinnamon underparts. **Voice:** Series of rapid *kuh* notes, dying away at end. Also rapid, rail-like *keks*. **Status:** Uncommon in summer (May-Sep); rare in winter (Oct-Apr). **Habitat:** Lake and pond margins, especially with tall reeds and cattails. Picacho Reservoir, Patagonia Lake, and Roper Lake are known locations. **Behavior:** Stalks prey in shallow water. If disturbed slinks away or flushes in short flights into deep reeds. **Noteworthy:** This is the smallest member of the heron and egret family in the U.S.

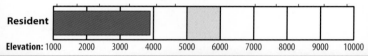

Resident

Elevation: 1000 2000 3000 4000 5000 6000 7000 8000 9000 10000

AMERICAN BITTERN, *Botaurus lentiginosus*

Description: 28". Heavy-set, **heavily-striped** heron with **prominent black moustache** continuing down sides of long neck. FLIGHT: Dark flight feathers above contrast with the brown upperparts. **Similar Species:** Immature Black-crowned Night-Heron (p. 71) lacks long black moustache stripes; in flight has unicolored wings. **Voice:** Flight call is nasal *squark*. Deep, hollow *LOONK-aloonk* song is almost never heard in SE Arizona. **Status:** Rare in winter (mid Sep-May). **Habitat:** Lake and pond margins, especially with tall reeds and cattails. Reported with some regularity from Picacho Reservoir and Patagonia Lake. **Behavior:** Captures prey by standing motionless. If disturbed, points bill skyward and imperceptibly sinks into reeds. **Noteworthy:** Most records of American Bittern in SE Arizona occur in October and November.

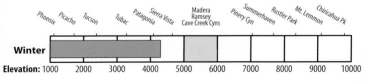

Winter

Elevation: 1000 2000 3000 4000 5000 6000 7000 8000 9000 10000

Description: 46″, wingspan 72″. **Very large, blue-gray heron** with long, dagger-like bill; cinnamon thighs; long, dark legs. ADULT: White stripe divides black crown; long black head plumes when breeding; black shoulders. JUVENILE: Solid dark crown; heavily streaked foreneck and breast; lacks black "shoulder" patch. FLIGHT: Ponderous and deliberate wing beats with head drawn inwards.

Similar Species: Sandhill Crane (p. 109) has solid gray plumage with a red crown; flies with shallow wing beats and an outstretched neck.

Voice: Loud, guttural *ruhh*.

Status: Fairly common resident. **Habitat:** Lakes and ponds, permanent rivers and streams, concentrated near nesting colonies while breeding from early spring to early fall. Wanders widely in valleys after the breeding season.

Behavior: Patiently stalks shoreline or shallow water areas for fish, crayfish, frogs, and other prey. Also hunts for rodents and reptiles in flooded fields. Often perches in trees. Nests colonially; builds large stick nests in tallest available trees, usually cottonwoods.

Noteworthy: Perhaps the easiest way to see a Tiger Salamander in Arizona is to watch a fishing Great Blue Heron. Great Blues are adept at catching the large larvae of Tiger Salamanders, which fishermen often refer to as "waterdogs."

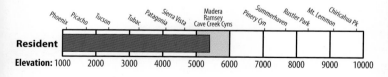

	Phoenix	Picacho	Tucson	Tubac	Patagonia	Sierra Vista	Madera Ramsey Cave Creek Cyns	Pinery Cyn	Summerhaven	Rustler Park	Mt. Lemmon	Chiricahua Pk
Resident												
Elevation:	1000	2000	3000	4000	5000	6000	7000	8000	9000	10000

Great Egret

Cattle Egret

Snowy Egret

GREAT EGRET, *Ardea alba*

Description: 39". **Large egret with yellow bill; black legs and feet.**
BREEDING: Nuptial plumes on back. **Similar Species:** Much smaller
Snowy Egret (below) has black stiletto bill and yellow feet. **Voice:** All
egrets give harsh, grating calls. **Status:** Uncommon resident. **Habitat:**
Lakes, ponds, rivers, and streams. **Behavior:** Spears fish and small
terrestrial vertebrates. **Noteworthy:** Slaughter of Great and Snowy
Egrets by plume hunters in the late 1800s led to formation of the
National Audubon Society.

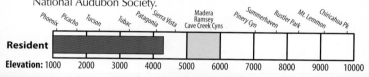

CATTLE EGRET, *Bubulcus ibis*

Description: 19". Short, thick, yellow bill; **short, thick neck; short legs
pastel-colored in summer and dusky in winter.** BREEDING: Buffy
crown, foreneck, and back. **Similar Species:** Snowy Egret (below) has
thin neck, black stiletto bill, and yellow feet. **Status:** Rare year-round.
Habitat: Valley fields, lakes, and ponds. Has bred on the Gila River near
Safford. **Behavior:** Follows cows, horses, and tractors to catch insects
disturbed by their activity. **Noteworthy:** First discovered in Arizona
near Phoenix in 1966.

SNOWY EGRET, *Egretta thula*

Description: 24". **Slender black bill;** mostly **black legs** that contrast with
yellow feet. BREEDING: Nuptial plumes on head, neck, and back.
Similar Species: Cattle Egret (above) has short neck, short yellow bill,
and short legs. **Status:** Uncommon in summer (Mar-Oct); casual in
winter (Nov-Feb). **Habitat:** Lakes and ponds, rivers and streams. Has
bred on the Gila River near Safford. **Behavior:** Spears fish, other small
aquatic vertebrates, and insects.

Little Blue Heron
Non-breeding

Little Blue Heron
Molting Juvenile

Tricolored Heron
Breeding

Reddish Egret
Juvenile

LITTLE BLUE HERON, *Egretta caerulea*

Description: 24". **Blue bill with black tip;** bluish body with maroon head and neck; greenish legs. JUVENILE: White or blue-mottled plumage. **Similar Species:** Much larger red morph immature Reddish Egret (below), the only morph and age recorded in Arizona, has pale yellow eyes, blackish bill, and usually feeds more actively. **Voice:** All usually silent in our area. **Status:** Casual in summer (primarily Apr-Sep). **Habitat:** Valley lakes and ponds. **Behavior:** Spears fish, small aquatic vertebrates, and insects. Hunts slowly and deliberately. **Noteworthy:** Only one white immature Little Blue Heron has been recorded in SE Arizona.

TRICOLORED HERON, *Egretta tricolor*

Description: 26". Very long, bicolored bill; **white belly and foreneck.** JUVENILE: Reddish neck and wings. **Similar Species:** Little Blue Heron (above) and much larger Reddish Egret (below) lack white belly and foreneck. **Status:** Casual in summer and early fall (primarily Apr-Oct). **Habitat:** Valley lakes and ponds. **Behavior:** Spears fish, small aquatic vertebrates, and insects.

REDDISH EGRET, *Egretta rufescens*

Description: 30". ADULT: Pink-based bill. JUVENILE: **Blackish bill; pale yellow eye;** reddish head and neck; gray body; **dark legs. Similar Species:** Much smaller Little Blue Heron (above) has bicolored bill and greenish legs. **Status:** Casual in summer and fall (late Jun-late Nov). **Habitat:** Valley lakes and ponds. **Behavior:** Active feeder that startles prey into open water. **Noteworthy:** Since the first record in 1996, only red morph immatures have been substantiated in SE Arizona.

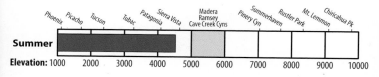

Green Heron

Juvenile

Black-crowned Night-Heron

Juvenile

GREEN HERON, *Butorides virescens*

Description: 18". Small, **thick-necked**, and short-legged heron. ADULT: **Rich chestnut neck**. Slate upperparts may have greenish gloss. JUVENILE: Streaked neck and breast. **Similar Species:** Smaller Least Bittern (p. 63) has bright buff shoulders and cinnamon underparts. **Voice:** Squawking *queowk!* alarm; also series of guttural *cuk-cuk-cuk-uh-uh-uh* calls. **Status:** Uncommon resident. **Habitat:** Valley ponds and lakes, and rivers and streams, especially with reeds and cattails and adjacent trees. **Behavior:** Perches motionlessly at water's edge for long periods before striking fish, frogs, insects, mice, or other vertebrates and invertebrates. **Noteworthy:** Green Herons drop food into water to attract small fish and other aquatic prey.

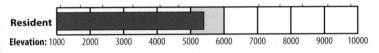

Resident

Elevation: 1000   2000   3000   4000   5000   6000   7000   8000   9000   10000

BLACK-CROWNED NIGHT-HERON, *Nycticorax nycticorax*

Description: 25". Medium-sized, stocky heron with **short, thick neck** and red eyes. ADULT: **Black bill, crown, and back**. JUVENILE: Heavily spotted white above and heavily streaked brown below; bill mostly olive-yellow (does not become black until third year). FLIGHT: Broad, pale underwings. **Similar Species:** American Bittern (p. 63) has long, dark moustache. In flight shows dark underwings. **Voice:** Quizzical *quock?* notes. **Status:** Uncommon but nomadic resident. **Habitat:** Valley ponds and lakes, especially with reeds and cattails and adjacent trees. **Behavior:** Sit-and-wait hunter striking unwary fish, frogs, snakes, or other aquatic prey. Primarily nocturnal. During the day typically roosts in dense cover near water. **Noteworthy:** Occurs on all continents except Antarctica. In midsummer roving flocks in SE Arizona may number more than 20.

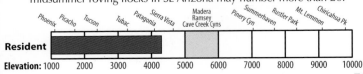

Phoenix   Picacho   Tucson   Tubac   Patagonia   Sierra Vista   Madera Ramsey Cave Creek Cyns   Pinery Cyn   Summerhaven   Rustler Park   Mt. Lemmon   Chiricahua Pk

Resident

Elevation: 1000   2000   3000   4000   5000   6000   7000   8000   9000   10000

White-faced Ibis

White-faced Ibis
Non-breeding

Roseate Spoonbill

WHITE-FACED IBIS, *Plegadis chihi*

Description: 23". Dark wading bird with a **long, decurved bill**. ADULT: Eyes red. BREEDING: Purple overall with **glossy green back and wings**; red face outlined by white; legs red. NON-BREEDING: Duller with finely streaked neck; pink facial skin. IMMATURE: Gray face and brown eyes.
Similar Species: Breeding adult Glossy Ibis (accidental) has slaty facial skin and dark eyes; short bluish-white lines above and below eye do not meet; gray legs with red confined to knees. Immatures probably not separable in field. Adult White Ibis (accidental) is all white with red bill.
Voice: Alarm call is low, quacking *waarr, waarr*. **Status:** Uncommon migrant (Apr-May and Aug-Oct); rare in midsummer (Jun-Jul); casual in winter (Nov-Mar). **Habitat:** Barren pond shores, flooded fields, and short grass pastures. **Behavior:** Probes with sickle bill for insects and invertebrates. Flocks may number 200 or more birds. **Noteworthy:** The closely related Glossy Ibis is a recent invader in SE Arizona, only arriving in 2005, and has always occurred as one or two birds in a flock of White-faced Ibis.

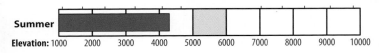

ROSEATE SPOONBILL, *Platalea ajaja*

Description: 32". Pink wading bird with a long, spatulate bill. ADULT: Deep pink with bald head and red shoulders. IMMATURE: White feathered head; pale pink overall. **Similar Species:** Unmistakable. The only large pink bird in our area. **Status:** Casual year-round. **Habitat:** Valley ponds and lakes.

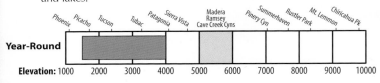

Black Vulture

Black Vulture

Turkey Vulture

Turkey Vulture

BLACK VULTURE, *Coragyps atratus*

Description: 25", wingspan 59". Large, chunky, raptor-like bird with **bare black head; black** overall with **short tail.** FLIGHT: **Outermost wingtips silvery,** contrasting with black inner wings; soars with wings in a flattened "M." **Similar Species:** Turkey Vulture (below) has smaller-headed, slimmer silhouette; adult has red head. In flight Turkey Vulture has longer, narrower two-toned wings, and longer tail. Soars with wings held in shallow "V." **Voice:** Silent. **Status:** Uncommon resident. **Habitat:** Valleys from Sonoita Creek west through the Tohono O'odham tribal lands; also Douglas. **Behavior:** Locates carrion by sight. **Noteworthy:** Black Vultures often cue on Turkey Vultures to find carrion. They were not recorded in Arizona until 1920.

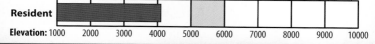

Resident									
Elevation: 1000	2000	3000	4000	5000	6000	7000	8000	9000	10000

TURKEY VULTURE, *Cathartes aura*

Description: 26", wingspan 66". Large **blackish-brown** raptor-like bird with **long tail.** ADULT: **Bare red head.** JUVENILE: Bare dark head. FLIGHT: **Two-toned wings** with pale flight feathers that contrast with black wing-linings; **"teeter-totters"** as it soars. **Similar Species:** Huskier Black Vulture (above) has black head, broad wings with silvery circles at the tips. Soaring Golden Eagle (p. 81) lacks bicolored wings. **Voice:** Silent. **Status:** Common in summer (mid Mar-mid Oct); uncommon in winter (mid Oct-mid Mar). **Habitat:** SUMMER: All habitats. WINTER: Primarily in western valleys; also Douglas. **Behavior:** Locates carrion by smell and by sight. Forms huge roosts with over 100 birds. **Noteworthy:** Summering Arizona Turkey Vultures migrate south; wintering birds probably originate from near the Canadian border.

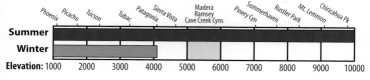

	Phoenix	Picacho	Tucson	Tubac	Patagonia	Sierra Vista	Madera Ramsey Cave Creek Cyns	Pinery Cyn	Summerhaven	Rustler Park	Mt. Lemmon	Chiricahua Pk
Summer												
Winter												
Elevation:	1000	2000	3000	4000	5000	6000	7000	8000	9000	10000		

75

OSPREY, *Pandion haliaetus*

Description: 23", wingspan 63". Large, brown, fish-eating hawk with **white head** and **dark eyestripe**. MALE: Unstreaked, clean white breast. FEMALE: Often shows a necklace of dark streaks across breast. JUVENILE: Scaled buff on the back and wings; buffy wash on the breast. FLIGHT: **Leading edge of wings sharply crooked at wrist** and down-bowed; soars like a gull.

Similar Species: Adult Bald Eagle (p. 81) is larger and stockier with big head that lacks dark eyestripe; has dark–not white–underparts, and adult has immaculate white tail.

Voice: Calls are short, chirping whistles.

Status: Uncommon migrant (mid Feb-mid May and mid Aug-mid Nov); rare in midwinter (mid Nov-mid Feb); casual in summer (mid May-mid Aug). **Habitat:** Usually found at lakes, large ponds, and along rivers, but migrants occur in all habitats, including waterless deserts and pine-clad mountain ridges. Often found at Agua Caliente Park in Tucson and Patagonia Lake near Nogales.

Behavior: Hunts by plunging feet-first into the water to capture fish, often hovering overhead before diving.

Noteworthy: An Osprey positions fish head forward to make flight more aerodynamic, before transporting it back to tree or utility pole perches for consumption.

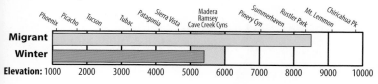

77

White-tailed Kite

White-tailed Kite

Mississippi Kite

Mississippi Kite

WHITE-TAILED KITE, *Elanus leucurus*

Description: 15″, wingspan 39″. Elegant gray and white raptor with **black shoulders**; long pointed wings; **long white tail**. JUVENILE: Buffy wash on neck and breast. FLIGHT: Buoyant, wings held high above body; frequently hovers. **Similar Species:** Adult Mississippi Kite (below) is gray overall with a black tail. **Voice:** Whistled *pity pity*. **Status:** Usually uncommon in summer (Apr-Sep) and rare in winter (Oct-Mar), but numbers fluctuate from year to year. **Habitat:** Flat or gently rolling valley grasslands, pastures, and fields with scattered trees. **Behavior:** Forages over open country for rodents, and less often snakes and lizards. Unlike most other raptors, usually produces two broods per year. **Noteworthy:** White-tailed Kite was not substantiated in Arizona until 1972.

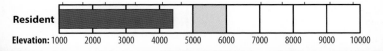

Resident

Elevation: 1000 2000 3000 4000 5000 6000 7000 8000 9000 10000

MISSISSIPPI KITE, *Ictinia mississippiensis*

Description: 14″, wingspan 31″. Gray raptor with **pearly head,** long narrow wings, and **long black tail**. MALE: Copper band in primaries. JUVENILE: Thick brown streaks below; banded tail. FLIGHT: Graduated wingtip; long, black, rectangular tail. Does not hover. **Similar Species:** White-tailed Kite (above) is mostly white with white tail. **Voice:** Whistled *kweer* notes. **Status:** Uncommon in summer (May-Sep). **Habitat:** River valley cottonwood groves, primarily along the San Pedro River between St. David and Winkelman. **Behavior:** Plucks insects, especially Apache cicadas, off the canopy of cottonwood trees. Small colonies of these kites nest high in cottonwood groves, and often forage together. **Noteworthy:** Mississippi Kite was unknown in Arizona until 1970.

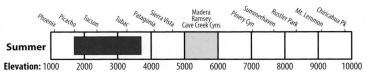

Summer

Elevation: 1000 2000 3000 4000 5000 6000 7000 8000 9000 10000

Bald Eagle

Bald Eagle Immature

Golden Eagle

Golden Eagle Immature

BALD EAGLE, *Haliaeetus leucocephalus*

Description: 31", wingspan 80". **Very large raptor** with big head and big bill. ADULT: **White head and tail**. IMMATURE: Blotchy plumage lacks pattern. FLIGHT: Long, rectangular wings held on horizontal plane. IMMATURE FLIGHT: Blotchy white underwings and white wingpits. **Similar Species:** Immature Golden Eagle (below) shows sharp black and white tail pattern and often sharp white wing patches. **Voice:** Usually silent. **Status:** Rare in summer (Apr-Oct); uncommon in winter (Nov-Mar). **Habitat:** SUMMER: Upper Gila River. WINTER: Large lakes; usually in valleys lacking dense human settlement, especially San Rafael Grasslands and Sulphur Springs Valley. **Behavior:** In winter eats carrion and hunts waterfowl. Breeding birds specialize on fish. **Noteworthy:** Virtually all fledged Arizona Bald Eagles that survive to adulthood return to breed. In 2012 there were 66 Arizona breeding territories.

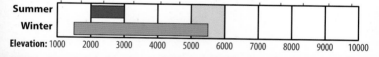

GOLDEN EAGLE, *Aquila chrysaetos*

Description: 30", wingspan 80". **Very large raptor** with relatively small head; **golden crown and nape**. ADULT FLIGHT: Long, all-dark wings held nearly flat. IMMATURE FLIGHT: White tail with broad black band at tip; usually large white wing "diamonds." **Similar Species:** Immature Bald Eagle (above) lacks crisp black terminal band on white tail and has mottled white wings. **Voice:** Usually silent. **Status:** Uncommon resident. **Habitat:** Deserts and valleys to mountain coniferous forest. **Behavior:** Hunts open country for rabbits and other small mammals. Builds and reuses large, bulky nests on cliff ledges. **Noteworthy:** Golden Eagles do not breed in drought years with limited rabbit availability.

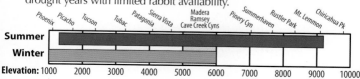

Female

Male

NORTHERN HARRIER, *Circus cyaneus*

Description: 18", wingspan 43". Small head with **owl-like facial disk**. MALE: Gull-like pattern of gray above and white below with some rusty spotting. FEMALE: Brown, with streaked underparts. JUVENILE: Brown; pale rusty underparts contrast with the dark head. FLIGHT: **Long wings held slightly above horizontal; white band across rump**.

Similar Species: Larger-headed Short-eared Owl (p. 173) lacks conspicuous white rump band; in flight wider wings not held above horizontal.

Voice: Usually silent in our area.

Status: Common in winter (Nov-Mar) and fairly common migrant (Apr-mid May and mid Jul-Oct); casual in summer (mid May-mid Jul). **Habitat:** Valley grasslands, pastures, fields, and marshes. Whitewater Draw Wildlife Area in the Sulphur Springs Valley probably hosts the largest wintering population.

Behavior: Usually flies very low and buoyantly over the ground while hunting for mice, small birds, and other vertebrates. Takes low perches on the ground, fence posts, or small trees. Highly nomadic species; population density is relative to prey abundance. Roosts communally on the ground in winter.

Noteworthy: Fledglings discovered east of the Chiricahua Mountains in 2005 represented the first proof of a successful nesting from SE Arizona since 1890. Research indicates that unlike other hawks, Northern Harriers rely on their acute sense of hearing, as well as keen vision, to locate prey.

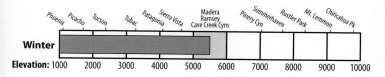

	Phoenix	Picacho	Tucson	Tubac	Patagonia	Sierra Vista	Madera Ramsey Cave Creek Cyns	Pinery Cyn	Summerhaven	Rustler Park	Mt. Lemmon	Chiricahua Pk
Winter												

Elevation: 1000 2000 3000 4000 5000 6000 7000 8000 9000 10000

Sharp-shinned Hawk

Sharp-shinned Hawk Juvenile

Cooper's Hawk

Cooper's Hawk Juvenile

SHARP-SHINNED HAWK, *Accipiter striatus*

Description: Male: 10″, female: 14″, wingspan 20-28″. Small-headed bird-hawk, **straw-thin legs, square-ended tail**. ADULT: Black cap does not contrast with slate-gray upperparts. JUVENILE: Coarse reddish-brown streaks below. FLIGHT: Head barely projects beyond wings. **Similar Species:** Male Cooper's Hawk (below) has proportionately larger head, thicker legs, and rounded tail tip. Immature has narrow streaks on breast. **Voice:** Series of *kew* notes. **Status:** Rare in summer (May-Jul); uncommon in winter (Aug-Apr). **Habitat:** SUMMER: Mountain coniferous forest and upper stream groves. WINTER: Valley groves and lower mountain canyons. **Behavior:** Cat-like when it hunts small birds, approaching stealthily, then capturing its prey with a burst of speed. **Noteworthy:** Female Sharp-shins weigh nearly twice as much as males.

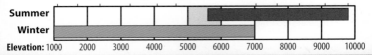

Summer									
Winter									
Elevation: 1000	2000	3000	4000	5000	6000	7000	8000	9000	10000

COOPER'S HAWK, *Accipiter cooperii*

Description: Male: 14″, female: 20″, wingspan 29-37″. Medium-sized bird-hawk with **rounded tail-tip**. ADULT: Black cap contrasts with blue-gray upperparts. JUVENILE: Thin dark streaks on white underparts. FLIGHT: Head projects well beyond wings. **Similar Species:** Female Sharp-shinned Hawk (above) has smaller head, thinner legs, and relatively shorter, square-ended tail. Immature is coarsely streaked. Larger Northern Goshawk (p. 87) has obvious white eyebrow. **Voice:** Series of *kek kek kek kek* notes. **Status:** Fairly common resident. **Habitat:** Urban areas; valley, foothill, and mountain canyon groves. **Behavior:** Small mammals constitute about 30 percent of diet in Arizona. **Noteworthy:** The Cooper's Hawk population in Tucson, over 300, is very high for the U.S.

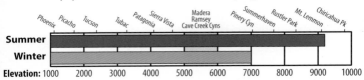

Phoenix	Picacho	Tucson	Tubac	Patagonia	Sierra Vista	Madera Ramsey Cave Creek Cyns	Pinery Cyn	Summerhaven	Rustler Park	Mt. Lemmon	Chiricahua Pk
Summer											
Winter											

Elevation: 1000	2000	3000	4000	5000	6000	7000	8000	9000	10000

Juvenile

NORTHERN GOSHAWK, *Accipiter gentilis*

Description: Male: 21", female: 26", wingspan 41-46". **Large**, long-tailed bird-hawk with **obvious white eyebrow**. ADULT: Thick white eyebrow bordered by dark crown and dark gray eyestripe; gray upperparts; finely gray-barred breast; long, indistinctly banded gray tail. JUVENILE: Pale brown head with bold white eyebrow; speckled brown upperparts; underparts buffy with dense, dark brown streaking; heavily streaked undertail coverts.

Similar Species: Smaller Cooper's Hawk (p. 85) lacks bold white eyebrow. Adult Cooper's is rusty-barred below and juvenile lacks undertail streaking. Similar-sized immature Red-tailed Hawk (p. 95) has much boxier profile, shorter tail, and lacks the white eyebrow.

Voice: Call at nest is deliberate, strident *gii gii gii gii gii* notes.

Status: Rare resident. **Habitat:** Mountain forests and canyon groves with tall timber. May hunt in the desert and grassland surrounding the mountains. Casual migrant through valleys. The Huachuca and Chiricahua Mountains produce the majority of Goshawk sightings in our area.

Behavior: Hunts large birds and mammals, including Band-tailed Pigeons, Mourning Doves, Steller's Jays, Northern Flickers, squirrels, and cottontails. Prefers mature forests with large trees and open understories for nesting. Aggressively defends nest and has injured humans who approached too near.

Noteworthy: Although primarily forest raptors, Goshawks may hunt a mile or more into the desert or grassland surrounding the mountains in SE Arizona. By weight Northern Goshawk is the largest accipiter in the world.

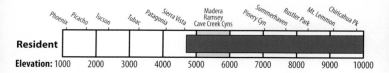

Common Black-Hawk

Adult

Juvenile

Zone-tailed Hawk

Adult

Juvenile

COMMON BLACK-HAWK, *Buteogallus anthracinus*

Description: 21", wingspan 50". Bulky with **long yellow legs**. ADULT: Black with **one broad white tail band**. JUVENILE: Thick black moustache; striped below. FLIGHT: "Flying umbrella" silhouette. **Similar Species:** Zone-tailed Hawk (below) lankier with multiple white tail bands. **Voice:** Whistled, complaining *wink wink wink oo-wink wink* in series. **Status:** Uncommon summer resident (Mar-Oct). **Habitat:** Valley, foothill, and mountain canyons with cottonwood and sycamore groves and permanent water. In SE Arizona most common in Aravaipa Canyon. In mid-March, Black-Hawk migration moves north along the Santa Cruz River past the Tubac Bridge. **Behavior:** Hunts frogs and small fish from stream banks. **Noteworthy:** Flight pattern reminiscent of Black Vulture.

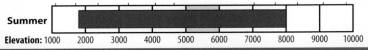

Summer									
Elevation: 1000	2000	3000	4000	5000	6000	7000	8000	9000	10000

ZONE-TAILED HAWK, *Buteo albonotatus*

Description: 20", wingspan 51". Slim and black with **multiple white tail bands**. ADULT: Two or three white tail bands. JUVENILE: Speckled white below; many thin tail bands. FLIGHT: Heavily checkered flight feathers. **Similar Species:** Common Black-Hawk (above) has very broad wings and much shorter, fan-shaped tail showing–in adults–one white tail band. **Voice:** Long *kreeeeeah* scream. **Status:** Uncommon in summer (mid Mar-mid Sep); rare in winter (mid Sep-mid Mar). **Habitat:** SUMMER: Desert washes to mountain coniferous forest, especially riparian groves. WINTER: Principally Tucson area. **Behavior:** Similarity to Turkey Vulture in flight seemingly lulls lizards, birds, and small mammals into complacency. Nests high in one of the tallest trees in its territory. **Noteworthy:** Occasionally soars with Turkey Vultures.

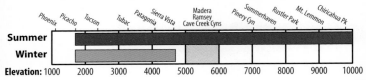

Phoenix	Picacho	Tucson	Tubac	Patagonia	Sierra Vista	Madera Ramsey Cave Creek Cyns	Pinery Cyn	Summerhaven	Rustler Park	Mt. Lemmon	Chiricahua Pk
Summer											
Winter											
Elevation: 1000	2000	3000	4000	5000	6000	7000	8000	9000	10000		

Harris's Hawk

Harris's Hawk
Juvenile

Harris's Hawk

Gray Hawk

Gray Hawk
Juvenile

Gray Hawk

HARRIS'S HAWK, *Parabuteo unicinctus*

Description: 21", wingspan 46". Chocolate-brown hawk with rufous shoulders and thighs; **white at base and tip of tail**. JUVENILE: Mottled chest and belly. FLIGHT: White base of tail; chestnut wing-linings. **Similar Species:** Zone-tailed Hawk (p. 89) is black and has multiple white tail bands. **Voice:** Sore-throated *kaarrrh* and *ayeh* notes. **Status:** Fairly common resident. **Habitat:** Sonoran and Chihuahuan Desert scrub and valley grasslands, less common farther east. Found in large city parks and on golf courses in Tucson and Phoenix. **Behavior:** Hunts reptiles, birds, and small mammals. Two or more Harris's may hunt cooperatively and use relays to run down rabbits. **Noteworthy:** Harris's Hawks form social aggregations in fall and winter that may number up to 18 birds.

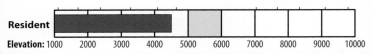

Resident

Elevation: 1000 2000 3000 4000 5000 6000 7000 8000 9000 10000

GRAY HAWK, *Buteo plagiatus*

Description: 17", wingspan 36". Small hawk with large, **dark eye** and striking **black and white tail bands**. ADULT: Entirely gray. JUVENILE: White face with bold black eyestripe and moustache. FLIGHT: Several flaps then a glide like Cooper's Hawk. **Similar Species:** Cooper's Hawk (p. 85) has lemon or orange-colored eyes and low contrast tail bands. **Voice:** Piercing whistle *wee-ah, wee-ah* and shrill, drawn-out *kreeeeeh*. **Status:** Fairly common in summer (Mar-mid Oct); rare in winter (mid Oct-Feb). **Habitat:** River valley and foothill canyon cottonwood groves. **Behavior:** Ambushes lizards and birds in trees. **Noteworthy:** Research indicates there are approximately 80 pairs of Gray Hawks in SE Arizona.

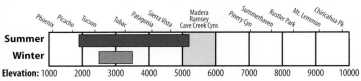

Summer

Winter

Elevation: 1000 2000 3000 4000 5000 6000 7000 8000 9000 10000

Swainson's Hawk light morph

Juvenile

Swainson's Hawk

Short-tailed Hawk

SWAINSON'S HAWK, *Buteo swainsoni*

Description: 21", wingspan 52". Hawk with **long, narrow, pointed wings**. ADULT: **Thick dark bib**. JUVENILE: Thick dark moustache extends to sides of chest. FLIGHT: **"Reversed" wing pattern** with dark flight feathers and either ivory or–less frequently–cinnamon wing linings. Wings held in shallow "V". **Similar Species:** Smaller Short-tailed Hawk (below) has compact shape, and rounded–not pointed–wings. **Voice:** Shrill *weee-a*. **Status:** Fairly common in summer (Mar-Oct). **Habitat:** Desertscrub mixed with grasses, valley grassland, and large fields and pastures. **Behavior:** Largely insectivorous but takes mammals and reptiles during breeding season. **Noteworthy:** Dark morphs are casual in SE Arizona.

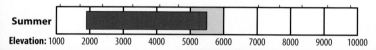

Summer									
Elevation: 1000	2000	3000	4000	5000	6000	7000	8000	9000	10000

SHORT-TAILED HAWK, *Buteo brachyurus*

Description: 17", wingspan 38". Small hawk with **big head**; off-white forehead and lores; wingtips reach to tail tip. LIGHT MORPH: **Dark helmet**. DARK MORPH: Blackish overall. FLIGHT: Often soars at great altitude on broad, black-trimmed wings with pale ovals at base of primaries; low contrast tail-barring with broad, dark subterminal band. **Similar Species:** Larger light morph Swainson's Hawk (above) has dark bib across chest. **Voice:** High, thin, dying *keee-h*. **Status:** Rare in summer (Apr-Oct); accidental in winter (Nov-Apr). **Habitat:** SUMMER: Mountain coniferous forest, especially Chiricahua Mountains. WINTER: Has occurred in Tucson. **Behavior:** Stoops from great heights on birds perched in treetops. **Noteworthy:** In Arizona most records pertain to light morph birds. First record of Short-tailed Hawk in Arizona came from Chiricahuas Mountains in 1985.

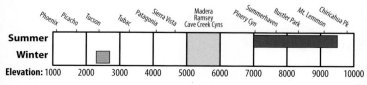

Phoenix	Picacho	Tucson	Tubac	Patagonia	Sierra Vista	Madera Ramsey Cave Creek Cyns	Pinery Cyn	Summerhaven	Rustler Park	Mt. Lemmon	Chiricahua Pk
Summer											
Winter											

Elevation: 1000	2000	3000	4000	5000	6000	7000	8000	9000	10000

"Fuertes's"
Adult

"Western"
Adult

"Western"
Juvenile

"Rufous"
Adult

Western

RED-TAILED HAWK, *Buteo jamaicensis*

Description: 20", wingspan 50". Common, bulky, broad-winged hawk with **broad tail, usually coppery-red in adults. Mottled upperparts** and **belly band** diagnostic when present. Many color morphs exist. "WESTERN" ADULT: Dark throat; plumage ground colors include whitish, buffy, rufous, and blackish morphs. Belly usually heavily streaked; solid black in dark morphs. "FUERTES'S" ADULT: Underparts and underwings whitish with belly streaking fine, faint, or absent. "RUFOUS" ADULT: Very dark overall with rufous chest and undertail coverts; typical red tail. "HARLAN'S" ADULT: Black with white streaks on chest; whitish tail with diffuse dusky tip. JUVENILE: Finely-barred tail. FLIGHT: All but blackest dark morphs show **dark shoulder bars** on the underwings.

Similar Species: Light morph Ferruginous Hawk (p. 97) has rufous shoulders and back, and fully feathered reddish leggings. Dark morph Ferruginous lacks white-streaked chest of "Harlan's" Red-tails.

Voice: Typical call is harsh, drawn-out scream *kreeeahh*.

Status: Common resident, most common in winter (Sep-Apr), when migrants augment resident population. "Harlan's" race rare in winter. **Habitat:** Most abundant in valleys, but widespread in all habitats from the desert floor to open mountain forests.

Behavior: Opportunistic; hunts either by pouncing on prey from an elevated perch or stooping from flight. Courting birds may fly in tandem with legs outstretched, lock talons, and perform acrobatic dives and rolls. Nests in trees, saguaros, utility poles, or on cliffs.

Noteworthy: During winter it is estimated that four Red-tails per mile occur along valley highways in SE Arizona.

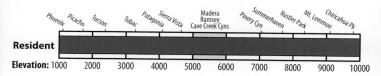

	Phoenix	Picacho	Tucson	Tubac	Patagonia	Sierra Vista	Madera Ramsey Cave Creek Cyns	Pinery Cyn	Summerhaven	Rustler Park	Mt. Lemmon	Chiricahua Pk
Resident												
Elevation:	1000	2000	3000	4000	5000	6000	7000	8000	9000	10000

Ferruginous Hawk

Light

Dark

**Rough-legged Hawk
Juvenile**

Rough-legged Hawk

FERRUGINOUS HAWK, *Buteo regalis*

Description: 23", wingspan 56". **Largest buteo**; large bill. Two color morphs. LIGHT ADULT: Gray head; **rufous back** and shoulders; **reddish leggings**; pale tail with reddish tinge. DARK ADULT: Entirely gray tail. IMMATURE: Like adult, but reduced red highlights. FLIGHT: Feathered red legs form contrasting "V" against white tail. **Similar Species:** Smaller Red-tailed Hawk (p. 95) usually has dark head, dark belly band, rufous tail–or finely banded tail in immatures, and lacks dark leggings. **Voice:** Shrill *keeerrrr*. **Status:** Uncommon in winter (Oct-Apr). **Habitat:** Valley grasslands and fields. **Behavior:** Usual prey is cotton rats and gophers. Often perches on the ground. **Noteworthy:** About 5% of Arizona Ferruginous Hawks are dark morph. Eliminating prairie dogs from SE Arizona in the 1930s seemingly spelled the end of breeding here.

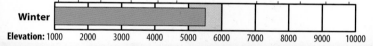

Winter									
Elevation: 1000	2000	3000	4000	5000	6000	7000	8000	9000	10000

ROUGH-LEGGED HAWK, *Buteo lagopus*

Description: 21", wingspan 53". **Large buteo**; small bill; **white tail with wide black subterminal band**. ADULT: Pale head; variably streaked pale breast; often a dark "cummerbund." JUVENILE: Like adult but subterminal tail band dusky. FLIGHT: Underwings white with **black wrist**. **Similar Species:** "Harlan's" Red-tailed Hawk (p. 95) and dark morph Ferruginous Hawk (above) lack large black wrist marks and broad black tail band. **Voice:** Usually silent in winter. **Status:** Rare in winter (Nov-Mar). **Habitat:** Desertscrub; valley grasslands and fields. **Behavior:** Primarily feeds on small rodents; will eat carrion. **Noteworthy:** SE Arizona is the southernmost limit of Rough-legged's usual winter range.

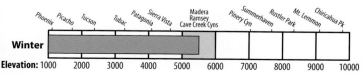

	Phoenix	Picacho	Tucson	Tubac	Patagonia	Sierra Vista	Madera Ramsey Cave Creek Cyns	Pinery Cyn	Summerhaven	Rustler Park	Mt. Lemmon	Chiricahua Pk
Winter												
Elevation: 1000	2000		3000	4000	5000		6000	7000	8000	9000		10000

Description: 23", wingspan 50". Large, brownish-black falcon of the subtropics. **Naked red foreface, long white neck**, and **long naked legs**. JUVENILE: Brown. FLIGHT: "Flying compass" with four points of white on the neck, near wingtips, and at base of tail.

Similar Species: Turkey Vulture (p. 75) has entirely naked red head, lacks short crest, and has no true white on body or wings.

Voice: Sputtering *purrrt purrrt, pur-rrtt.*

Status: Uncommon resident. **Habitat:** Lower western valleys of the Sonoran Desert. Best locations include the Santa Cruz Flats and Tohono O'odham tribal lands west of Tucson. Strays occur annually along the upper Santa Cruz River south of Tucson; accidental in the southern Sulphur Springs Valley.

Behavior: With bare facial skin and long legs, Caracaras are well adapted for scavenging. They are even capable of driving vultures off carrion. Caracaras are known to follow highways, especially early in the morning, apparently looking for overnight road kills. Flies low, and may take reptiles and small mammals by surprise. Prey remains at some nests in Arizona show a strong predilection for a diet of Horned Lizards. Nests are frequently located in the lower arms of a saguaro cactus, usually below a height of 15 feet.

Noteworthy: Researchers have estimated the Crested Caracara population in Arizona numbers only 20-25 pairs. Winter flocks in the Santa Cruz Flats often number from 5-10 Caracaras and are sometimes larger.

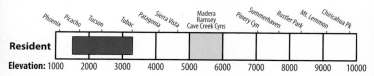

	Phoenix	Picacho	Tucson	Tubac	Patagonia	Sierra Vista	Madera Ramsey Cave Creek Cyns	Pinery Cyn	Summerhaven	Rustler Park	Mt. Lemmon	Chiricahua Pk
Resident												
Elevation:	1000	2000	3000	4000	5000	6000	7000	8000	9000	10000

American Kestrel
Male

American Kestrel
Female

"Prairie" Merlin
Male

"Taiga" Merlin
Female

AMERICAN KESTREL, *Falco sparverius*

Description: 10″, wingspan 21″. Slim little falcon with **two vertical face stripes; red tail**. MALE: Blue-gray wings. FEMALE: Larger; rusty-barred wings, back, and tail. FLIGHT: Frequently hovers; underwings whitish. **Similar Species:** Merlin (below) shows only one facial stripe and lacks red tail. **Voice:** Rapid *kli kli kli* notes. **Status:** Uncommon in summer (mid Apr-mid Aug); common when migrants swell population in winter (mid Aug-mid Apr). **Habitat:** Open deserts; valley fields, pastures, and grasslands; mountain burns. **Behavior:** Takes open perches; often hovers hunting insects, small birds, and mice. Nests in holes in saguaros and trees, burrows in banks, cracks in cliffs, and under palm fronds. **Noteworthy:** Most abundant falcon in Arizona and North America.

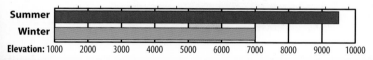

Summer									
Winter									
Elevation: 1000	2000	3000	4000	5000	6000	7000	8000	9000	10000

MERLIN, *Falco columbarius*

Description: 11″, wingspan 23″. Boxy little falcon with **thin eyebrow** and **one indistinct vertical face stripe**; narrowly gray-banded dark tail. MALE: Upperparts gray. FEMALE: Upperparts brown. FLIGHT: Powerful, direct, and rapid; underwings dark. **Similar Species:** Sharp-shinned Hawk (p. 85) has round head and wings, broadly gray-banded dark tail. **Voice:** Usually silent in winter. **Status:** Uncommon in winter (mid Sep-Apr). **Habitat:** Valley grasslands and farms, especially near ponds. **Behavior:** Perches within trees. Overtakes birds and small mammals with speed. Hunts bats at dusk. **Noteworthy:** Two races winter in SE Arizona: pale blue male or brown female "Prairie," *F. c. richardsonii*, and slate-gray male or dark brown female "Taiga," *F. c. columbarius*.

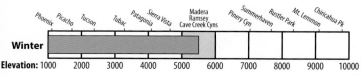

Phoenix	Picacho	Tucson	Tubac	Patagonia	Sierra Vista	Madera Ramsey Cave Creek Cyns	Pinery Cyn	Summerhaven	Rustler Park	Mt. Lemmon	Chiricahua Pk

Winter									
Elevation: 1000	2000	3000	4000	5000	6000	7000	8000	9000	10000

Peregrine Falcon

Peregrine Falcon Juvenile

Prairie Falcon

Prairie Falcon Juvenile

PEREGRINE FALCON, *Falco peregrinus*

Description: 17", wingspan 41". Husky, **helmet-headed** falcon. ADULT: Slate-gray above; black-barred below. JUVENILE: Sooty brown above; heavily streaked below. FLIGHT: Uniform gray underwings concolor with breast. **Similar Species:** Sandy-brown Prairie Falcon (below) has pale eyebrow; thin moustache; black "wingpits" in flight. **Voice:** Strident, harsh *weh weh weh*. **Status:** Uncommon in summer (mid Apr-Aug); more numerous but still uncommon in winter (Sep-mid Apr). **Habitat:** SUMMER: Mountains, especially in cliff areas near water. WINTER: Deserts and valleys, especially near water. **Behavior:** Aerial hunter, power-diving on birds at speeds exceeding 100 mph. Nests on cliff ledges. **Noteworthy:** Although perhaps half of the approximately 300 pairs nesting in Arizona are found within the Grand Canyon, a large concentration also occurs in SE Arizona.

Summer									
Winter									
Elevation: 1000	2000	3000	4000	5000	6000	7000	8000	9000	10000

PRAIRIE FALCON, *Falco mexicanus*

Description: 16", wingspan 40". Lanky, long-tailed falcon with **pale eyebrow** and **thin moustache.** ADULT: Sandy-brown above; spotted below. JUVENILE: Dark brown above; streaked below. FLIGHT: **Black "wingpits"** contrast with pale breast. **Similar Species:** Peregrine Falcon (above) has solid black "helmet"; lacks black "wingpits" in flight. **Voice:** Strident *kree kree kree*. **Status:** Rare in summer (May-Jul); uncommon in winter (Aug-Apr). **Habitat:** SUMMER: Cliffs near desert and valley grassland. WINTER: Open desertscrub; valley grasslands and fields, especially near water. **Behavior:** Hunts for birds and small mammals by overtaking them with speed. **Noteworthy:** Prairies tend to nest on lower cliffs in more arid areas than Peregrine Falcons.

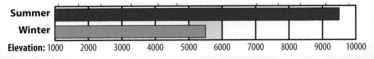

Phoenix	Picacho	Tucson	Tubac	Patagonia	Sierra Vista	Madera Ramsey Cave Creek Cyns	Pinery Cyn	Summerhaven	Rustler Park	Mt. Lemmon	Chiricahua Pk

Summer									
Winter									
Elevation: 1000	2000	3000	4000	5000	6000	7000	8000	9000	10000

Virginia Rail

Sora

VIRGINIA RAIL, *Rallus limicola*

Description: 9.5". Small marsh bird with **long, thin, slightly downcurved bill**; red legs. ADULT: Red bill; cinnamon underparts. JUVENILE: Blackish bill; sooty breast. **Similar Species:** Sora (below) has short, thick yellow bill and olive legs. **Voice:** Male gives hard *gik gik gik gidik gidik gidik* notes followed by accelerating series *wep wepwepwepwepppprrr.* **Status:** Uncommon resident, more widespread in winter. **Habitat:** Marshes and ponds and lakes with reeds and cattails. **Behavior:** Eats aquatic invertebrates, small fish, and seeds. May feed on open mudflats, but usually shy and hidden. Slinks through reeds when disturbed; seldom flies. **Noteworthy:** Rails are indeed "thin as a rail," having a narrow shape and flexible vertebrae adapted for maneuvering through reeds.

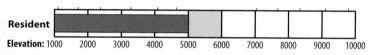

Resident

Elevation: 1000   2000   3000   4000   5000   6000   7000   8000   9000   10000

SORA, *Porzana carolina*

Description: 8.75". Plump little marsh bird with **stubby yellow bill**; olive legs. ADULT: Black foreface surrounding bill; gray breast. JUVENILE: Dull buffy breast. **Similar Species:** Virginia Rail (above) has long, curved bill and red legs. **Voice:** A rising *ko-WEE* followed by long squealing whinny. **Status:** Fairly common fall, winter, and spring (Aug–mid May); rare in summer (mid May–Jul). **Habitat:** Marshes and ponds and lakes with reeds and cattails. **Behavior:** Feeds primarily on seeds. May feed on mudflats and open shorelines, but usually shy and hidden. Slinks through reeds when disturbed; seldom flies. **Noteworthy:** Rails are usually first detected–and identified–by their distinctive calls.

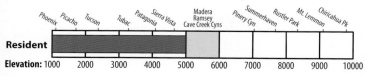

Phoenix   Picacho   Tucson   Tubac   Patagonia   Sierra Vista   Madera Ramsey Cave Creek Cyns   Pinery Cyn   Summerhaven   Rustler Park   Mt. Lemmon   Chiricahua Pk

Resident

Elevation: 1000   2000   3000   4000   5000   6000   7000   8000   9000   10000

Purple Gallinule

American Coot

Common Moorhen
Breeding

Common Moorhen
Juvenile

PURPLE GALLINULE, *Porphyrio martinicus*

Description: 12.5". Glossy purple and green marsh bird with **baby-blue frontal shield**; white undertail coverts; yellow legs. JUVENILE: Thick olive bill; buffy overall with bluish-green tinge on wings. **Similar Species:** Larger Common Moorhen (below) has white flank line and bright red frontal shield. **Status:** Casual in summer (mid Jun-early Oct). **Habitat:** Marshes and ponds with reedy edges, primarily in Tucson basin.

AMERICAN COOT, *Fulica americana*

Description: 15". Stocky, dull **black** aquatic bird with stout **white bill**. ADULT: Small, diamond-shaped maroon frontal shield. JUVENILE: Pale gray below; downy young have blood-red head markings. **Similar Species:** Pied-billed Grebe (p. 53) is colored plain, tawny-brown. **Status:** Common resident; abundant in winter. **Habitat:** Ponds or lakes with permanent water. **Behavior:** Forages in water, on mudflats, and grazes on land adjacent to water. Nests in marshes. **Noteworthy:** American Coots dominate Common Moorhens and Purple Gallinules.

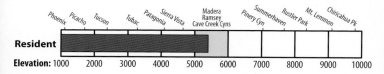

	Phoenix	Picacho	Tucson	Tubac	Patagonia	Sierra Vista	Madera Ramsey Cave Creek Cyns	Pinery Cyn	Summerhaven	Rustler Park	Mt. Lemmon	Chiricahua Pk
Resident												
Elevation:	1000	2000	3000	4000	5000	6000	7000	8000	9000	10000

COMMON GALLINULE, *Gallinula Galeata*

Description: 14". Brown-backed marsh bird with **bright red frontal shield** and mostly red bill; **broken white line on flank**. JUVENILE: No frontal shield; dusky bill. **Similar Species:** American Coot (above) lacks white flank line and bright red frontal shield. **Status:** Fairly common but local resident. **Habitat:** Marshes and ponds with reeds and cattails. **Behavior:** Forages in water and on mudflats, and grazes on land adjacent to water. **Noteworthy:** Unlike Coots, Moorhens and Gallinules spend most of their time under cover.

SANDHILL CRANE, *Grus canadensis*

Description: 41-46", wingspan 72-84". **Very tall** wading bird with **long feathers on lower back forming a "bustle."** ADULT: Entirely gray with red crown; white cheek patch; most variably stained rusty on body. JUVENILE: Lacks red crown and whitish cheek. FLIGHT: Neck and legs fully extended.

Similar Species: Smaller Great Blue Heron (p. 65) lacks red crown, lacks "bustle," flies with neck folded back on body. Larger Whooping Crane is all white with a red crown and black moustache. All wandering Whoopers in SE Arizona were reported prior to 2000, and apparently stemmed from now defunct USFWS reintroduction efforts.

Voice: Loud, gurgling *hgarrrr hgarrr* bugles often carry for several miles.

Status: Common in winter (Oct-Mar). **Habitat:** Principally the Sulphur Springs Valley, especially at Whitewater Draw Wildlife Area, Lake Cochise, and Apache Station Wildlife Area.

Behavior: Sandhills primarily forage for waste corn in stubble fields during their stay in SE Arizona. Daily routine includes loafing from mid-day to late afternoon at the same shallow ponds used for evening roosts. Migrating flocks occasionally soar above 10,000' over Chiricahua Mountains.

Noteworthy: Even in midwinter Sandhill Cranes perform elaborate courtship displays. Paired birds face each other, bow, and then leap repeatedly into the air while calling with wings spread. First Sulphur Springs Valley census in 1970 showed approximately 850 birds; by January 2010 population had grown to 40,500 Sandhills.

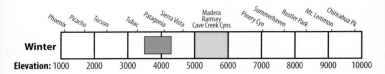

Black-bellied Plover
Juvenile

American Golden-Plover
Non-breeding

BLACK-BELLIED PLOVER, *Pluvialis squatarola*

Description: 11.5". Largest plover; big head, thick bill, and **white tail**. BREEDING: Ermine cape divides frosted white back from coal black face and underparts. NON-BREEDING: Neutral gray upperparts, white belly. FLIGHT: **Bold white wingstripe, black "armpits,"** white rump and tail. **Similar Species:** In flight smaller American Golden-Plover (below) lacks strong white wingstripe, black "armpits," and pure white rump. **Voice:** High, plaintive whistle *plee-oo-EE*. **Status:** Uncommon to rare migrant (Apr-May, Aug-Oct), usually seen as singles. **Habitat:** Valley ponds and lakes with sandy or muddy shorelines. **Behavior:** Feeds by sight; sprints, stops, and stabs for food. **Noteworthy:** Usually seen in drab non-breeding plumage, Black-bellied Plovers are known as Gray Plovers in the eastern hemisphere.

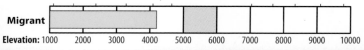

Migrant

Elevation: 1000   2000   3000   4000   5000   6000   7000   8000   9000   10000

AMERICAN GOLDEN-PLOVER, *Pluvialis dominica*

Description: 10.25". Delicate, small-headed, thin-billed plover; **gray tail**. BREEDING: White "question marks" on face end in blobs on chest; golden-shingled back. NON-BREEDING: Pale fringes on back feathers. FLIGHT: Faint white wingstripe, **smoky-gray underwings, dark rump and tail**. **Similar Species:** Black-bellied Plover (above) has white tail; in flight shows black "armpits" and white wingstripe. Pacific Golden-Plover (accidental) shows three—not four—primary tips. **Voice:** Sharp *kee-ee?* queries. **Status:** Casual migrant (mid May-Jun, mid Sep-mid-Nov), usually seen as singles. **Habitat:** Valley ponds and lakes with sandy or muddy shorelines. Most often reported from Lake Cochise. **Behavior:** Feeds by sight; sprints, stops, and stabs for food. **Noteworthy:** Arizona birds are usually in non-breeding plumage.

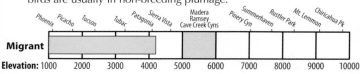

Migrant

Elevation: 1000   2000   3000   4000   5000   6000   7000   8000   9000   10000

Snowy Plover Non-breeding

Snowy Plover Breeding

Semipalmated Plover Non-breeding

Semipalmated Plover Breeding

SNOWY PLOVER, *Charadrius nivosus*

Description: 6.5". Small **pale** plover with **thin black bill; incomplete breast band; dark legs.** BREEDING: Black forehead, ear patches, and black "lapels." NON-BREEDING: Lacks black accents. **Similar Species:** Semipalmated Plover (below) has brown upperparts, complete dark breast band, and orange legs. **Voice:** Clear *peep* notes and soft *chew-y* calls. **Status:** Rare and irregular in summer (Apr-mid Oct). **Habitat:** Valley ponds and lakes with sandy, muddy, or barren shorelines. **Behavior:** Uses run-and-stop technique to catch insects. **Noteworthy:** Snowy Plovers are most apt to breed in Arizona after a very wet winter. Has bred at Lake Cochise. In 2012 Snowy Plovers were splt as a full species from Old World Kentish Plovers.

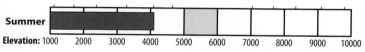

Summer									
Elevation: 1000	2000	3000	4000	5000	6000	7000	8000	9000	10000

SEMIPALMATED PLOVER, *Charadrius semipalmatus*

Description: 7.25". Small **brown** plover with stubby, **orange-based bill; complete breast band; orange legs.** BREEDING: Black headband envelops eye; black-tipped, bright orange bill. NON-BREEDING: White eyebrow; dull orange-based bill. **Similar Species:** Snowy Plover (above) has gray upperparts, incomplete breast band, black bill, and dark legs. Young Killdeer (p. 115) with a single breast band has very long bill and bluish legs. **Voice:** Silent in our area. **Status:** Uncommon migrant (Apr-mid May and Aug-Oct). **Habitat:** Valley ponds and lakes with sandy, muddy, or barren shorelines. **Behavior:** Uses run-and-stop technique to catch insects. **Noteworthy:** Arizona migrants breed in northern Canada and winter south along the Pacific coast from Mexico to southern South America.

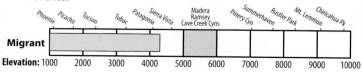

	Phoenix	Picacho	Tucson	Tubac	Patagonia	Sierra Vista	Madera Ramsey Cave Creek Cyns	Pinery Cyn	Summerhaven	Rustler Park	Mt. Lemmon	Chiricahua Pk
Migrant												
Elevation: 1000	2000		3000	4000		5000	6000	7000	8000		9000	10000

113

Killdeer

Mountain Plover
Non-breeding

KILLDEER, *Charadrius vociferus*

Description: 10.5". Dark brown plover with long bill; **two black breast bands**; long tail. FLIGHT: White stripe full length of long wing; **orange rump**. **Similar Species:** JUVENILE: One chest band; absurdly long black legs. Smaller, stubby-billed Semipalmated Plover (p. 113) has only one breast band. **Voice:** Often heard, strident *kee-e or kil-lee* calls. **Status:** Common resident. **Habitat:** Valley fields and pastures, golf courses, ponds and lakes, and broad, sandy riverbeds with water. Population is augmented in winter by northern migrants. **Behavior:** Eats insects it catches on the ground. Nests in gravel, even on Tucson rooftops. Feigns broken wing to distract intruders from nest. **Noteworthy:** Black mottled Killdeer eggs are often invisible against background pebbles.

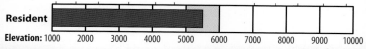

Resident									
Elevation: 1000	2000	3000	4000	5000	6000	7000	8000	9000	10000

MOUNTAIN PLOVER, *Charadrius montanus*

Description: 9". **Plain, tan**, dry-country plover; **long white eyebrows** merge with white forehead. BREEDING: Black forecrown. FLIGHT: White underwings. **Similar Species:** Larger, browner Killdeer (above) has longer tail, double chest bands, and shows orange rump in flight. **Voice:** Usually silent in our area. **Status:** Uncommon in winter (Nov-Mar); flocks range from a few to 200. **Habitat:** Broad, barren valley deserts, tilled fields, and pastures with low, new growth. Best areas are the central Sulphur Springs Valley near Elfrida and sod farms in the Santa Cruz Flats. **Behavior:** Feeds by sight; sprints, stops, and stabs for insects. **Noteworthy:** Mountain Plover is the only North American shorebird that typically never forages, roosts, or breeds on any shore.

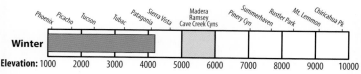

	Phoenix	Picacho	Tucson	Tubac	Patagonia	Sierra Vista	Madera Ramsey Cave Creek Cyns	Pinery Cyn	Summerhaven	Rustler Park	Mt. Lemmon	Chiricahua Pk
Winter												
Elevation: 1000		2000	3000	4000	5000	6000	7000	8000	9000	10000		

Black-necked Stilt Male

American Avocet Breeding Male

American Avocet Non-breeding Male

BLACK-NECKED STILT, *Himantopus mexicanus*

Description: 14″. Black and white shorebird with **needle bill and very long red legs**. **Similar Species:** American Avocet (below) has upturned bill and blue-gray legs. **Voice:** Yapping, often incessant, *wik wik* and *pleunk* notes. **Status:** Fairly common summer resident (Apr-Sep); uncommon, especially in Tucson area, in winter (Oct-Mar). **Habitat:** Valley rivers, ponds and lakes with sandy, muddy, or barren shorelines. **Behavior:** Feeds by picking and probing along open muddy edges of ponds and lakes. Prefers to nest on islands. **Noteworthy:** Populations of Stilts in SE Arizona are growing with increase of man-made habitats. Has bred along the Santa Cruz River at Tucson and at Lake Cochise near Willcox.

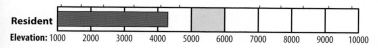

AMERICAN AVOCET, *Recurvirostra americana*

Description: 18″. Black and white shorebird with long, thin **up-turned bill** and long, **blue-gray legs**. BREEDING: Head and neck rich tawny. NON-BREEDING: Head and neck pale gray. **Similar Species:** Black-necked Stilt (above) has straight bill and red legs. **Voice:** Loud resonant *kweep* notes. **Status:** Common local summer resident (Apr-Nov); rare, especially in Tucson area, in winter (Dec-Mar). **Habitat:** Valley rivers, ponds and lakes with sandy, muddy, or barren shorelines. **Behavior:** Filter feeds by sweeping curved bill back and forth underwater. Nests colonially. **Noteworthy:** The first known Arizona nest of American Avocet was at Lake Cochise in 1965, where the present summer population sometimes exceeds 150 birds.

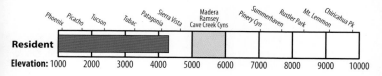

117

Juveniles

Description: 9.5". Yellow-billed tropical shorebird; spindly-legged with **extremely long toes**. ADULT: Black head with bright orange-yellow frontal shield and pale blue patch just above the bill; black neck and underparts; rich chestnut back and wings. JUVENILE: Lacks frontal shield; white eyebrow, face, foreneck, and underparts; dull brown back. FLIGHT: Flashes brilliant **lime-yellow flight feathers**; legs trail behind. Usually lifts both wings simultaneously upon landing.

Similar Species: Juvenile told from other shorebirds by unmarked brown upperparts, lime-yellow flight feathers, and extremely long toes. Adult unmistakable.

Voice: Screechy *eep* notes. Apt to call if startled or put to flight.

Status: Accidental; widely-spaced records for every month but May. **Habitat:** Valley and canyon ponds and lakes with aquatic plants and weedy or grassy banks. Four records for birds seen at Kino Springs and Guevavi Ranch near Nogales (same bird), Arivaca Lake, Casa Grande at a golf course pond, and at the spillway of Patagonia Lake.

Behavior: Forages by walking on lily pads and water hyacinths, distributing its weight over a wide area with its long toes. Frequently lifts both wings and flashes its lime-yellow flight feathers.

Noteworthy: Jacanas have proportionately the longest toes of any bird. Once detected in Arizona, a vagrant Northern Jacana often stays for several weeks or even half a year. Seemingly the same Casa Grande bird returned at least two consecutive winters.

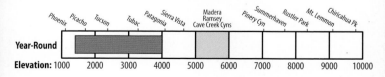

Spotted Sandpiper
Breeding

Spotted Sandpiper
Non-breeding

Solitary Sandpiper
Breeding

Solitary Sandpiper
Juvenile

SPOTTED SANDPIPER, *Actitis macularius*

Description: 7.5". Shorebird with **white eyebrow** and **white shoulder bar; bobs** as it walks. BREEDING: Orange bill; heavy black spotting below. NON-BREEDING: Unspotted underparts. FLIGHT: Stiff, bowed wing beats; white wingstripe. **Similar Species:** Larger, darker Solitary Sandpiper (below) has longer legs and bold white eye-ring; in flight lacks wingstripe and shows barred outer tail. **Voice:** Call is loud whistled *puip*. **Status:** Common migrant (Apr-May and Jul-Oct); uncommon in winter (Nov-Mar); casual in midsummer (Jun). **Habitat:** Desert, valley, foothill, and mountain canyon ponds, lakes, streams, and rivers. **Behavior:** Patrols shorelines searching for insect prey, bobbing almost constantly. **Noteworthy:** Migrant Spotted Sandpipers in breeding plumage are seen in April-May and July-August; fall and winter Spotted Sandpipers in SE Arizona are typically unspotted.

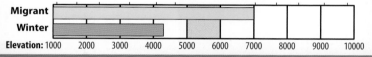

SOLITARY SANDPIPER, *Tringa solitaria*

Description: 8.5". Shorebird with **white eye-ring**; dark **back dotted white**. FLIGHT: Black and white **barred outer tail feathers**; lacks wingstripe. **Similar Species:** Smaller, paler Spotted Sandpiper (above) has shorter legs, white shoulder bar, white eyestripe; in flight shows white wingstripe and lacks barred outer tail. **Voice:** Call is shrill *pee-weet*. **Status:** Uncommon migrant (Apr-May and Jul-Sep). **Habitat:** Valley ponds, small lakes, seasonally flooded puddles, and marshes. **Behavior:** Wades in shallows and stirs mud to bring insects to surface. Bobs less than a Spotted Sandpiper. **Noteworthy:** Usually migrates singly, but aggregations of a dozen or more may appear at limited habitat available in Arizona.

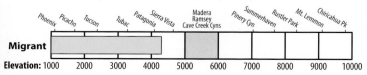

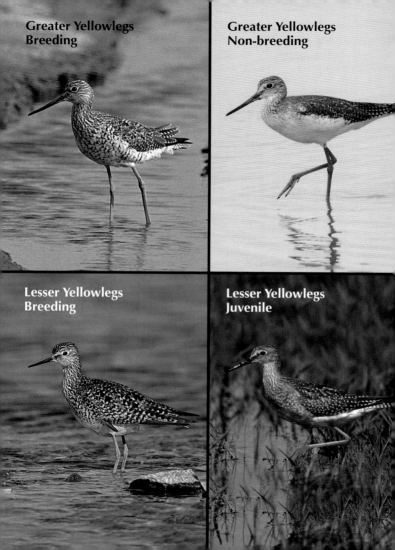

Greater Yellowlegs
Breeding

Greater Yellowlegs
Non-breeding

Lesser Yellowlegs
Breeding

Lesser Yellowlegs
Juvenile

Description: 14". Large, long-necked shorebird with **medium-long, thick-based, subtly upturned bill**; long, yellow legs. FLIGHT: Mostly white rump and tail. **Similar Species:** Smaller Lesser Yellowlegs (below) has short, thin, very straight bill. **Voice:** Emphatic, descending three-noted whistle *TEW-Tew-tew*. **Status:** Uncommon spring (Mar-Apr) and fairly common fall (Jul-Oct) migrant; rare in winter (Nov-Feb). **Habitat:** Valley ponds, lakes, and rivers with sandy, muddy, or barren shorelines. **Behavior:** Active feeder, chases small fish and aquatic invertebrates in shallows. **Noteworthy:** Migrating Greater Yellowlegs, rarely up to about 20 birds, occasionally congregate at the few ponds and lakes in SE Arizona's water-poor valleys.

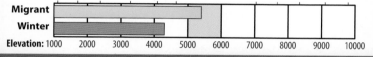

Migrant
Winter
Elevation: 1000 2000 3000 4000 5000 6000 7000 8000 9000 10000

Description: 10.5". Midsized, long-necked shorebird with **short, thin, very straight bill**; long, yellow legs. FLIGHT: Mostly white rump and tail. **Similar Species:** Larger Greater Yellowlegs (above) has longer, slightly upturned bill. Smaller Solitary Sandpiper (p. 121) has bold white eye-ring, shorter, greenish legs; in flight dark rump and central tail. **Voice:** Fluting two-note whistle *tu-tu*, often strung together in a series. **Status:** Uncommon spring (mid Mar-mid Apr) and fairly common fall (mid Jul-mid Oct) migrant. **Habitat:** Valley ponds, lakes, and rivers with sandy, muddy, or barren shorelines. **Behavior:** Although less active than Greater Yellowlegs, often chases small fish and aquatic invertebrates in shallows. **Noteworthy:** In SE Arizona during migration, flocks of Lessers are almost as apt to occur as flocks of Greater Yellowlegs.

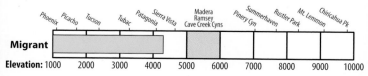

Phoenix Picacho Tucson Tubac Patagonia Sierra Vista Madera Ramsey Cave Creek Cyns Pinery Cyn Summerhaven Rustler Park Mt. Lemmon Chiricahua Pk

Migrant
Elevation: 1000 2000 3000 4000 5000 6000 7000 8000 9000 10000

123

Willet
Non-breeding

Willet

Marbled Godwit

WILLET, *Tringa semipalmata inornata*

Description: 15". Stocky gray shorebird with **stout, straight gray bill** and gray legs. BREEDING: Barred, spotted, and mottled pattern. FLIGHT: **Striking black and white wings**. **Similar Species:** Greater Yellowlegs (p. 123) has bright yellow legs. **Voice:** Excited *pa-whee-whee-whee! pa-whee-whee-whee!* **Status:** Uncommon migrant (Apr-May and mid Jul-Aug). **Habitat:** Valley ponds, lakes, and rivers with sandy, muddy, or barren shorelines. **Behavior:** Forages for aquatic insects and other invertebrates on sandy shores and mudflats. **Noteworthy:** Our larger "Western" Willet (*T. s. inornata*) differs from the eastern subspecies (*T. s. semipalmata*) that breeds on Atlantic and Gulf coasts in having much less patterned breeding plumage.

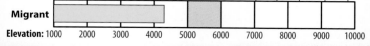

Migrant									
Elevation: 1000	2000	3000	4000	5000	6000	7000	8000	9000	10000

MARBLED GODWIT, *Limosa fedoa*

Description: 18". Large shorebird with pale eyestripe and **long, bicolored, upcurved bill**. BREEDING: Heavily barred below. NON-BREEDING: Pale buff below. FLIGHT: **Cinnamon underwings** and orange inner flight feathers on upperwings. **Similar Species:** Larger Long-billed Curlew (p. 127) has very long, downcurved bill. Similar-sized Whimbrel (p. 127) is much grayer, has bold head stripes, and a downcurved bill. **Voice:** Repeated *ka-wheck* notes. **Status:** Rare spring (mid Apr-May) and uncommon fall migrant (mid Jul-Oct). **Habitat:** Valley ponds and lakes with sandy, muddy, or barren shorelines. **Behavior:** Probes so deeply in shallow water for aquatic insects and other invertebrates that it occasionally submerges its head. **Noteworthy:** Usually seen in flocks along coast in winter, but in SE Arizona often occurs singly or in twosomes.

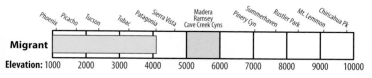

	Phoenix	Picacho	Tucson	Tubac	Patagonia	Sierra Vista	Madera Ramsey Cave Creek Cyns	Pinery Cyn	Summerhaven	Rustler Park	Mt. Lemmon	Chiricahua Pk
Migrant												
Elevation: 1000	2000		3000	4000		5000	6000	7000		8000	9000	10000

Whimbrel

Long-billed Curlew

WHIMBREL, *Numenius phaeopus*

Description: 17". **Large** shorebird with **boldly striped crown** and broad dusky eye-line; **long, downcurved bill**. JUVENILE: Shorter bill. FLIGHT: Underwings dark. **Similar Species:** Larger Long-billed Curlew (below) has unmarked face, longer bill, and cinnamon underwings in flight. Similar-sized Marbled Godwit (p. 125) lacks head stripes and has long, slightly upcurved bill. **Voice:** Vibrato whistle *whi-pi-pi-pi-pi-pi-pi*. **Status:** Casual migrant (Apr-mid Jun and Aug-mid Sep). **Habitat:** Valley ponds and lakes with sandy, muddy, or barren shorelines. **Behavior:** Forages on land in flat open areas for insects and in water for small invertebrates on the surface. **Noteworthy:** Extremely widespread, Whimbrels are known from six continents.

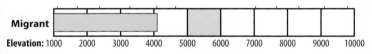

LONG-BILLED CURLEW, *Numenius americanus*

Description: 23". North America's largest shorebird. **Very large**, plain-faced with **very long, downcurved bill**; long-legged. JUVENILE: Shorter bill. FLIGHT: **Underwings bright cinnamon**. **Similar Species:** Smaller Whimbrel (above) has bold crown stripes and shorter bill; lacks cinnamon underwings in flight. **Voice:** Call is loud *cur-lee*. **Status:** Uncommon migrant and winter visitor (July-mid May); rare in early summer (mid May-Jun). **Habitat:** Valley ponds and lakes with sandy, muddy, or barren shorelines. Feeds in barren desert pastures and newly plowed valley fields. **Behavior:** Walks briskly, poking well in front of its shadow with long bill; may probe mud or clods of soft earth. **Noteworthy:** Female curlews are noticeably larger and longer-billed than males.

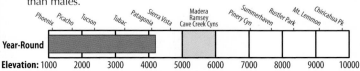

Western Sandpiper
Breeding

Western Sandpiper
Non-breeding

Semipalmated Sandpiper
Non-breeding

Least Sandpiper
Non-breeding

WESTERN SANDPIPER, *Calidris mauri*

Description: 6.5". Small sandpiper with **blackish legs; relatively long bill with slight droop toward fine tip**. BREEDING: Red tints on crown, ears, and base of "shoulder" feathers. **Similar Species:** Semipalmated Sandpiper (below) has short, straight bill; lacks red tints. **Voice:** Tinkling calls or high, scratchy *djeeet* notes. **Status:** Fairly common spring (Apr-mid May) and common fall (Jul-Oct) migrant; casual in winter (Nov-Mar). **Habitat:** Valley ponds, lakes, and rivers with barren shorelines. **Behavior:** Feeds along shorelines probing for small invertebrates. **Noteworthy:** Small *Calidris* sandpipers are collectively known as "peeps."

SEMIPALMATED SANDPIPER, *Calidris pusilla*

Description: 6.25". Small sandpiper with **blackish legs; short, straight bill with blunt tip. Similar Species:** Western Sandpiper (above) has long bill with slight droop toward fine tip; often shows red tints. **Voice:** Rough *churt*. **Status:** Rare migrant (late Apr-May and Jul-mid Sep). **Habitat:** Valley ponds and lakes with barren shorelines. **Behavior:** Feeds along shorelines probing for small invertebrates. **Noteworthy:** Singles join mixed flocks with Western and Least Sandpipers.

LEAST SANDPIPER, *Calidris minutilla*

Description: 6". Small sandpiper with **yellowish legs;** short and thin, slightly arched bill; brownish breast. **Similar Species:** Larger Western (above) and Semipalmated Sandpipers (above) both have black legs. **Voice:** Shrill *jeeet*. **Status:** Common migrant and winter visitor (Jul-May). **Habitat:** Valley ponds, lakes, and rivers with barren shorelines. **Behavior:** Feeds along shorelines probing for small invertebrates. **Noteworthy:** Least is the world's smallest sandpiper.

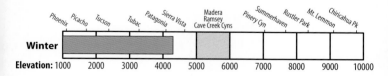

	Phoenix	Picacho	Tucson	Tubac	Patagonia	Sierra Vista	Madera Ramsey Cave Creek Cyns	Pinery Cyn	Summerhaven	Rustler Park	Mt. Lemmon	Chiricahua Pk
Winter												
Elevation:	1000	2000	3000	4000	5000	6000	7000	8000	9000	10000

129

**Baird's Sandpiper
Juvenile**

**Pectoral Sandpiper
Adult**

BAIRD'S SANDPIPER, *Calidris bairdii*

Description: 7.5" Midsized sandpiper with **very long wings extending beyond tail**; dark legs. BREEDING: Big black spots on pale back. JUVENILE: Back appears scaly; breast strongly washed with buff. **Similar Species:** Smaller Semipalmated and Western Sandpipers (p. 129) lack Baird's scaly upperparts, buffy breast, and very long wings. White-rumped Sandpiper (casual May-Jun), similar in size and structure, has red fringes on back, white rump, and streaked flanks. **Voice:** Squealing *kreeeel*. **Status:** Rare spring (mid Apr-mid May) and fairly common fall (Jul-mid Oct) migrant. **Habitat:** Valley ponds and lakes with barren shorelines. **Behavior:** Feeds slowly and deliberately on mudflats and in shallow water. **Noteworthy:** Baird's Sandpipers breed in the high Arctic and winter in southern South America, placing them among the world's longest-distance migrants.

Migrant									
Elevation: 1000	2000	3000	4000	5000	6000	7000	8000	9000	10000

PECTORAL SANDPIPER, *Calidris melanotos*

Description: 8.75". Midsized sandpiper with **heavily streaked breast contrasting sharply with white belly; yellowish legs**. **Similar Species:** Least Sandpiper (p. 129) similar to female Pectoral, but much smaller. Larger Ruff (accidental Oct-Jan) shows pale fringes on black-centered back feathers and has unmarked breast. **Voice:** Rolling *churrrk*. **Status:** Casual spring (Apr-mid May) and uncommon fall (mid Aug-Oct) migrant. **Habitat:** Ponds and lakes, especially with grassy or weedy margins. **Behavior:** Probes for insects in shallow water and on weedy shorelines. **Noteworthy:** The name Pectoral comes from the male's inflatable breast sacs, which it inflates as it hoots over the tundra, flying like a toy schooner.

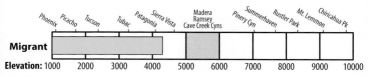

	Phoenix	Picacho	Tucson	Tubac	Patagonia	Sierra Vista	Madera Ramsey Cave Creek Cyns	Pinery Cyn	Summerhaven	Rustler Park	Mt. Lemmon	Chiricahua Pk
Migrant												
Elevation: 1000	2000		3000	4000		5000	6000	7000		8000	9000	10000

Dunlin Breeding

Dunlin Non-breeding

Stilt Sandpiper Breeding

Stilt Sandpiper Juvenile

DUNLIN, *Calidris alpina*

Description: 8.5". Stocky, midsized sandpiper with long, **stout, drooping bill**; blackish legs. BREEDING: Reddish back; black belly. NON-BREEDING: Drab with **brownish breast**. **Similar Species:** Smaller non-breeding Western Sandpiper (p. 129) has shorter bill and cleaner white breast. **Voice:** Flight call is harsh *kreee*. **Status:** Uncommon fall migrant (mid Sep-Nov); rare in winter and spring (Dec-mid May). **Habitat:** Valley ponds, lakes, and rivers with sandy, muddy, or barren shorelines. **Behavior:** Probes and "stitch-feeds" like a miniature sewing machine on shoreline and shallows. **Noteworthy:** Because Dunlins remain in the Arctic to molt after breeding, they arrive in Arizona relatively late in fall in very dull plumage.

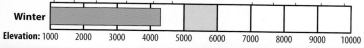

Winter									
Elevation: 1000	2000	3000	4000	5000	6000	7000	8000	9000	10000

STILT SANDPIPER, *Calidris himantopus*

Description: 8.5". Delicate, midsized sandpiper with **thin, drooping bill** and **long, yellow-green legs**. BREEDING: Chestnut ear; scaly, blackish back; heavily barred flanks. NON-BREEDING: Pale unpatterned gray above. JUVENILE: Like non-breeding adult, but back scaly black. **Similar Species:** Larger dowitchers (p. 135) have much straighter and longer bills, and proportionately shorter legs. **Voice:** Flight call is harsh *kreee*. **Status:** Rare spring (mid Apr-mid May) and uncommon fall (mid Jul-mid Oct) migrant. **Habitat:** Valley ponds and lakes with barren shorelines. **Behavior:** Feeds like a dowitcher, but longer legs force its head down lower and its tail up higher. **Noteworthy:** Early fall migrants in Arizona are usually adults in breeding plumage, but by September Stilt Sandpipers lack flank bars.

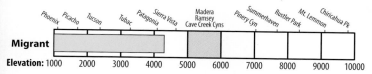

	Phoenix	Picacho	Tucson	Tubac	Patagonia	Sierra Vista	Madera Ramsey Cave Creek Cyns	Pinery Cyn	Summerhaven	Rustler Park	Mt. Lemmon	Chiricahua Pk
Migrant												
Elevation:	1000	2000	3000	4000	5000	6000	7000	8000	9000	10000		

133

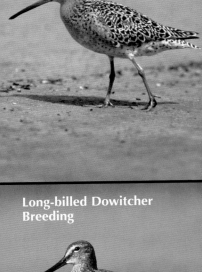

Short-billed Dowitcher Breeding

Short-billed Dowitcher Juvenile

Long-billed Dowitcher Breeding

Long-billed Dowitcher Non-breeding

SHORT-BILLED DOWITCHER, *Limnodromus griseus hendersoni*

Description: 11". Bulky shorebird with **very long, straight bill**. BREEDING: Face and underparts largely chestnut with variably white lower belly; **unmarked foreneck; breast spotted**. NON-BREEDING: Unpatterned gray. JUVENILE: Broad coppery fringes on upperpart feathers; **"tiger" barring on longest visible wing feathers**. FLIGHT: White wedge up lower back. **Similar Species:** Long-billed Dowitcher (below) very similar, but gives sharp *keek* notes. **Voice:** Rapid series of *tu-tu-tu* calls. **Status:** Casual spring (mid Apr-May) and rare fall (mid Jun-mid Oct) migrant. **Habitat:** Valley ponds and lakes with barren shorelines. **Behavior:** Dowitchers employ a distinctive rapid "sewing-machine" probing motion to find invertebrates. **Noteworthy:** In Arizona, most adults migrate June-July; juveniles migrate in August-September.

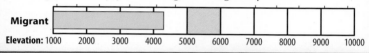

Migrant									
Elevation: 1000	2000	3000	4000	5000	6000	7000	8000	9000	10000

LONG-BILLED DOWITCHER, *Limnodromus scolopaceus*

Description: 11.5". Bulky shorebird with **very long, straight bill**. BREEDING: Face and underparts entirely chestnut; **barred sides of foreneck and breast**. NON-BREEDING: Unpatterned gray. JUVENILE: Narrow rusty fringes on upperpart feathers. FLIGHT: White wedge up lower back. **Similar Species:** Short-billed Dowitcher (above) very similar, but gives rapid *tu-tu-tu* call. **Voice:** Sharp *keek* notes, often in rapid series. **Status:** Fairly common migrant (Apr-May and Aug-Oct); uncommon in winter (Nov-Mar). **Habitat:** Valley ponds, lakes, and rivers with sandy, muddy, or barren shorelines. **Behavior:** Dowitchers employ a distinctive rapid "sewing-machine" probing motion to find invertebrates. **Noteworthy:** In Arizona, most juvenile Long-bills arrive in September. After mid-October all Arizona dowitchers are Long-billed.

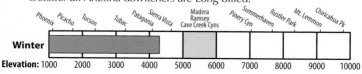

	Phoenix	Picacho	Tucson	Tubac	Patagonia	Sierra Vista	Madera Ramsey Cave Creek Cyns	Pinery Cyn	Summerhaven	Rustler Park	Mt. Lemmon	Chiricahua Pk
Winter												
Elevation: 1000	2000		3000	4000		5000	6000	7000		8000	9000	10000

135

Wilson's Snipe

Red Phalarope
Breeding

Red Phalarope
Non-breeding

WILSON'S SNIPE, *Gallinago delicata*

Description: 10.5". Stocky, heavily-striped, **short-legged** shorebird with a **long, straight bill**; longitudinal **white back stripes**. FLIGHT: Zigzags up, then abruptly drops into cover. **Similar Species:** Dowitchers (p. 135) have a white rump and longer legs; lack back stripes. **Voice:** When flushed, gives raspy *scaaip* call. **Status:** Common migrant and winter resident (Aug-mid May). **Habitat:** Valley marshes, flooded fields, rivers, streams, ponds, and lakes with grassy or weedy shores. **Behavior:** Secretive, usually motionless within short marshy vegetation; sometimes feeds more openly on mudflats, but rarely far from concealing vegetation. Usually solitary, but in migration several or more may occur together. **Noteworthy:** Flexible, sensitive bill-tip enables Snipe to find worms in mud.

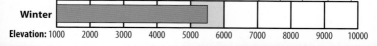

Winter									
Elevation: 1000	2000	3000	4000	5000	6000	7000	8000	9000	10000

RED PHALAROPE, *Phalaropus fulicarius*

Description: 8.5". **Short-billed phalarope.** BREEDING: Yellow bill; **entirely chestnut neck and underparts.** NON-BREEDING: Black bill; **white forehead and forecrown**; blackish ear; unmarked gray back. **Similar Species:** Larger Wilson's Phalarope (p. 139) has longer bill, gray forehead and forecrown. Smaller Red-necked Phalarope (p. 139) shows strong "V" stripes on back. **Voice:** Trilled *chrrrt!* **Status:** Rare migrant, primarily fall (mid Sep-Nov) with records every month but March. **Habitat:** Valley ponds and lakes. **Behavior:** Like all phalaropes, Red Phalaropes often feed by spinning rapidly in tight circles to create upwellings that bring small food items to the water's surface. **Noteworthy:** In Arizona, Red Phalarope usually occurs singly and in non-breeding plumage.

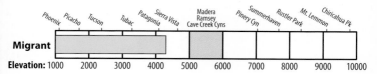

	Phoenix	Picacho	Tucson	Tubac	Patagonia	Sierra Vista	Madera Ramsey Cave Creek Cyns	Pinery Cyn	Summerhaven	Rustler Park	Mt. Lemmon	Chiricahua Pk
Migrant												
Elevation: 1000	2000		3000	4000		5000	6000	7000		8000	9000	10000

**Wilson's Phalarope
Breeding Female**

**Wilson's Phalarope
Molting Juvenile**

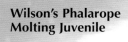

**Red-necked Phalarope
Breeding Female**

**Red-necked Phalarope
Juvenile**

WILSON'S PHALAROPE, *Phalaropus tricolor*

Description: 9.25". Long-bodied phalarope with **needle bill** and yellow legs. BREEDING: **Eyestripe widens down sides of neck.** NON-BREEDING: **Gray forehead and crown**, pale gray upperparts. **Similar Species:** Smaller Red-necked Phalarope (below) has strong "V" stripes on its back. Lesser Yellowlegs (p. 123) has much longer legs and white-spotted wings and back. **Voice:** Guttural *whuh*. **Status:** Common migrant (Apr-mid Jun and mid Jul-mid Oct); irregular in midsummer (mid Jun-mid Jul). **Habitat:** Valley lakes, ponds, and rivers pools with barren shorelines. **Behavior:** Spins in circles to bring tiny food items to surface. More apt to be seen feeding on mudflats than other phalaropes. **Noteworthy:** Female Wilson's Phalaropes are larger and brighter than males.

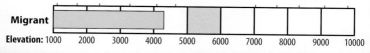

Migrant

Elevation: 1000   2000   3000   4000   5000   6000   7000   8000   9000   10000

RED-NECKED PHALAROPE, *Phalaropus lobatus*

Description: 7.75". Small phalarope with **bold "V" stripes on its back**. BREEDING: **Red yoke around white throat**. NON-BREEDING: Dark back accentuates "V" pattern. **Similar Species:** Larger Wilson's Phalarope (above) has longer bill, unmarked back, white rump, yellow legs. Breeding Red Phalarope (p. 137) has yellow bill, red underparts; non-breeding lacks "V" stripes on back. **Voice:** Hard *chit* notes. **Status:** Uncommon migrant (mid May-mid Jun and mid Jul-mid Oct). **Habitat:** Valley lakes and ponds with barren shorelines. **Behavior:** Like all species of phalaropes, Red-necked females court multiple males and may lay eggs in several nests; males provide all care for eggs and young. **Noteworthy:** Red-necked Phalaropes winter on southern seas.

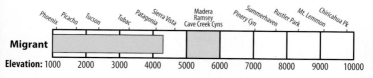

Phoenix   Picacho   Tucson   Tubac   Patagonia   Sierra Vista   Madera Ramsey Cave Creek Cyns   Pinery Cyn   Summerhaven   Rustler Park   Mt. Lemmon   Chiricahua Pk

Migrant

Elevation: 1000   2000   3000   4000   5000   6000   7000   8000   9000   10000

Heermann's Gull
Breeding

Heermann's Gull
1st Year

Sabine's Gull
Breeding

Sabine's Gull
Juvenile

HEERMANN'S GULL, *Larus heermanni*

Description: 19", wingspan 51". **Dark-mantled**, medium-sized gull with **long bill** and long wings. ADULT BREEDING: White head; red bill; gray body. IMMATURES: Sooty black overall. FLIGHT: **Dark wings concolor with back** with narrow white trailing edge. **Similar Species:** Same-sized Ring-billed Gull (p. 145) has pale gray mantle. **Voice:** Silent in our area. **Status:** Casual in winter and spring (Oct-Jun). **Habitat:** Valley ponds and lakes, usually with barren shorelines. **Behavior:** Primarily eats fish, often robbing them from other birds, especially pelicans. **Noteworthy:** In SE Arizona, Heermann's Gulls usually arrive singly and only stay part of one day. Most records come from the Tucson area.

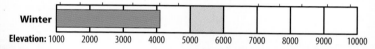

Winter								
Elevation: 1000 2000 3000 4000 5000 6000 7000 8000 9000 10000

SABINE'S GULL, *Xema sabini*

Description: 13.5", wingspan 33". Small gull with **very short bill** and long wings. BREEDING: **Gray hood; yellow-tipped black bill**. JUVENILE: Soft gray-brown nape; back with narrow wavy bands; black bill. FLIGHT: Striking, **tricolored wings with white inner triangles**. **Similar Species:** Same-sized Bonaparte's Gull (p. 143) breeding adult has thin white eye-arcs; longer bill lacking yellow tip. Immature Bonaparte's has dark ear spot; in flight lacks tricolored wings. **Voice:** Silent in our area. **Status:** Rare and irregular fall migrant (Sep-mid Oct). **Habitat:** Valley ponds and lakes, usually with barren shorelines. **Behavior:** May pick food off the water surface in tern-like flight or while swimming. **Noteworthy:** Usually migrates from its Arctic breeding grounds well out to sea. Most Arizona records are of juveniles.

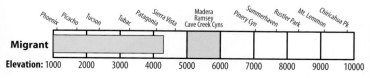

Phoenix Picacho Tucson Tubac Patagonia Sierra Vista Madera Ramsey Cave Creek Cyns Pinery Cyn Summerhaven Rustler Park Mt. Lemmon Chiricahua Pk

Migrant

Elevation: 1000 2000 3000 4000 5000 6000 7000 8000 9000 10000

**Bonaparte's Gull
Breeding**

**Bonaparte's Gull
First Winter**

**Franklin's Gull
Breeding**

**Franklin's Gull
Non-breeding**

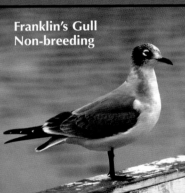

**Laughing Gull
Breeding**

**Laughing Gull
Non-breeding**

BONAPARTE'S GULL, *Croicocephalus philadelphia*

Description: 13.5", wingspan 33". **Small**, tern-like gull with **slender black bill**. BREEDING: Black hood; red legs. NON-BREEDING: **Black spot behind eye**. FLIGHT: **White wedge on outer wing**. **Similar Species:** Breeding Franklin's Gull (below) has deep red bill and non-breeding has almost solid black hind-hood. **Status:** Rare migrant (late Mar-May and Oct-Nov); casual otherwise. **Habitat:** Valley ponds and lakes with barren shorelines. **Behavior:** Plucks food from water surface or dives like tern.

FRANKLIN'S GULL, *Leucophaeus pipixcan*

Description: 14.5", wingspan 36". Small gull with **thick white eye-arcs**. BREEDING: Black hood; red bill; variably pinkish on breast. NON-BREEDING: Dark half-hood; black bill. FLIGHT: Pale underwings; narrow **black crescents on white wingtips**. **Similar Species:** Breeding Bonaparte's Gull (above) has black bill and bright red legs; non-breeding Bonaparte's has black ear spot. **Status:** Uncommon in spring (late Mar-May); rare in fall (Oct-mid Nov); casual in summer. **Habitat:** Valley ponds and lakes with barren shorelines. **Behavior:** Forages for water insects.

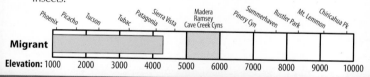

LAUGHING GULL, *Leucophaeus atricilla*

Description: 16.5", wingspan 40". Medium-sized gull with **long bill**. BREEDING: Black hood; narrow white eye-arcs; red bill. NON-BREEDING: Sooty hindcrown and nape; black legs. FLIGHT: **Black wingtips**. **Similar Species:** Smaller Franklin's Gull (above) has short bill, broad white eye-arcs, and adult shows white wingtips in flight. **Status:** Casual migrant (May-Jun and late Jul-Aug). **Habitat:** Valley ponds and lakes, usually with barren shorelines. **Behavior:** Eats carrion, insects, eggs, and fish.

Ring-billed Gull
Non-breeding

Ring-billed Gull
First Winter

California Gull
Breeding

California Gull
First Year

RING-BILLED GULL, *Larus delawarensis*

Description: 18″, wingspan 48″. Medium-sized gull with short bill and **pale mantle**; takes three years to attain adult plumage. BREEDING: Black ring on bill; **pale yellowish eye; yellow legs**. NON-BREEDING: Head and neck flecked with brown. FIRST-WINTER: Pink bill with black tip; dark eye; gray back with blackish shoulders; pink legs. **Similar Species:** Larger adult California Gull (below) has dark eye and red spot near tip of its longer bill. **Voice:** Squealing *wheeah*. **Status:** Uncommon spring (Mar-May) and fall (Aug-mid Dec) migrant; rare in midsummer and midwinter. **Habitat:** Valley ponds and lakes, usually with barren shorelines. **Behavior:** Scavenges on water and shore. **Noteworthy:** Arizona's most common gull.

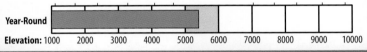

Year-Round

Elevation: 1000 2000 3000 4000 5000 6000 7000 8000 9000 10000

CALIFORNIA GULL, *Larus californicus*

Description: 21″, wingspan 54″. **Large gull** with **dark eye** and **medium-gray mantle**; takes four years to mature. BREEDING: Yellow bill with small black ring and **red spot** near tip; **yellow-green legs**. NON-BREEDING: Head and chest streaked with brown. FIRST-WINTER: Lacks gray mantle. SECOND-WINTER: Black-banded bluish bill and blue legs; gray back and mottled gray shoulders. **Similar Species:** First-winter Ring-billed (above), unlike second-winter California Gull, has pink–not bluish–bill and legs. **Voice:** Usually silent. **Status:** Rare spring (Apr-May) and fall (Aug-Nov) migrant; casual in summer. **Habitat:** Valley ponds and lakes, usually with barren shorelines. **Behavior:** Scavenges on water and shore. **Noteworthy:** In 1848 credited with saving Mormons from a plague of grasshoppers.

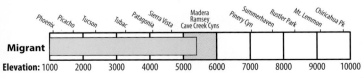

Phoenix Picacho Tucson Tubac Patagonia Sierra Vista Madera Ramsey Cave Creek Cyns Pinery Cyn Summerhaven Rustler Park Mt. Lemmon Chiricahua Pk

Migrant

Elevation: 1000 2000 3000 4000 5000 6000 7000 8000 9000 10000

145

Least Tern

**Black Tern
Breeding**

**Black Tern
Non-breeding**

LEAST TERN, *Sternula antillarum*

Description: 8.5". **Smallest tern** in North America. Distinctive **yellow bill and white forehead**. FLIGHT: Quick, deep wing beats reveal ink-black outermost primaries. **Similar Species:** All other Arizona terns are larger and lack yellow bill. **Voice:** Usually silent in our area. **Status:** Rare spring migrant (late Apr-Jun). **Habitat:** Valley ponds and lakes with barren shorelines. Most records are from Lake Cochise, Willcox, but possible anywhere. **Behavior:** Dives for insects and small fish swimming on or just below the surface. **Noteworthy:** Least Tern records in SE Arizona are of adult-plumaged birds.

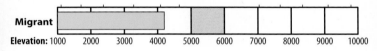

Migrant									
Elevation: 1000	2000	3000	4000	5000	6000	7000	8000	9000	10000

BLACK TERN, *Chlidonias niger*

Description: 10". Small **short-tailed tern** with thin, black bill. BREEDING: **Black head and body**. NON-BREEDING: White head with black crown and ear muffs; upperparts dark gray; dark smudges on sides of breast. FLIGHT: Bouncy and erratic with silvery underwings. **Similar Species:** All other Arizona terns have pale gray upperparts and lack "ear muffs." **Voice:** Quick raspy *cheep chep chep*. **Status:** Rare spring (May-Jun) and uncommon fall (mid Jul-Sep) migrant. **Habitat:** Valley ponds and lakes with barren shorelines. **Behavior:** Seldom dives like other terns; sorties rapidly across lakes chasing insects and snatching prey items from the surface. **Noteworthy:** While Black Terns may appear singly in our area, more often they number from a few to more than 20. Most birds seen after mid-August are transitioning from black to white underparts.

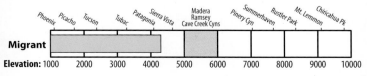

Phoenix	Picacho	Tucson	Tubac	Patagonia	Sierra Vista	Madera Ramsey Cave Creek Cyns	Pinery Cyn	Summerhaven	Rustler Park	Mt. Lemmon	Chiricahua Pk

Migrant									
Elevation: 1000	2000	3000	4000	5000	6000	7000	8000	9000	10000

**Common Tern
Breeding**

**Common Tern
Juvenile**

**Forster's Tern
Breeding**

**Forster's Tern
First Winter**

COMMON TERN, *Sterna hirundo*

Description: 14". Medium-sized tern with **pale gray underparts, short tail** only extends to end of wing. BREEDING: Black cap; red bill with black tip (may lose black tip in midsummer); red legs. NON-BREEDING: **Black half-hood**, black or mostly black bill and legs; most have **black shoulder bar**. FLIGHT: **Dark wedge** in outer flight feathers **on gray upperwing**. **Similar Species:** Forster's Tern (below) has long tail extending well beyond wings; in flight shows silvery primaries. **Voice:** Harsh *kee-rrr*. **Status:** Rare spring (mid Apr-May) and fall (mid Jul-Oct) migrant. **Habitat:** Valley ponds and lakes with barren shorelines. **Behavior:** Plunge-dives for small fish and insects. **Noteworthy:** Like Forster's Tern, Common Tern in SE Arizona is usually seen as singles or twosomes.

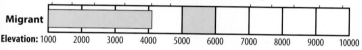

Migrant

Elevation: 1000 2000 3000 4000 5000 6000 7000 8000 9000 10000

FORSTER'S TERN, *Sterna forsteri*

Description: 14.5". Medium-sized tern with **white underparts; long tail** extends well beyond wings. BREEDING: Black cap; orange-red bill with black tip; orange legs. NON-BREEDING: **Jet black ear** on white face; black bill and legs. FLIGHT: **Silvery outer flight feathers on snowy upperwing**. **Similar Species:** Common Tern (above) has short tail not extending beyond wings; in flight shows blackish wedge on upper side of gray outer wings. **Voice:** Burry *yurrrh*. **Status:** Rare spring (Apr-early Jun) and fall (Aug-early Nov) migrant. **Habitat:** Valley ponds and lakes with barren shorelines. **Behavior:** Plunge-dives for small fish and insects. **Noteworthy:** Forster's Tern is more common than Common Tern in SE Arizona.

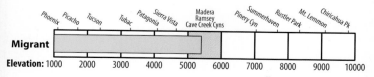

Migrant

Elevation: 1000 2000 3000 4000 5000 6000 7000 8000 9000 10000

Rock Pigeon

Rock Pigeon

Band-tailed Pigeon

ROCK PIGEON, *Columba livia*

Description: 13″. Introduced pigeon with **black bill** and white cere; iridescent neck; **pink legs**. TYPICAL: **Pale gray body** with **two black wingbars**; gray tail with black terminal band. **Many other plumages**. FLIGHT: **White underwings**. **Similar Species:** Band-tailed Pigeon (below) has yellow bill and feet, white hindneck crescent and lacks black wingbars. **Voice:** Gruff cooing notes and gurgles. Wings clap on take-off. **Status:** Common resident. **Habitat:** Cities, towns, and farms. Flocks often roost under highway overpasses. **Behavior:** Eats seeds, fruits, and a wide variety of human waste foods. **Noteworthy:** Rock Pigeons first colonized southern Arizona towns about 1900.

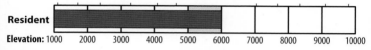

Resident

Elevation: 1000   2000   3000   4000   5000   6000   7000   8000   9000   10000

BAND-TAILED PIGEON, *Patagioenas fasciata*

Description: 14″. Native pigeon with **yellow bill; white crescent on hindneck; dark body** and dark-banded gray tail; **yellow legs**. JUVENILE: Lacks white collar. FLIGHT: **Gray underwings**. **Similar Species:** Rock Pigeon (above) has black bill and pink legs, usually pale gray body, and two bold black wingbars. **Voice:** Owl-like hooting *to-who? to-who? who-o-o?* Wings clap on take-off. **Status:** Usually fairly common but irregular in summer (mid Apr-Oct); casual in winter (Nov-mid Apr). **Habitat:** Mountain forests and canyon groves. Wanders to valley river groves. **Behavior:** Flocks in Arizona roam up to 20 miles per day in search of acorns, pinyon nuts, mulberries, manzanita berries, and seeds. **Noteworthy:** During major forest fires, an entire population of Band-tails may abandon a SE Arizona mountain range.

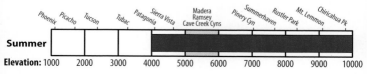

Phoenix   Picacho   Tucson   Tubac   Patagonia   Sierra Vista   Madera Ramsey Cave Creek Cyns   Pinery Cyn   Summerhaven   Rustler Park   Mt. Lemmon   Chiricahua Pk

Summer

Elevation: 1000   2000   3000   4000   5000   6000   7000   8000   9000   10000

Eurasian Collared-Dove

White-winged Dove

Mourning Dove

EURASIAN COLLARED-DOVE, *Streptopelia decaocto*

Description: 12.5″. Introduced **large, pale dove** with **black hindcollar** and dark flight feathers. **Similar Species:** Smaller, darker White-winged Dove (below) has white wing crescents. **Voice:** Trisyllabic *coo COOO cup*. **Status:** Fairly common resident. **Habitat:** Desert and valley farms and small towns; uncommon around Tucson. **Behavior:** All three species of doves on this page forage for seeds on the ground and use conspicuous perches. **Noteworthy:** First detected in Arizona in 2000, its population is still expanding.

WHITE-WINGED DOVE, *Zenaida asiatica*

Description: 12″. Bulky dove with **bold white wing crescents; square tail with white corners**. **Similar Species:** Similar-sized Mourning Dove (below) has black spots on wings and long, pointed tail. **Voice:** Usually rendered *who cooks for you?* **Status:** Common in summer (Mar-Sep); rare in winter (Oct-Feb). **Habitat:** Deserts, valleys, foothills, and lower mountain canyons. Common in towns and cities. **Behavior:** Diet includes saguaro nectar and fruits. **Noteworthy:** Arrival of Sonoran Desert population seems timed to take advantage of newly flowering saguaros.

MOURNING DOVE, *Zenaida macroura*

Description: 12″. Slender dove with **black-spotted wings and long, pointed tail**. **Similar Species:** Similar-sized White-winged Dove (above) has bold white crescents in the wings and on corners of its square tail. **Voice:** Mournful *oah-oo-oo-ooo*. **Status:** Common resident. Primarily in valleys during winter (Nov-Mar). **Habitat:** Deserts, valleys, foothills, and lower mountain canyons. Common in towns and cities. **Noteworthy:** Mourning Dove is considered the most abundant breeding bird in Arizona.

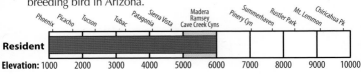

153

Inca Dove

Inca Dove

Common Ground-Dove
Male

Ruddy Ground-Dove
Male

Ruddy Ground-Dove
Female

INCA DOVE, *Columbina inca*

Description: 8.5". Little, **long-tailed** town dove; head and **upperparts entirely "scaled."** FLIGHT: Chestnut wings; **white outer tail feathers. Similar Species:** Smaller Common Ground-Dove (below) has short tail with black outer tail feathers. **Voice:** Blowy *no hope*. **Status:** Fairly common resident. **Habitat:** Desert and valley farms and small towns; usually uncommon to fairly common around Tucson, depending on the year. **Noteworthy:** Inca Dove is almost never found far from people.

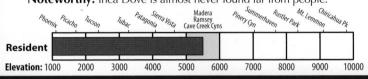

	Phoenix	Picacho	Tucson	Tubac	Patagonia	Sierra Vista	Madera Ramsey Cave Creek Cyns	Pinery Cyn	Summerhaven	Rustler Park	Mt. Lemmon	Chiricahua Pk
Resident												
Elevation:	1000	2000	3000	4000	5000	6000	7000	8000	9000	10000

COMMON GROUND-DOVE, *Columbina passerina*

Description: 6.5". Little, **short-tailed** dove; only scaled on head and breast; **bill red or pink**. MALE: Blue-gray crown; rosy breast. FEMALE: Uniform gray. FLIGHT: Chestnut wings; **black outer tail feathers. Similar Species:** Inca Dove has longer tail and its upperparts are scaled. Both Inca (above) and Ruddy-Ground Doves (below) have slaty bills–not red. **Voice:** Deliberate *wu-u wu-u wuoop*. **Status:** Uncommon resident. **Habitat:** Desert and valley openings and fields adjacent to brush and permanent water. **Noteworthy:** Usually does not associate with Ruddy Ground-Dove.

RUDDY GROUND-DOVE, *Columbina talpacoti*

Description: 6.75". Little dove with **medium-length tail; bill slaty**. MALE: Bluish head; ruddy upperparts. FEMALE: Rump may be tinged reddish. FLIGHT: Chestnut wings; **black outer tail feathers. Similar Species:** Common Ground-Dove (above) has scaly head and breast and red-based bill. **Voice:** Almost identical to Common Ground-Dove but much faster *wuoop wuoop* notes. **Status:** Rare and irregular resident. **Habitat:** Desert and valley farms and feedlots adjacent to brush and permanent water. **Noteworthy:** First recorded in Arizona in 1981, Ruddy's often associate with Inca Doves.

Yellow-billed Cuckoo

Groove-billed Ani

YELLOW-BILLED CUCKOO, *Coccyzus americanus*

Description: 12". Sleek brown bird with arched, mostly **yellow bill**; long, **black and white tail**. JUVENILE: Bill lacks yellow. FLIGHT: Like small falcon with **rusty flight feathers**. **Similar Species:** Black-billed Cuckoo (accidental Aug-Oct) has black bill, red eye-ring, mostly gray undertail, and lacks red in the flight feathers. **Voice:** Staccato *cuk-cuk-cuk* ending in *kowlp kowlp*. **Status:** Fairly common summer resident (Jun-Sep). **Habitat:** Valley and foothill canyon river groves, especially with permanent water. The upper Santa Cruz and San Pedro Rivers are proven locations, along with Arivaca Cienaga, Sonoita Creek, and San Bernardino Ranch. **Behavior:** Dines on caterpillars, helping control tent caterpillar outbreaks. Yellow-billed typically does not lay eggs in other bird's nests. **Noteworthy:** Recorded infrequently in May, most arrive after mid June, giving Yellow-billed Cuckoo the distinction of being the last breeding bird to arrive in Arizona.

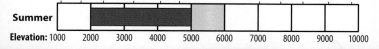

Summer									
Elevation: 1000	2000	3000	4000	5000	6000	7000	8000	9000	10000

GROOVE-BILLED ANI, *Crotophaga sulcirostris*

Description: 13.5". Awkward, disheveled-looking black bird with long, floppy tail. Cleaver-like **bill shows lateral grooving**. **Similar Species:** Male Great-tailed Grackle (p. 405) has much thinner bill and yellow eyes. **Voice:** Whiny, repeated calls of *treach-e-ry*. **Status:** Casual, primarily in summer (May-Nov) but records throughout year. **Habitat:** Valley areas with thick, rank brush and vines, usually near still or stagnant water. **Behavior:** Eats mostly big, slow-moving insects. In Mexico adults from several pairs known to share communal nest. **Noteworthy:** In SE Arizona shows a tendency to arrive during the summer rainy season.

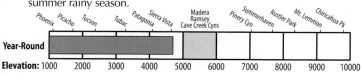

	Phoenix	Picacho	Tucson	Tubac	Patagonia	Sierra Vista	Madera Ramsey Cave Creek Cyns	Pinery Cyn	Summerhaven	Rustler Park	Mt. Lemmon	Chiricahua Pk
Year-Round												
Elevation: 1000		2000	3000	4000	5000	6000	7000	8000	9000	10000

GREATER ROADRUNNER, *Geococcyx californianus*

Description: 23". Big, **bushy-crested, heavily-streaked ground cuckoo** with long, expressive tail. The crest can be elevated or lowered at will. An inch-long patch of bare, mostly blue skin extends behind the eye. When agitated or in courtship the rear-most end of this skin may turn bright orange.

Similar Species: Distinctive; similarly shaped thrashers are much smaller birds, with unstreaked upperparts.

Voice: Piteous series of *wuah wuah wuah* moans like a sorry puppy, fading at end; also a loud bill chatter.

Status: Fairly common resident. **Habitat:** Deserts, valley grasslands, and open foothill woodlands and chaparral. Common around Tucson and other lowland urban areas, especially near parks or golf courses, or where homes are widely spaced and retain some native plants. Rarely wanders above 7,000' into open Ponderosa pine forest.

Behavior: Although famous for occasionally dining on rattlesnake, staples are primarily smaller snakes and lizards. Hunts prey on the ground and opportunistically catches young quail or doves, other birds, small rodents, and large insects with bursts of speed. Has been timed running parallel to roads at 15 mph. Also eats some cactus fruit. Courting Roadrunners present potential mates with a stick or lizard. Displaying birds may fly 50 feet or higher to the tops of trees or utility poles.

Noteworthy: In southern Arizona Greater Roadrunners typically nest twice: once in spring and again during the midsummer monsoons.

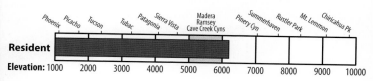

BARN OWL, *Tyto alba*

Description: 16". Medium-large **gold and white owl** with **dark eyes** and **heart-shaped face.** MALE: Underparts white. FEMALE: Underparts usually buff. FLIGHT: Both sexes appear ghostly white at night.

Similar Species: Pale—but not white—Short-eared owl (p.173) is mostly active at dawn and dusk, has yellow—not deep brown—eyes, and a striped breast.

Voice: Rasping, hair-raising screech, often given in flight.

Status: Fairly common resident. Winter population is usually larger, augmented by migrants from the north. **Habitat:** Open deserts and valleys with suitable dark roosting and nesting sites. In SE Arizona, rarely wanders into mountain Ponderosa pine forests.

Behavior: Nocturnal; hunts rodents with long, coursing flights. Arizona Barn Owls spend the daylight hours sequestered under palm fronds, inside dense trees, abandoned buildings, old wells, mine shafts, under highway bridges, within crevices in stacks of baled hay, and on shaded cliff ledges. Barn Owls often nest in the same places they roost. They are also known to excavate three- to six-foot-long burrows into the sides of steep arroyo banks. More than 10 percent of male Barn Owls in the Southwest are thought to be polygamous, with two or even three mates.

Noteworthy: Barn Owls occur on every continent except Antarctica, and are the most widely distributed land birds in the world.

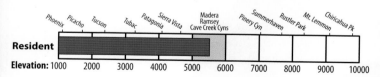

	Phoenix	Picacho	Tucson	Tubac	Patagonia	Sierra Vista	Madera Ramsey Cave Creek Cyns	Pinery Cyn	Summerhaven	Rustler Park	Mt. Lemmon	Chiricahua Pk
Resident												
Elevation:	1000	2000	3000	4000	5000	6000	7000	8000	9000	10000		

Northern Saw-whet Owl

Flammulated Owl

NORTHERN SAW-WHET OWL, *Aegolius acadicus*

Description: 8″. **Big-headed**, little mountain owl with **whitish goggles**; short tail. JUVENILE: Unmarked buffy belly. **Similar Species:** Flammulated Owl (below) has ear tufts and dark eyes. **Voice:** Long rhythmic series of mellow toots. Calls infrequently after June. **Status:** Rare resident. **Habitat:** Mountain coniferous forest, especially with some Gambel's oak or aspen; casual in winter (Nov-Mar) in desert and valley towns and oases. **Behavior:** Nocturnal; hunts rodents at night from low perches. Occasionally migrates southward or down-slope in the fall. If detected but left undisturbed in the daytime, usually just snoozes. **Noteworthy:** Most reports of wintering Saw-whets in SE Arizona come from desert towns and oases, perhaps owing to the concentration of observers in these areas.

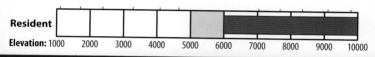

Resident									
Elevation: 1000	2000	3000	4000	5000	6000	7000	8000	9000	10000

FLAMMULATED OWL, *Otus flammeolus*

Description: 6.5″. Small, **dark-eyed** forest owl with variably **red-tinted facial disk**; short, relaxable ear tufts; red-edged line of buff spots delineates shoulder. **Similar Species:** Larger Western Screech-Owl (p. 165) has yellow eyes; lacks any reddish tints. **Voice:** Low, soft, widely-spaced *boop* notes; becomes quiet in July. **Status:** Fairly common in summer (mid Mar-Sep). **Habitat:** Mountain coniferous forests, especially mixed with Gambel's oaks, and in tall canyon groves within Sierra Madrean pine-oak woodland. **Behavior:** Feeds almost exclusively on insects, especially moths. Most active just after dark and just before dawn. Usually perches next to tree trunks. **Noteworthy:** Flammulated Owl is considered Arizona's most common forest-dwelling owl in summer.

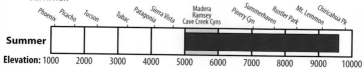

	Phoenix	Picacho	Tucson	Tubac	Patagonia	Sierra Vista	Madera Ramsey Cave Creek Cyns	Piney Cyn	Summerhaven	Rustler Park	Mt. Lemmon	Chiricahua Pk
Summer												
Elevation: 1000		2000	3000	4000	5000	6000	7000	8000	9000	10000		

Western Screech-Owl

Whiskered Screech-Owl

WESTERN SCREECH-OWL, *Megascops kennicottii*

Description: Description: 8.5". Small "eared" owl of the lowlands and foothills with yellow eyes and **black bill;** relatively **large feet.** Best identified by voice. **Similar Species:** Smaller Flammulated Owl (p. 163) has dark eyes. Whiskered Screech-Owl (below) has greenish bill. **Voice:** "Bouncing ball" series of short, accelerating whistles. Calls infrequently after July. **Status:** Fairly common resident. **Habitat:** Suburbs, Saguaro desert, river cottonwood groves, foothill canyon groves, and open oak woodland. **Behavior:** Ambushes prey from perches on lower limbs. Eats small rodents, birds, and large insects. **Noteworthy:** In SE Arizona, Western is replaced by Whiskered Screech-Owl at higher elevations where stream cottonwood groves and open oak woodlands transition into denser sycamore groves and pine-oak woodlands.

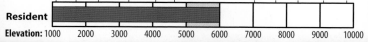

Resident

Elevation: 1000 2000 3000 4000 5000 6000 7000 8000 9000 10000

WHISKERED SCREECH-OWL, *Megascops trichopsis*

Description: 7.25". Small "eared" owl of the mountains with yellow eyes and **greenish bill;** relatively **small feet.** Best identified by voice. **Similar Species:** Smaller Flammulated Owl (p. 163) has dark eyes. Western Screech-Owl (above) has black bill. **Voice:** Syncopated "Morse Code" series of short and long toots. Calls infrequently after July. **Status:** Fairly common resident. **Habitat:** Mountain canyon sycamore groves and Sierra Madrean pine-oak woodland. Most nests have been in sycamore trees. **Behavior:** Ambushes prey from perches on lower limbs. Eats small rodents, birds, and large insects. **Noteworthy:** Except for Sycamore Canyon in the Atascosa Mountains, Whiskered Screech-Owl is confined to SE Arizona mountain ranges which exceed elevations of 7,000'.

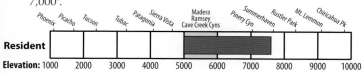

Resident

Elevation: 1000 2000 3000 4000 5000 6000 7000 8000 9000 10000

Great Horned Owl

"Mexican" Spotted Owl

GREAT HORNED OWL, *Bubo virginianus*

Description: 22", wingspan 44". **Big, boxy, ear-tufted owl** with **yellow eyes**.
Similar Species: Smaller, lankier Long-eared Owl (p. 173) has longer,
more closely-spaced ear tufts. **Voice:** Song is rolling *hoo h'HOOO hoo
hoo*. **Status:** Common resident. **Habitat:** Saguaro desert, urban areas,
valley and foothill groves, and open woodlands. May wander up to limits
of open Ponderosa pine forest. **Behavior:** Ambushes rodents, rabbits,
skunks, and snakes from perches overlooking open areas. Nests
"borrowed" from large hawks, herons, and ravens; also in tree hollows,
under bridges, inside old buildings. **Noteworthy:** Desert Great Horned
Owls are early breeders, initiating courtship in December; in SE Arizona
mountains some fledglings do not leave their nest until mid-May.

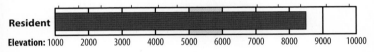

Resident

Elevation: 1000 2000 3000 4000 5000 6000 7000 8000 9000 10000

"MEXICAN" SPOTTED OWL, *Strix occidentalis lucida*

Description: 18", wingspan 40". Bulky, **big-headed forest owl** with **dark eyes**
and **no ear tufts**. **Similar Species:** Larger Great Horned Owl (above) has
yellow eyes and obvious ear tufts. **Voice:** Hooted *hoo hoo wa-hoooh*.
Status: Uncommon resident. **Habitat:** Mountain canyon groves, tall
pine-oak woodland, and shady coniferous forest. **Behavior:** Ambushes
mice, woodrats, bats, small birds, and insects from open perches. Day
roosts in large trees are usually on lower limb, well away from tree trunk,
or in a small tree. Most nests are in potholes in cliffs. **Noteworthy:**
"Mexican" race Spotted Owls are somewhat paler and more spotted on
upperparts than Pacific Northwest race; ranges do not overlap.

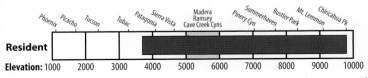

Resident

Elevation: 1000 2000 3000 4000 5000 6000 7000 8000 9000 10000

Northern Pygmy-Owl

"Cactus" Ferruginous Pygmy-Owl

NORTHERN PYGMY-OWL, *Glaucidium gnoma*

Description: 6.75". Mountain gnome with **spotted crown**; long, white-barred tail. Large "eye-spots" on hindcrown. **Similar Species:** Northern Saw-whet Owl (p. 163) has big head with streaked crown and shorter tail, and larger Whiskered Screech-Owl (p. 165) has ear tufts. Lower elevation, desert-dwelling Ferruginous Pygmy-Owl (below) has streaked crown and rusty-barred tail. **Voice:** Repeated single toots (northern form) or double toots (Mexican form of the border ranges); low, rapid *popopopopopo, too, too, too* if very excited. **Status:** Uncommon resident. **Habitat:** Mountain canyon groves, pine-oak woodland, and open coniferous forest. **Behavior:** Chases down birds, rodents, and lizards at dawn and dusk. Aggressively defends territories. **Noteworthy:** Northern Pygmy-Owls sometimes kill birds and mammals larger than themselves.

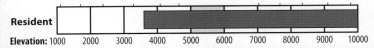

Resident									
Elevation: 1000	2000	3000	4000	5000	6000	7000	8000	9000	10000

"CACTUS" FERRUGINOUS PYGMY-OWL, *Glaucidium brasilianum cactorum*

Description: 6.75". Desert gnome with **streaked crown**; long, rusty or gray-barred tail. Large "eye-spots" on hindcrown. **Similar Species:** Larger Western Screech-Owl (p. 165) has ear tufts. Mountain-dwelling Northern Pygmy-Owl (above) has spotted crown and white-barred tail. **Voice:** Long, monotonous series of toots. **Status:** Rare resident. **Habitat:** Saguaro cactus desert and foothill thorn forest canyon groves. **Behavior:** Chases down birds, rodents, lizards, and scorpions at dawn and dusk. Nests almost exclusively in saguaro cavities. **Noteworthy:** Habitat loss owing to urban sprawl and eradication of valley cottonwood groves is a serious threat to the continued presence of Ferruginous Pygmy-Owls in SE Arizona. In 2006 researchers documented only 26 individuals in Arizona.

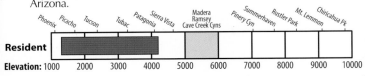

	Phoenix	Picacho	Tucson	Tubac	Patagonia	Sierra Vista	Madera Ramsey Cave Creek Cyns	Pinery Cyn	Summerhaven	Rustler Park	Mt. Lemmon	Chiricahua Pk
Resident												
Elevation: 1000	2000		3000	4000	5000		6000	7000	8000		9000	10000

Elf Owl

Burrowing Owl

ELF OWL, *Micrathene whitneyi*

Description: 5.75". **Tiny**, round-headed, **short-tailed owl**. **Similar Species:** Both Ferruginous and Northern Pygmy-Owls are much larger and have long tails. **Voice:** Wild, giggling chirps and winnies *he-ha-ha-he-he*. Descending, whistled *feeoh*. Usually silent after mid July. **Status:** Common summer resident (mid Mar-Aug). **Habitat:** Saguaro cactus desert, and valley, foothill, and lower mountain canyon groves. **Behavior:** Forages for moths, scorpions, and other small invertebrates. Most nest in old woodpecker holes in saguaros, cottonwoods, sycamores, and utility poles. **Noteworthy:** Weighing only slightly more than an ounce, Elf Owl is the smallest member of its family in the world.

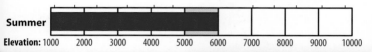

Summer									
Elevation: 1000	2000	3000	4000	5000	6000	7000	8000	9000	10000

BURROWING OWL, *Athene cunicularia*

Description: 9.5". **Long-legged**, round-headed, diurnal **ground owl** of open terrain. JUVENILE: Unmarked buffy underparts. **Similar Species:** Much larger Short-eared Owl (p. 173) has boldly-streaked underparts. **Voice:** Hollow, laughter-like *huh-huh* or *hoh-hoh*; rapid, raspy *kwik-kwik-kwik*. **Status:** Uncommon in summer (mid Mar-Oct) and rare in winter (Nov-mid Mar). **Habitat:** Open deserts, barren fields and pastures, golf courses, cemeteries, and valley grasslands. **Behavior:** Forages for insects and rodents, primarily at dawn and dusk. Often perches most of the day on rocks, mounds, cemetery monuments, or low, dead stumps. Nests in abandoned rodent burrows or—where available—in old drainage pipes and under cement slabs. **Noteworthy:** Elimination of Black-tailed Prairie Dogs in the late 1930s and the subsequent loss of their burrows for nests severely reduced Burrowing Owl populations in Arizona.

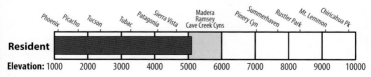

Resident									
Elevation: 1000	2000	3000	4000	5000	6000	7000	8000	9000	10000

Long-eared Owl

Long-eared Owl

Short-eared Owl

Short-eared Owl

LONG-EARED OWL, *Asio otus*

Description: 15", wingspan 36". **Long, slim owl with long, close-set "ears;"** barred belly. FLIGHT: Broad wings buff below with orange crescents on upperwing. **Similar Species:** Larger, boxier Great Horned Owl (p. 167) has widely spaced ear tufts. Paler Short-eared Owl (below) has miniscule ear tufts and striped underparts. **Voice:** Regularly spaced *boo boo boo* hoots at three-second intervals. **Status:** Rare and irregular, primarily in winter (Oct-Mar). **Habitat:** Desert mesquite, valley willow, and foothill juniper and oak thickets, especially adjacent to open areas. **Behavior:** Quarters across open, usually flat terrain at night, flying low as it searches for small rodents; often perches near ground in dense thickets. In winter, most join communal roosts of up to 30 birds. **Noteworthy:** These nomadic owls materialize when plagues of small rodents develop, and disappear almost as suddenly.

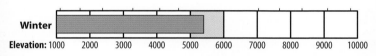

Winter									
Elevation: 1000	2000	3000	4000	5000	6000	7000	8000	9000	10000

SHORT-EARED OWL, *Asio flammeus*

Description: 15", wingspan 38". **Pale, open country owl with tiny "ears;"** streaked underparts. FLIGHT: Moth-like; very long wings with large **buffy patches on upper side**. **Similar Species:** Female Northern Harrier (p. 83) has smaller head, white rump, and longer tail. **Voice:** Silent in our area. **Status:** Rare in winter (mid Oct-Mar). **Habitat:** Valley grasslands, farmlands, and seasonal marshes. **Behavior:** Flies near ground, hunting rodents at dawn and dusk. Perches on ground. **Noteworthy:** In Arizona, may occur in small, seemingly loosely associated groups of five or more birds.

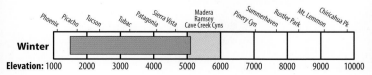

Phoenix · Picacho · Tucson · Tubac · Patagonia · Sierra Vista · Madera Ramsey Cave Creek Cyns · Pinery Cyn · Summerhaven · Rustler Park · Mt. Lemmon · Chiricahua Pk

Winter									
Elevation: 1000	2000	3000	4000	5000	6000	7000	8000	9000	10000

Lesser Nighthawk

Lesser Nighthawk

Common Nighthawk

Common Nighthawk

LESSER NIGHTHAWK, *Chordeiles acutipennis*

Description: 9". Slim, falconate nightbird with—when perched—visible **white wing patch below rump**; long, notched tail. MALE: White throat; white bar midway out in primaries. FEMALE: Buff throat; buff bar midway out in primaries. **FLIGHT: Rounded wingtips. Similar Species:** In flight Common Nighthawk (below) has pointed wingtips. **Voice:** Very long purring trill. **Status:** Common in summer (mid Apr-Oct). **Habitat:** Desert and valley grasslands, especially over stock tanks, sewage ponds, irrigated fields, rivers, dirt roads, and around parking lot and stadium lights. **Behavior:** Performs intricate ballets while capturing flying insects on the wing; often active well into morning or in late afternoon. **Noteworthy:** In late afternoon flocks may number over 100 birds at strategic watering areas before they disperse to feed.

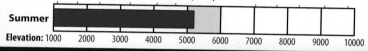

Summer									
Elevation: 1000	2000	3000	4000	5000	6000	7000	8000	9000	10000

COMMON NIGHTHAWK, *Chordeiles minor*

Description: 9.5". Slim, falconate nightbird with—when perched—visible **white wing patch below back**; long, notched tail. MALE: White throat; white bar near base of primaries. FEMALE: Buff throat; buff bar near base of primaries. **FLIGHT: Pointed wingtips. Similar Species:** In flight Lesser Nighthawk (above) has rounded wingtips. **Voice:** Nasal bleat *peeent*. Males produce a loud bellow with wings in display dives. **Status:** Uncommon in summer (mid May-mid Sep). **Habitat:** Higher valley grasslands and oak savanna on mountain steppes. **Behavior:** Captures flying insects, often higher above ground than Lesser Nighthawks. **Noteworthy:** In SE Arizona, migrating Common Nighthawks may follow mountain crests.

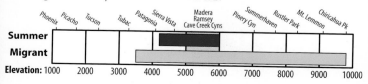

Phoenix	Picacho	Tucson	Tubac	Patagonia	Sierra Vista	Madera Ramsey Cave Creek Cyns	Pinery Cyn	Summerhaven	Rustler Park	Mt. Lemmon	Chiricahua Pk
Summer											
Migrant											
Elevation: 1000		2000		3000		4000	5000	6000	7000	8000	9000	10000

Common Poorwill

Buff-collared Nightjar

Mexican Whip-poor-will

COMMON POORWILL, *Phalaenoptilus nuttallii*

Description: 7.75". **Small** nightjar with **short tail**. MALE: White tail corners. FEMALE: Buffy tail tips. **Similar Species:** Larger Buff-collared Nightjar (below) has longer tail extending beyond wingtips. **Voice:** Evocative *poorwill!* **Status:** Fairly common in summer (Mar-Oct); rarely detected in winter (Nov-Feb). **Habitat:** Deserts with broken terrain and foothills with open woodland, often in canyons. **Behavior:** Usually captures flying insects from ground perches. **Noteworthy:** Perhaps as common in winter as summer, but Common Poorwill is the only bird known to hibernate.

BUFF-COLLARED NIGHTJAR, *Antrostomus ridgwayi*

Description: 8.75". Nightjar with **cinnamon hindcollar**. MALE: Extensive white tail corners. FEMALE: Buffy tail tips. **Similar Species:** Larger Whip-poor-will (below) has longer tail and lacks crisp cinnamon hindcollar. **Voice:** Piano-like up-scale notes often rendered *presta-me-tu-cuchillo* in Spanish. **Status:** Rare in summer (mid Apr-mid Sep). **Habitat:** Foothill thornscrub. **Behavior:** Usually captures flying insects from short treetops. **Noteworthy:** Discovered in SE Arizona in 1960.

MEXICAN WHIP-POOR-WILL, *Antrostomus arizonae*

Description: 9.75". Nightjar with dark **median crown stripe**. MALE: Bold white tail corners. FEMALE: Buffy tail tips. **Similar Species:** Smaller Buff-collared Nightjar (above) has shorter tail and lacks median crown stripe. **Voice:** Burry *uh-purple-whip! purple-whip! purple-whip!* **Status:** Fairly common in summer (mid Apr-mid Oct). **Habitat:** Mountain pine-oak and coniferous forest, especially in canyon groves. **Behavior:** Usually captures flying insects from tree perches. **Noteworthy:** Arizona birds have different song from Eastern Whip-poor-wills, and were split as a separate species in 2010.

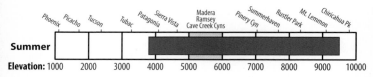

Vaux's Swift

White-throated Swift

VAUX'S SWIFT, *Chaetura vauxi*

Description: 4.75". Small aerialist often described as a "cigar with wings." **Dusky overall**, with paler gray throat, breast, and rump; **short, squared tail**. **Similar Species:** Long-tailed White-throated Swift (below) has contrasting black and white plumage. Swallows have shorter, broader-based wings. **Voice:** Thin chittering usually not heard in our area. **Status:** Rare spring (Apr-mid May) and uncommon fall (Sep-mid Oct) migrant. **Habitat:** Deserts and valleys to mountain canyons and crests. **Behavior:** Forages for flying insects. In Arizona occurs both singly and in loose flocks up to 200 or more birds. **Noteworthy:** SE Arizona represents the easternmost limits of Vaux's Swift regular occurrence.

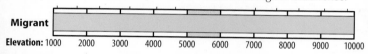

WHITE-THROATED SWIFT, *Aeronautes saxatalis*

Description: 6.5". **Black and white** aerialist with white "V" on breast and white sides of rump; **long, notched tail** often appears pointed. **Similar Species:** Smaller Vaux's Swift (above) has a stubby tail and lacks white markings. Larger Black Swift (casual mid May-Aug) shows no white markings. **Voice:** Scratchy, shrill, and rapid series of *jee-jee-jee* notes delivered in flight. **Status:** Common in summer (Mar-Sep); uncommon in winter (Oct-Feb). **Habitat:** SUMMER: Near mountain cliffs and canyons. WINTER: Primarily lowland areas west of Tucson. **Behavior:** Flocks forage for flying insects. Nests colonially in cliff crevices. **Noteworthy:** Among North America's fastest fliers, easily zooming to speeds over 100 mph; nonetheless in SE Arizona frequently taken by Peregrine Falcons.

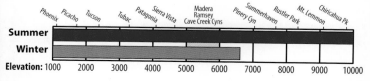

Broad-billed Hummingbird
Male

Broad-billed Hummingbird
Female

White-eared
Hummingbird Male

White-eared
Hummingbird Female

Male

BROAD-BILLED HUMMINGBIRD, *Cynanthus latirostris*

Description: 4″. **Red-billed** hummingbird with notched **blue-black tail**. MALE: Rich blue throat and breast; deep green below. FEMALE: "Bandito mask" behind eyes; red-based bill; gray underparts; blackish tail with white corners. **Similar Species:** Female White-eared Hummingbird (below) has broad white eyestripe, green dots on throat and flanks. **Voice:** Dry chattering *t-dik* notes. **Status:** Common in summer (mid Mar-mid Sep); rare in winter (mid Sep-mid Mar). **Habitat:** Upper river valley, foothills stream, and lower mountain canyon groves; most abundant west of the San Pedro River. **Behavior:** Feeds on nectar and gnats. May nest twice during spring and summer. **Noteworthy:** Broad-billed Hummingbirds live up to their name with very wide-based bills.

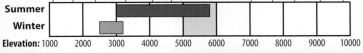

Summer									
Winter									
Elevation: 1000	2000	3000	4000	5000	6000	7000	8000	9000	10000

WHITE-EARED HUMMINGBIRD, *Hylocharis leucotis*

Description: 3.75″. **Red-billed** hummingbird with **broad white eyestripe**, central tail green. MALE: Purple foreface; forest green throat. FEMALE: Red-based bill; green-dotted throat and flanks; white belly; black outer tail with white corners. **Similar Species:** Female Broad-billed Hummingbird (above) has dusky "bandito mask" behind the eyes, uniform gray underparts. **Voice:** Doubled *tsk-tsk* chips; hard chatter. **Status:** Rare in summer (May-Sep); casual earlier in spring and later in fall. **Habitat:** Mountain canyon groves and coniferous forest slopes mixed with some oaks. **Behavior:** Feeds on nectar and gnats. Nests are low in oak or other deciduous tree between 4 and 10′ above the ground. **Noteworthy:** Known SE Arizona nests have been between 7,200 and 7,600′ in elevation.

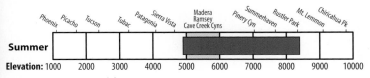

Phoenix Picacho Tucson Tubac Patagonia Sierra Vista Madera Ramsey Cave Creek Cyns Pinery Cyn Summerhaven Rustler Park Mt. Lemmon Chiricahua Pk

Summer									
Elevation: 1000	2000	3000	4000	5000	6000	7000	8000	9000	10000

Berylline Hummingbird
Male

Berylline Hummingbird
Female

Cinnamon Hummingbird

Violet-crowned Hummingbir

BERYLLINE HUMMINGBIRD, *Amazilia beryllina*

Description: 4″. **Red-billed** hummingbird with red primarily on lower mandible, rarely bill may appear black; glittering green throat and breast; **rufous wings and rump**; **purplish-bronze tail**. MALE: Buffy belly. FEMALE: Gray belly. **Similar Species:** Larger (4.3″) Cinnamon Hummingbird (photo lower left) accidental: 1 record July 1992 in Patagonia) has bright red, black-tipped bill, entirely cinnamon-buff underparts, and lacks rufous wing panels. **Voice:** Toy trumpet *ta-do-ta-tee-ta-teet;* harsh chatter. **Status:** Rare in summer (May-Sep). **Habitat:** Mountain canyon groves. **Behavior:** Feeds on nectar and gnats. May nest twice during spring and summer. **Noteworthy:** The first U.S. record of Berylline Hummingbird came from Madera Canyon in 1964.

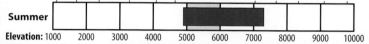

Summer									

Elevation: 1000   2000   3000   4000   5000   6000   7000   8000   9000   10000

VIOLET-CROWNED HUMMINGBIRD, *Amazilia violiceps*

Description: 4.5″. **Red-billed** hummingbird with **immaculate white underparts**; back is olive-brown. MALE: Slightly brighter purple crown than female. JUVENILE: Lacks purple crown. **Similar Species:** Smaller female Black-chinned Hummingbird (p. 187) lacks red bill, violet crown, and snow-white underparts. **Voice:** Popping *tchk* notes, given singly or in scolding bursts. **Status:** Uncommon in summer (Apr-Sep); rare in winter (Oct-Mar). **Habitat:** Foothill and lower mountain canyon groves. Casual in Tucson. **Behavior:** Feeds on nectar and gnats. Nests are ordinarily in sycamore trees, rarely in other broadleaf trees. **Noteworthy:** Peak Violet-crowned Hummingbird nesting activity in July seems timed to coincide with the summer rainy season when both flower nectar and tiny insects are most available. The first Arizona nest was in Guadalupe Canyon in 1958.

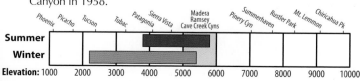

Phoenix Picacho Tucson Tubac Patagonia Sierra Vista Madera Ramsey Cave Creek Cyns Pinery Cyn Summerhaven Rustler Park Mt. Lemmon Chiricahua Pk

Summer									
Winter									

Elevation: 1000   2000   3000   4000   5000   6000   7000   8000   9000   10000

Blue-throated Hummingbird
Male

Blue-throated Hummingbird
Female

Plain-capped
Starthroat

Magnificent Hummingbird
Male

Magnificent Hummingbird
Female

BLUE-THROATED HUMMINGBIRD, *Lampornis clemenciae*

Description: 5.25". Big, **husky** hummingbird with **medium-length bill**; gray rump; uniform gray underparts; **broad blue-black tail** with **bold white corners**. MALE: Blue throat. FEMALE: Gray throat. **Similar Species:** Female Magnificent Hummingbird (below) has much longer bill, scaly green sides. **Voice:** Penetrating high thin *seep* notes. **Status:** Fairly common in summer (Apr-Oct); rare in winter (Nov-Mar). **Habitat:** Mountain canyon groves with perennial water. **Noteworthy:** Blue-throateds are the largest hummingbird species in the U.S.

PLAIN-CAPPED STARTHROAT, *Heliomaster constantii*

Description: 4.9". Large, **olive-brown** hummingbird with **very long bill**; thick white facial stripes; long gorget with red-flecked bottom edge; **white ovals on back and flanks**. **Similar Species:** Female Magnificent Hummingbird (below) lacks white flank and back ovals. **Voice:** Juicy *wheeck* and *whick* chips. **Status:** Casual in summer (mid May-early Oct). **Habitat:** Foothill canyons and hillside agave stands. **Noteworthy:** At 1.5", Starthroat bill is longest of any U.S. hummingbird.

MAGNIFICENT HUMMINGBIRD, *Eugenes fulgens*

Description: 5.1". Large, **dark** hummingbird with **long bill**; oily green back. MALE: Iridescent purple cap; white dot behind eye; iridescent green throat; black velvet below. FEMALE: Scaly green sides. JUVENILE MALE: Uniform green scaling below. **Similar Species:** Female Blue-throated Hummingbird (above) has smooth gray underparts. **Voice:** Imperious *chik!* or *tchik!* chips. **Status:** Common in summer (Apr-Oct); rare in winter (Nov-Mar). **Habitat:** SUMMER: Mountain canyon groves; openings within coniferous forest. WINTER: Lower mountain canyons. **Noteworthy:** Only subordinate to Blue-throated Hummingbird at feeders.

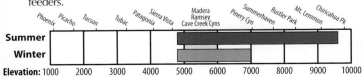

Lucifer Hummingbird
Male

Lucifer Hummingbird
Female

Black-chinned Hummingbird
Male

Black-chinned Hummingbird
Female

LUCIFER HUMMINGBIRD, *Calothorax lucifer*

Description: 3.75". Relatively **long, deeply-arched bill**. MALE: Elongated, pointed purple gorget; long, thin tail. FEMALE: Broad apricot stripe behind eye; apricot and cream underparts; extensively rufous tail base.
Similar Species: Female Black-chinned Hummingbird (below) lacks broad, apricot stripe behind eye and never shows rufous at base of tail.
Voice: Lightly smacking *cheat cheat* notes, sometimes run together into a thin stutter. **Status:** Rare in summer (Apr-mid Oct). **Habitat:** Foothill canyons; hillside agave and ocotillo stands. **Behavior:** Male performs courtship display over the head of female as she sits on nest.
Noteworthy: Now annual, it was 69 years from Arizona's first recorded Lucifer Hummingbird in 1874 until the next sighting in 1963.

Summer
Elevation: 1000   2000   3000   4000   5000   6000   7000   8000   9000   10000

BLACK-CHINNED HUMMINGBIRD, *Archilochus alexandri*

Description: 3.75". **Lanky**, green-backed hummer with medium-long bill; **tail projects beyond wingtips**. MALE: Black chin; violet throat band (often looks black); white spot behind eye; broad white collar below throat. FEMALE: Throat finely stippled; pale gray underparts; green-based tail. **Similar Species:** Female Anna's (p. 189) has diffuse stripe behind eye, heavily dotted throat, dark gray breast, with iridescent green flank spotting. **Voice:** Soft *tchup* notes, sometimes doubled or repeated in a series. **Status:** Common summer resident (Mar-mid Oct). **Habitat:** Deserts, valleys, foothills, and mountains, especially urban areas, oases, river and stream groves, and woodlands. **Behavior:** Wags tail as it feeds on nectar and gnats. **Noteworthy:** Black-chinned is Arizona's most abundant summering hummingbird.

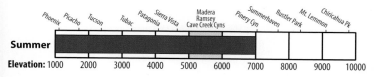

Summer
Elevation: 1000   2000   3000   4000   5000   6000   7000   8000   9000   10000

Anna's Hummingbird
Male

Anna's Hummingbird
Female

Costa's Hummingbird
Male

Costa's Hummingbird
Female

ANNA'S HUMMINGBIRD, *Calypte anna*

Description: 3.75". **Stocky** hummingbird with **short bill**. MALE: Rose-red, square-cut hood. FEMALE: Diffuse stripe behind eye; spotted throat often with central "beard;" iridescent green flank discs. **Similar Species:** Lanky female Black-chinned Hummingbird (p. 187) has white spot–not stripe– behind eye, finely stippled throat, and lacks green flank discs. **Voice:** Scratchy *zzzt-zzt-zz-zzt* song; call is emphatic *tsik*. **Status:** Common resident. **Habitat:** Deserts, valleys, foothills, and mountains, especially in urban areas, desert oases, and river and stream groves; common from Tucson west in winter, and in Santa Rita and Huachuca Mountains in late summer and fall. **Behavior:** Feeds on nectar and gnats without obvious tail-wagging. **Noteworthy:** Anna's is Arizona's most abundant wintering hummingbird.

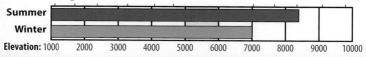

Elevation:	1000	2000	3000	4000	5000	6000	7000	8000	9000	10000
Summer										
Winter										

COSTA'S HUMMINGBIRD, *Calypte costae*

Description: 3.5". **Chubby** hummingbird with **short bill and tail**; wings extend to tail tip. MALE: Purple hood with flaring gorget. FEMALE: Tiny dots on throat; uniform pale gray underparts. **Similar Species:** Larger, darker female Anna's Hummingbird (above) often has "bearded" throat and green flank spots; larger, lankier female Black-chinned Hummingbird (p. 187) has white dot behind eye. **Voice:** Tiny, tinny *sit* chips; very high, thin, continuous *iiiii* song, rising and fading in volume. **Status:** Uncommon in summer-fall (Jun-Nov) and fairly common in winter-spring (Dec-May). **Habitat:** Desert, valley groves, and foothill canyons, especially west of San Pedro River. **Behavior:** Wags tail as it feeds on nectar and gnats. **Noteworthy:** During May, after the spring wildflower season ends, most Costa's probably migrate to California and Baja.

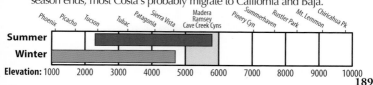

	Phoenix	Picacho	Tucson	Tubac	Patagonia	Sierra Vista	Madera Ramsey Cave Creek Cyns	Pinery Cyn	Summerhaven	Rustler Park	Mt. Lemmon	Chiricahua Pk

Elevation:	1000	2000	3000	4000	5000	6000	7000	8000	9000	10000
Summer										
Winter										

Calliope Hummingbird Male

Calliope Hummingbird Female

Broad-tailed Hummingbird Male

Broad-tailed Hummingbird Female

CALLIOPE HUMMINGBIRD, *Selasphorus calliope*

Description: 3.1". **Tiny; very short bill** and **very short tail**. Wings extend beyond tail. MALE: Rays of magenta radiate from chin. FEMALE: Loose rows of green flecks radiate from chin; apricot wash below; tail tipped snow white. **Similar Species:** Larger female Costa's Hummingbird (p. 189) has whitish underparts. **Voice:** Usually silent in our area. **Status:** Rare spring (late Mar-early May) and uncommon fall (mid Jul-Oct) migrant. **Habitat:** Foothill canyons; hillside agave and ocotillo, and mountain canyons and meadows. Late fall females and immatures also visit flower beds in valley groves and oases. **Behavior:** Feeds on nectar and gnats. **Noteworthy:** Calliope Hummingbird is the smallest bird in the United States and Canada.

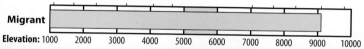

Migrant									
Elevation: 1000	2000	3000	4000	5000	6000	7000	8000	9000	10000

BROAD-TAILED HUMMINGBIRD, *Selasphorus platycercus*

Description: 3.75". **Long-tailed** with irregular **white eye-ring**. MALE: Deep red, square-cut gorget; white collar; narrow rufous tail edging. FEMALE: Throat spotted green; buffy flanks; green rump; limited red at base of outer tail. **Similar Species:** Female Rufous and Allen's Hummingbirds (p. 193) have rufous edges on rump feathers and more extensive red at tail bases, including center. **Voice:** Sibilant *ch-dip ch-dip ch-dip*. Wingtips of male Broad-tail produce trill. **Status:** Common in summer (Mar-Sep); uncommon migrant (mid Feb-May and mid Jul-Oct). **Habitat:** SUMMER: Mountain canyons and meadows. MIGRATION: Deserts and valleys to mountain tops. **Behavior:** Feeds on nectar and gnats. **Noteworthy:** Broad-tails are the most common breeding high-elevation hummingbird in Arizona.

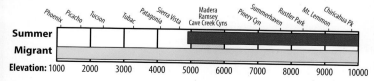

	Phoenix	Picacho	Tucson	Tubac	Patagonia	Sierra Vista	Madera Ramsey Cave Creek Cyns	Pinery Cyn	Summerhaven	Rustler Park	Mt. Lemmon	Chiricahua Pk
Summer												
Migrant												
Elevation: 1000		2000	3000	4000	5000	6000	7000		8000	9000	10000	

Rufous Hummingbird
Male

Rufous Hummingbird
Female

Allen's Hummingbird
Male

RUFOUS HUMMINGBIRD, *Selasphorus rufus*

Description: 3.5″. **Small** hummingbird with **orange flanks** and **rufous tail**. MALE: Fiery orange-red gorget; mostly **copper-red upperparts**. FEMALE: Rusty edging on rump feathers. **Similar Species:** Adult male Allen's Hummingbird (below) has green back and its outermost two tail feathers are toothpick-thin. Female and immature Rufous/Allen's cannot be separated in the field. **Voice:** Angry *tzchk tzchk* and *tzchup* chips; male's distinctive wing trill seems higher-pitched than male Broad-tailed Hummingbird's. **Status:** Uncommon in spring (Mar–early May); common in fall (Jul–Oct). **Habitat:** SPRING: Primarily in western lowlands. FALL: Foothill canyons, hillside agave stands, and mountain canyons and meadows. **Behavior:** Feeds on nectar and gnats. Often dominates larger hummingbird species at feeders. **Noteworthy:** If migration distance is divided by body length, the 2,000-mile migration of Rufous Hummingbirds is among the longest in the animal kingdom.

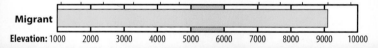

Migrant

Elevation: 1000   2000   3000   4000   5000   6000   7000   8000   9000   10000

ALLEN'S HUMMINGBIRD, *Selasphorus sasin*

Description: 3.35″. Like fractionally larger Rufous Hummingbird (above), but adult male has almost solid **green upperparts**. **Similar Species:** See Rufous Hummingbird (above). **Voice:** See Rufous Hummingbird (above). **Status:** Uncommon in summer and fall (late Jun–mid Oct); accidental in winter. Adult males depart by mid-August. **Habitat:** Foothill canyons, hillside agave stands, and mountain canyons and meadows. **Behavior:** Feeds on nectar and gnats. **Noteworthy:** Banding studies have shown that Allen's constitutes about five percent of migrant summer and fall Rufous/Allen's in the Santa Rita and Huachuca Mountains, and only about one percent in the Chiricahua Mountains.

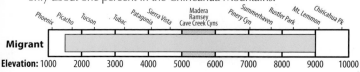

Migrant

Elevation: 1000   2000   3000   4000   5000   6000   7000   8000   9000   10000

Elegant Trogon
Male

Elegant Trogon
Female

ELEGANT TROGON, *Trogon elegans*

Description: 12″. Medium-large tropical bird of border range canyons with **yellow bill, orange eye-ring, white breast band**, and **long tail barred black and white**. MALE: Emerald green above, scarlet red below; uppertail coppery green and underside finely barred with wavy black lines. FEMALE: White "teardrop" behind eye; neutral olive-brown upperparts; brownish vest; pink abdomen; uppertail bronze and undertail heavily barred black. JUVENILE: Like female but with rows of large white spots on the wing coverts. New bob-tailed fledgling requires a month to grow full length tail.

Similar Species: Larger Eared Quetzal (p. 197) has relatively smaller head, black bill, lacks orange eye-ring, lacks white breast band, and has blue uppertail with white underside.

Voice: Croaking series of typically 4-6 *koink* or *koa* notes; alarm call is *w-kkkk*. Becomes mostly silent after July.

Status: Fairly common in summer (mid Apr-Oct); rare in winter (Nov-mid Apr). **Habitat:** SUMMER: Major mountain canyons with sycamore groves near the Sonoran border. Sycamore, Madera, Garden, Huachuca, Cave Creek, and South Fork Canyons are most accessible locations. WINTER: Foothill and lower mountain canyon groves near the border. Sonoita Creek above Patagonia Lake has been reliable.

Behavior: Although males may advertise for mates and announce territorial boundaries from treetops, foraging trogons hover-pluck berries and insects from under the canopy. Most nests are in sycamore cavities that have been excavated by woodpeckers, even those appearing natural.

Noteworthy: In recent summers census efforts sponsored by the Tucson Audubon Society have found approximately 100 Elegant Trogons in SE Arizona. Usually 3-6 birds are detected during Christmas Bird Counts.

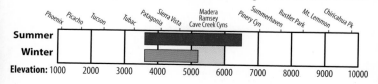

**Eared Quetzal
Male**

**Eared Quetzal
Female**

Description: 14". Large bodied, **small-headed** trogon of the border ranges with small **black bill**, iridescent green back, **green wing coverts**, flame-red belly, and **broad tail, rich blue above** and white below. Wispy, elongated ear feathers usually not visible. MALE: Black head and foreneck; emerald green hindneck and breast. FEMALE: Grayish-brown head, neck, and breast. JUVENILE: Like female but with rows of large white spots on the wing coverts.

Similar Species: Smaller Elegant Trogon (p. 195) has relatively larger head, yellow bill, bold orange eye-ring, white breast band, and proportionately longer tail lacking blue.

Voice: Loud, usually repeated squeal-chuck *wEEE-k* call; flight call a cackled *kac-ka-k-kac*; song is ascending bisyllabic whistle.

Status: Casual and irregular, primarily in fall and early winter (Oct-Dec).
Habitat: Upper mountain canyon groves with adjacent pine-oak forest, usually near the border with Mexico. Most records come from Madera and Gardner Canyon in the Santa Ritas; Ramsey, Carr, and Miller Canyons in the Huachucas; and Cave Creek and South Fork Cave Creek in the Chiricahua Mountains.

Behavior: Eared Quetzals court in spring and early summer but delay nesting until after the summer rains begin in midsummer, when berries and insects are most abundant. In Mexico, young fledge in late summer and early fall.

Noteworthy: The first record of Eared Quetzal in the United States came from South Fork Cave Creek in 1977.

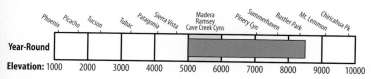

Belted Kingfisher Male

Belted Kingfisher Female

Green Kingfisher Male

Green Kingfisher Female

BELTED KINGFISHER, *Megaceryle alcyon*

Description: 13". Stocky, big-billed, bull-headed plunge-diving bird with a **bushy crest** and white collar. **Blue-gray above** with **blue-gray chest band**. MALE: Single blue-gray chest band. FEMALE: Two chest bands, bottom band rusty. FLIGHT: White upperwing patch. **Similar Species:** Much smaller Green Kingfisher (below) has green upperparts. **Voice:** Long and loud staccato rattle. **Status:** Uncommon migrant (Apr-mid May and Aug-Oct); more uncommon in winter (Nov-Mar). **Habitat:** Desert, valley, and foothill streams and rivers, ponds, and lakes with fairly clear waters. **Behavior:** Often takes open perches overlooking water. Hovers before plunging for fish or other prey. **Noteworthy:** Arizona population has undoubtedly increased as a consequence of artificial impoundments with introduced fish and crayfish.

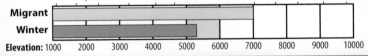

Migrant									
Winter									
Elevation: 1000	2000	3000	4000	5000	6000	7000	8000	9000	10000

GREEN KINGFISHER, *Chloroceryle americana*

Description: 8.75". Small, plunge-diving bird with very long, heron-like bill and white collar. **Oily green above** with **white wing spots**. MALE: Broad rufous chest band. FEMALE: Two splotchy green chest bands. FLIGHT: White outer tail feathers. **Similar Species:** Much larger Belted Kingfisher (above) is blue-gray overall. **Voice:** Insect-like *ch-dit ch-dit*; harsh *chrrrt* notes. **Status:** Rare and irregular year-round. **Habitat:** Woodland ponds, rivers, and streams with sluggish, fairly clear waters. **Behavior:** Often takes low perches overlooking water. Plunges to catch tiny fish and other prey without hovering. **Noteworthy:** SE Arizona population fluctuates in response to drought, floods, and human activities that clear stream groves, reduce stream flow, or increase water turbidity.

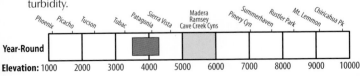

Phoenix	Picacho	Tucson	Tubac	Patagonia	Sierra Vista	Madera Ramsey Cave Creek Cyns	Pinery Cyn	Summerhaven	Rustler Park	Mt. Lemmon	Chiricahua Pk

Year-Round									
Elevation: 1000	2000	3000	4000	5000	6000	7000	8000	9000	10000

Lewis's Woodpecker

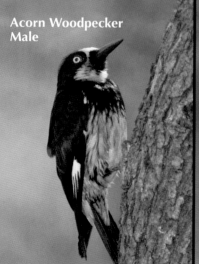

Acorn Woodpecker
Male

Acorn Woodpecker
Female

LEWIS'S WOODPECKER, *Melanerpes lewis*

Description: 10.75". Large, dark, **glossy green woodpecker**. ADULT: Raspberry-red face inside black bonnet and gray macintosh; **pink belly**. JUVENILE: Lacks red face and gray mac¹. FLIGHT: Broad wings; slow, crow-like flapping. **Similar Species:** Acorn Woodpecker (below) lacks red face, gray macintosh, and pinkish underparts. **Voice:** Usually silent in our area. **Status:** Rare migrant and irregular in winter (mid Oct-mid May). **Habitat:** Pecan groves; desert, valley, foothill, and lower mountain canyon groves. **Behavior:** Harvests pecans, acorns, and berries and stores them in crevices; flycatches from high, exposed perches. **Noteworthy:** Tall perching trees or utility poles are important component of Lewis's Woodpecker winter habitat in SE Arizona.

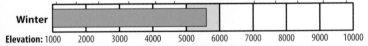

Winter									
Elevation: 1000	2000	3000	4000	5000	6000	7000	8000	9000	10000

ACORN WOODPECKER, *Melanerpes formicivorus*

Description: 9". Black woodpecker with **white iris** and **white clown face**. MALE: Red cap borders white forehead. FEMALE: Black bar separates red cap from white forehead. JUVENILE: Dark iris. FLIGHT: White rump and wing patches. **Similar Species:** Larger Lewis's Woodpecker (above) lacks white face and rump. **Voice:** Aggravated, nasal *drat-it, drat-it, drat-it!* **Status:** Common resident; rare in lowlands in winter (mid Sep-May). **Habitat:** Foothill and mountain canyon groves, exceptionally Ponderosa pine forest and old burns with nearby oaks. **Behavior:** Small groups harvest acorns and store them until winter in "granary trees"– dead snags peppered with small holes. **Noteworthy:** Nests colonially on West Coast with multiple adults sharing one chamber, but group nesting presently remains unrecorded in Arizona.

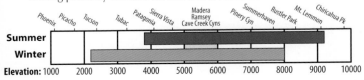

Phoenix	Picacho	Tucson	Tubac	Patagonia	Sierra Vista	Madera Ramsey Cave Creek Cyns	Pinery Cyn	Summerhaven	Rustler Park	Mt. Lemmon	Chiricahua Pk
Summer											
Winter											
Elevation: 1000	2000	3000	4000	5000	6000	7000	8000	9000	10000		

Ladder-backed
Woodpecker
Male

Gilded Flicker
Male

Gila Woodpecker
Female

Gila Woodpecker
Male

LADDER-BACKED WOODPECKER, *Picoides scalaris*

Description: 7.25". Small, bar-backed woodpecker with **black facial bridle**. MALE: Red cap. **Similar Species:** Larger Gila Woodpecker (below) has unmarked face and underparts. **Voice:** Well-spaced *peach* notes; whinnies run-on *quick* notes. **Status:** Common resident. **Habitat:** Saguaro desert, valley and foothill canyon groves, and hillside agave stands. **Behavior:** Pecks for insects. Preferred nest tree, where available, is paloverde. **Noteworthy:** Most nest cavities are on the underside of branches or "lean" side of agave stalks.

GILDED FLICKER, *Colaptes chrysoides*

Description: 11.5". Large, brown, bar-backed woodpecker with **black chest band**; yellow wing and tail shafts. MALE: Red moustache. FLIGHT: **Yellow underwings and undertail**; white rump. **Similar Species:** Northern Flicker (p. 209) has salmon-pink underwings and undertail. **Voice:** Poignant clear *wika-wika-wika* series. **Status:** Fairly common resident. **Habitat:** Saguaro desert; rare in cottonwood groves in western valleys. **Behavior:** Mostly eats ants. Nests almost exclusively in saguaros. **Noteworthy:** Largely confined to the range of saguaro cactus in southern Arizona and adjacent California.

GILA WOODPECKER, *Melanerpes uropygialis*

Description: 9.25". Bar-backed woodpecker with **unmarked tan underparts**. MALE: Red cap. **Similar Species:** Larger Gilded (above) and Northern Flickers (p. 209) have black chest bands. **Voice:** Squealed *wheek* and *slurrr* calls. **Status:** Common resident. **Habitat:** Saguaro desert, valley cottonwoods, and towns. **Behavior:** Seldom drills for fruits and insects. Most nests are in saguaros and cottonwoods. **Noteworthy:** Its "cactus boot" nest cavities in saguaros are used by many other birds.

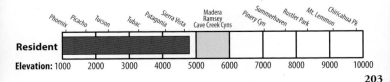

203

Hairy Woodpecker
Male

Hairy Woodpecker
Female

Arizona Woodpecker
Male

Arizona
Woodpecker
Female

HAIRY WOODPECKER, *Picoides villosus*

Description: 9". Black and white woodpecker of high mountains. Diagnostic **long white back stripe**; white underparts; **white outer tail feathers**. MALE: Red bar on the nape. FEMALE: All black nape. **Similar Species:** Much smaller Downy Woodpecker (accidental Apr-Aug in SE Arizona mountains) has small bill and black barring on outer tail feathers. **Voice:** Sharp *peek*. Also a hard rattle *chitchitchitchit*. **Status:** Fairly common resident. **Habitat:** Upper mountain canyons and coniferous forest, especially in recent burns. **Behavior:** Pecks and scales bark searching for insects and grubs on trunks and large limbs. **Noteworthy:** Post-breeding wandering can take these woodpeckers down almost to mountain canyon outlets in desert grassland, well below coniferous forest.

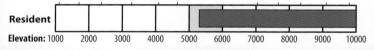

Resident									
Elevation:	1000	2000	3000	4000	5000	6000	7000	8000	9000	10000

ARIZONA WOODPECKER, *Picoides arizonae*

Description: 8". The only woodpecker in the United States with **solid brown upperparts**. MALE: Red hindcrown. FEMALE: Entirely brown crown. **Similar Species:** Acorn Woodpecker has black back with white rump. **Voice:** Loud *keek!* Rattle is harsh *whawhawhawha* rolled into rapid series. **Status:** Fairly common. **Habitat:** Sierra Madrean pine-oak woodland, especially in major canyons. **Behavior:** Pecks and scales bark searching for insects and grubs on trunks and large limbs. **Noteworthy:** Becomes quiet after fledging young, and many move up roadless ridges where they are difficult to detect. Arizona Woodpeckers below an elevation of 4,000' in Sycamore Canyon are about 1,000' lower than other populations in the state.

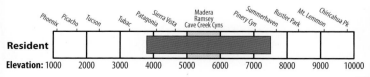

Resident									
Elevation:	1000	2000	3000	4000	5000	6000	7000	8000	9000	10000

Yellow-bellied Sapsucker
Juvenile

Yellow-bellied
Sapsucker
Male

Red-breasted
Sapsucker

Red-naped Sapsucker
Male

YELLOW-BELLIED SAPSUCKER, *Sphyrapicus varius*

Description: 8.5". Red crown; **white nape**; long **black whisker fuses with black bib**. MALE: Red throat. FEMALE: White throat. JUVENILE: Muted pattern of adult superimposed over brownish ground color persists through March. **Similar Species:** Red-naped Sapsucker (below) shows a red nape; black whisker does not fuse with black bib. **Voice:** Plaintive *weea* and rubber stopper squeal are similar for all sapsuckers. **Status:** Casual in winter (mid Oct-mid Mar). **Habitat:** Desert, valley, and canyon orchards and groves. **Behavior:** All sapsuckers eat sap and insects. **Noteworthy:** Most records of Yellow-bellied Sapsuckers in SE Arizona pertain to juveniles.

RED-NAPED SAPSUCKER, *Sphyrapicus nuchalis*

Description: 8.5". Red crown; **red nape**; thin **black whisker does not fuse with black bib**. MALE: Red throat. FEMALE: White chin; red throat. JUVENILE: Lacks solid black breast band. By October young Red-naped Sapsuckers look like adults. **Similar Species:** See Yellow-bellied Sapsucker (above). **Status:** Fairly common in migration (Mar-Apr and Sep-Oct); uncommon in winter (Nov-Feb). **Habitat:** Desert oases to open forests, especially orchards. **Noteworthy:** Any juvenile-plumaged sapsucker in Arizona from October to April is probably Yellow-bellied.

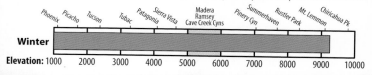

RED-BREASTED SAPSUCKER, *Sphyrapicus ruber*

Description: 8.5". **Red head and breast;** white moustache. **Similar Species:** Red-naped Sapsucker (above) has bold head stripes. **Status:** Casual in winter (late Sep-early Mar). **Habitat:** Desert oases to lower mountain canyon groves. **Noteworthy:** In SE Arizona, hybrids with Red-naped Sapsuckers outnumber pure Red-breasted Sapsuckers. These show suffusion of red over black hind-crown and breast band.

Williamson's Sapsucker Male

Williamson's Sapsucker Juvenile

Northern Flicker "Red-Shafted" Male

Northern Flicker "Red-Shafted" Female

WILLIAMSON'S SAPSUCKER, *Sphyrapicus thyroideus*

Description: 9". Large **black-breasted** sapsucker. MALE: White facial stripes; red throat; **solid black back.** FEMALE: Brown head; **barred back and flanks.** **Similar Species:** Larger Gilded (p. 203) and Northern Flickers (below) resemble female Williamson's, but have boldly spotted underparts. **Voice:** Silent in our area. **Status:** Uncommon in migration (Mar-Apr and Sep-Nov); casual in summer (May-Aug); rare in winter (Dec-Feb). **Habitat:** MIGRATION: Mountain canyon groves and coniferous forest. WINTER: Desert oases and towns; valley groves; mountain canyon groves and coniferous forest. **Behavior:** Eats sap, insects, and fruit. Drills distinctive horizontal rows of small holes in tree trunks called "sapsucker wells." **Noteworthy:** Female Williamson's Sapsucker looks so different from the male that for 20 years–until 1873–they were thought to be two species.

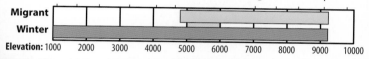

Migrant									
Winter									
Elevation: 1000	2000	3000	4000	5000	6000	7000	8000	9000	10000

"RED-SHAFTED" NORTHERN FLICKER, *Colaptes auratus collaris*

Description: 12.5". Large, **brown**, bar-backed woodpecker with **black chest crescent**. MALE: Red moustache. FLIGHT: **Salmon-pink underwings and undertail**; white rump. **Similar Species:** Gilded Flicker (p. 203) has yellow underwings and undertail and entirely cinnamon crown. "Yellow-shafted" Northern Flicker, casual in winter (Oct-Apr) in valley and lower canyon groves, has yellow underwings and tail, gray crown with red crescent on hindhead. **Voice:** Poignant *clear*; also *wika-wika-wika* series. **Status:** Common resident. **Habitat:** SUMMER (Mar-Sep): Woodlands and coniferous forest. WINTER (Sep-Apr): Desert oases to open pine forests. **Behavior:** Mostly eats ants. **Noteworthy:** Occurs in more habitats than any other woodpecker in Arizona.

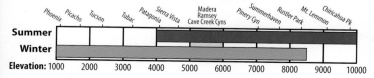

Phoenix	Picacho	Tucson	Tubac	Patagonia	Sierra Vista	Madera Ramsey Cave Creek Cyns	Pinery Cyn	Summerhaven	Rustler Park	Mt. Lemmon	Chiricahua Pk

Summer										
Winter										
Elevation: 1000	2000	3000	4000	5000	6000	7000	8000	9000	10000	

Northern Beardless-Tyrannulet

Olive-sided Flycatcher

NORTHERN BEARDLESS-TYRANNULET, *Camptostoma imberbe*

Description: 4.5". **Tiny flycatcher with bushy crest** and stubby, orange-based bill; **short, faint eyebrow**; grayish wingbars. Orange mouth sometimes visible when calling. **Similar Species:** Larger Gray Flycatcher (p. 217) may share same habitat, lacks crest, has eye-ring and long bill; long tail has obvious white edges. Frequently dips tail down. **Voice:** Descending series of four (usually) clear notes *peer peer peer peer*. **Status:** Fairly common in summer (Mar-Sep); rare in winter (Oct-Feb). **Habitat:** Valley and foothill canyon cottonwood groves, mesquite bosques, and hackberry thickets–or any combination of them. **Behavior:** Forages actively low in the subcanopy for insects. **Noteworthy:** Northern Beardless-Tyrannulet is the smallest U.S. flycatcher.

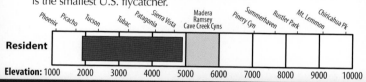

OLIVE-SIDED FLYCATCHER, *Contopus cooperi*

Description: 7.5". **Bulky, bull-headed** flycatcher with white "zipper" down center of breast; white ovals may show above wings when perched; short tail. **Similar Species:** Greater Pewee (p. 213) has smaller, crested head, lacks white mid-stripe on breast, and has a longer tail. **Voice:** Call is *pip-pip-pip*; song is loud *pip-WEE-deer* ("Quick, three beers!"). Usually silent in migration. **Status:** Uncommon migrant (mid Apr-mid Jun and Aug-mid Oct). **Habitat:** Valley and foothill groves; mountain woodlands and forests from canyon bottom to crest. **Behavior:** Sallies from exposed–often dead–treetop perches to capture flying insects, and frequently returns to its original perch. **Noteworthy:** Competition with Greater Pewees seems to force nesting Olive-sided Flycatchers into forests north of SE Arizona.

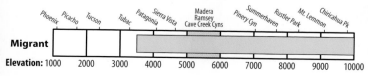

Greater Pewee

Western Wood-Pewee

GREATER PEWEE, *Contopus pertinax*

Description: 8". Slim, peak-headed flycatcher with **short crest**; long bill with **orange lower mandible**. **Similar Species:** Smaller, more compact Western Wood-Pewee (below) lacks crest and has shorter, orange-based bill; wingbars show greater contrast than Greater Pewee's. **Voice:** Pleasant, whistled *José Maria*; call consists of *pip* notes. **Status:** Uncommon in summer (Apr-Sep); rare in winter (Oct-Mar). **Habitat:** SUMMER: Upper mountain canyons, pine-oak woodland, and Ponderosa pine forest. WINTER: Desert oases; valley, foothill and lower mountain canyon groves. **Behavior:** Usually sallies from perches at mid-height to treetops to capture flying insects, and often returns to same perch. **Noteworthy:** This Sierra Madre highland species reaches its northern limits in central Arizona.

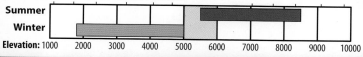

Summer									
Winter									
Elevation: 1000	2000	3000	4000	5000	6000	7000	8000	9000	10000

WESTERN WOOD-PEWEE, *Contopus sordidulus*

Description: 6.25". Compact, peak-headed flycatcher with short, orange-based bill; faint eye-ring; **long wings** with gray wingbars. **Similar Species:** Willow Flycatcher (p. 217) has entirely orange lower mandible, shorter wings, and flicks its tail up. Eastern Wood-Pewee (accidental in SE Arizona), essentially identical, only safely identified by its slow *pee-a-wee* song. **Voice:** Burry descending *bee-zee*; clear *p-pe-pee* and *p'weet* notes. **Status:** Common in summer (May-Sep); uncommon migrant (Apr and Oct). **Habitat:** Valley, foothill and mountain canyon groves, and open Ponderosa pine forest. **Behavior:** Perches from low to high and sallies out to capture flying insects, often returning to original perch. **Noteworthy:** Wintering in South America, Western Wood-Pewees perform the longest migration flight of any Arizona passerine.

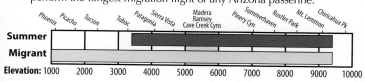

Phoenix	Picacho	Tucson	Tubac	Patagonia	Sierra Vista	Madera Ramsey Cave Creek Cyns	Pinery Cyn	Summerhaven	Rustler Park	Mt. Lemmon	Chiricahua Pk

Summer									
Migrant									
Elevation: 1000	2000	3000	4000	5000	6000	7000	8000	9000	10000

Tufted Flycatcher

Buff-breasted Flycatcher

TUFTED FLYCATCHER, *Mitrephanes phaeocercus*

Description: 5". **Small, cinnamon-colored** flycatcher with conspicuous **crest. Similar Species:** Buff-breasted Flycatcher (below) has rounded crown–not crested head–and obvious wingbars. **Voice:** Clear *pweep* similar to Hammond's Flycatcher (p. 219); slightly burry *treee-tweee.* **Status:** Accidental; present two weeks in May 2008 in upper Cave Creek Canyon, Chiricahua Mountains. **Habitat:** Canyon riparian in pine-oak woodland. **Behavior:** Sallies from high, exposed perches, and often returns to its original perch. **Noteworthy:** Arizona's first Tufted Flycatcher was recorded at Lake Mohave on the Colorado River in February 2005; another was observed in early July 2011 in central AZ at Boyce Thompson Arboretum.

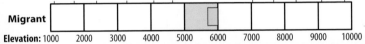

Migrant

Elevation: 1000   2000   3000   4000   5000   6000   7000   8000   9000   10000

BUFF-BREASTED FLYCATCHER, *Empidonax fulvifrons*

Description: 4.7". Small flycatcher with **cinnamon-buff underparts**; oval eye-ring; small bill with entirely orange lower mandible; wingbars tinged buff. **Similar Species:** Similarly-colored and sized Tufted Flycatcher (above), accidental in May 2008 in Chiricahua Mountains, has tall crest and lacks well-defined wingbars. **Voice:** High, sharp *pit!* Also *chidew chdip* song. **Status:** Fairly common in summer (late March-mid Sep). **Habitat:** Open stands of Chihuahua and Apache pines, primarily in a handful of canyons in the Santa Catalina, Huachuca, and Chiricahua Mountains. **Behavior:** Often flycatches below canopy. Often constructs nests well out on lower limbs of Chihuahua Pine. **Noteworthy:** Buff-breasted Flycatchers usually nest in loose colonies of two or more pairs along canyon bottoms. Estimated Arizona population in 2000 was about 75.

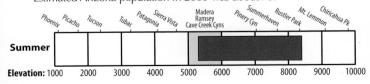

Summer

Elevation: 1000   2000   3000   4000   5000   6000   7000   8000   9000   10000

215

"Southwestern" Willow Flycatcher

Gray Flycatcher

Description: 5.75". **Large brownish** *Empidonax* flycatcher **without obvious eye-ring**; long, broad **bill with lower mandible entirely orange**; flips tail up. **Similar Species:** Mostly gray Gray Flycatcher (below) shows white eye-ring, has narrow lower mandible tipped black, and drops white-edged tail down. **Voice:** Sharp *whit*; burry *witz-beeer* or *fitz-bew* song. **Status:** Rare summer resident (May-mid Oct); fairly common migrant (May and Sep). **Habitat:** Valley and foothill subcanopy thickets. Breeding birds confined to San Pedro and Gila Rivers. Migrants use all wetland thickets, including desert pond edges and lower mountain canyons. **Behavior:** Forages for insects in understory thickets. Flicks tail up. **Noteworthy:** Fewer than 600 "Southwestern" Willow Flycatchers survive in Arizona and are classified as endangered by the U.S. Fish & Wildlife Service.

Summer									
Migrant									
Elevation: 1000	2000	3000	4000	5000	6000	7000	8000	9000	10000

Description: 6". **Large grayish** *Empidonax* flycatcher **with narrow eye-ring**; long, narrow orange **bill with ink-black tip; dips long, white-edged tail down.** **Similar Species:** Mostly brown Willow Flycatcher (above) lacks obvious eye-ring, has lower mandible wholly orange, and flips its tail up. **Voice:** Sharp, dry *wit*; sibilant *chi-lip* song. **Status:** Rare summer resident (May-mid Aug); fairly common in winter (mid Aug-Apr). **Habitat:** SUMMER: Foothill pinyon-juniper woodlands in Chiricahua and Pinaleno Mountains. WINTER: Valley and foothill mesquite thickets and adjacent riparian groves. **Behavior:** Forages for insects in understory thickets. Drops tail down. **Noteworthy:** Below 4,500', Gray is the most common wintering *Empidonax* flycatcher in SE Arizona.

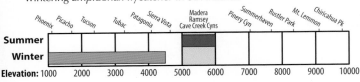

	Phoenix	Picacho	Tucson	Tubac	Patagonia	Sierra Vista	Madera Ramsey Cave Creek Cyns	Pinery Cyn	Summerhaven	Rustler Park	Mt. Lemmon	Chiricahua Pk
Summer												
Winter												
Elevation: 1000		2000	3000	4000	5000	6000	7000	8000	9000	10000

217

Hammond's Flycatcher

Dusky Flycatcher

HAMMOND'S FLYCATCHER, *Empidonax hammondii*

Description: 5.5″. Small, **bull-headed *Empidonax*** flycatcher, with an oval eye-ring; very **short, dark bill**; long primary extension; **tail looks short**. **Similar Species:** Small-headed, slimmer Dusky Flycatcher (below) has longer tail, shorter wings. **Voice:** High, moist *puip* call; does not sing in our area. **Status:** Common migrant (Apr-mid May and mid Aug-Sep); uncommon in winter (Oct-Mar). **Habitat:** Valley, foothill, and mountain canyon groves; uncommon migrant in mountain pine-oak and Ponderosa pine forest in spring. **Behavior:** Usually forages for insects high in canopy. Flicks tail up and often simultaneously flicks wings. **Noteworthy:** Hammond's undergoes its molt on breeding grounds, and is dullest in spring and brightest in fall.

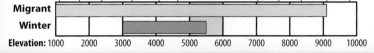

DUSKY FLYCATCHER, *Empidonax oberholseri*

Description: 5.75″. Slender, **small-headed *Empidonax*** flycatcher with a round **eye-ring connected to pale lore**; short, **orange-based bill**; short wing extension; **tail looks long**. **Similar Species:** Hammond's Flycatcher (above) is more compact with proportionately bigger head, longer wings, shorter tail. Distinctive *puip* call helps separate from Dusky. **Voice:** Husky *whit* call, similar to call of Gray Flycatcher; does not sing in our area. **Status:** Fairly common migrant (Apr-mid May and Aug-mid Oct); rare in winter (Oct-Mar). **Habitat:** Valley, foothill, and mountain canyon groves; also migrates through mountain pines. **Behavior:** Usually sallies from low perches to catch insects on the wing. Flicks its tail up. **Noteworthy:** Dusky Flycatcher molts after fall migration, so fall birds have dull plumage and spring migrants are bright.

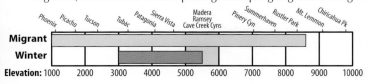

Cordilleran Flycatcher

Pacific-slope Flycatcher

Pacific-slope Flycatcher

CORDILLERAN FLYCATCHER, *Empidonax occidentalis*

Description: 5.6". **Yellow-throated** *Empidonax* flycatcher with teardrop-shaped eye-ring; spade-shaped bill with orange lower mandible; olive above and yellowish below. Best identified by voice. **Similar Species:** See Pacific-slope Flycatcher (below). **Voice:** High *seep* and *pdip* calls; male uses *wh-seeet!*, accented on second syllable. **Status:** Fairly common in summer (late Apr–late Sep). **Habitat:** Wet mountain canyon groves and coniferous forest. **Behavior:** Nests in niches in boulders in major canyons, as well as tree cavities and cabin porch eaves at higher elevations. **Noteworthy:** "Western Flycatcher" was not split into Pacific-slope and Cordilleran Flycatcher until 1989, when DNA analysis established they were different species.

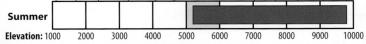

Summer

Elevation: 1000   2000   3000   4000   5000   6000   7000   8000   9000   10000

PACIFIC-SLOPE FLYCATCHER, *Empidonax difficilis*

Description: 5.5". **Yellow-throated** *Empidonax* flycatcher with teardrop-shaped eye-ring; spade-shaped bill with orange lower mandible; olive above and yellowish below. Best identified by voice. **Similar Species:** Virtually identical Cordilleran Flycatcher should be distinguished by voice, but habitat is a valuable clue. In SE Arizona Cordilleran is nearly always confined to mountain canyon groves and mixed coniferous forest, whereas Pacific-slope is a valley and foothill grove species. **Voice:** Tiny, bell-like *tink*; also *pdip* calls; male uses up-slurred *s-weeet*. **Status:** Fairly common migrant (mid Mar–May and Aug–mid Oct); casual in winter (mid Oct–mid Mar) **Habitat:** Valley and foothill groves. **Behavior:** Sallies for insects at all levels from ground to canopy. **Noteworthy:** In SE Arizona, all winter "Western Flycatcher" records seem to pertain to Pacific-slope Flycatchers.

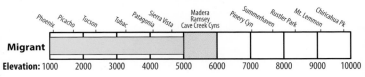

Migrant

Elevation: 1000   2000   3000   4000   5000   6000   7000   8000   9000   10000

Black Phoebe

Eastern Phoebe

Say's Phoebe

BLACK PHOEBE, *Sayornis nigricans*

Description: 6.75". **Black and white** wetlands flycatcher. **Similar Species:** Rare Eastern Phoebe (below), in same riparian habitats in winter, is brown above with whitish throat. **Voice:** Whistled *pdeee*; dying *cheer* call. **Status:** Common resident. **Habitat:** Desert oases, valley rivers, ponds, and lakes, and foothill and mountain canyon streams. **Behavior:** Forages low over water or adjacent grasses, shrubs, or boulders. All three U.S. phoebes often dip and spread tails and all frequently nest on man-made structures. **Noteworthy:** Most birds and wildlife are darker above and paler below, but none exemplifies the biological precept of "counter-shading" better than Black Phoebe.

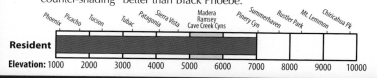

	Phoenix	Picacho	Tucson	Tubac	Patagonia	Sierra Vista	Madera Ramsey Cave Creek Cyns	Pinery Cyn	Summerhaven	Rustler Park	Mt. Lemmon	Chiricahua Pk
Resident												
Elevation:	1000	2000	3000	4000	5000	6000	7000	8000	9000	10000

EASTERN PHOEBE, *Sayornis phoebe*

Description: 6.75". **Brown and white** wetlands flycatcher with dusky chest and yellow-tinged belly. **Similar Species:** Black Phoebe (above) has black throat, chest, and flanks. **Voice:** Husky, whistled *fee-bee*; also *chep* calls. **Status:** Rare in winter (Oct-mid May). **Habitat:** Desert oases to mountain canyon streams.

SAY'S PHOEBE, *Sayornis saya*

Description: 7.75". **Gray**, open-country flycatcher with **apricot belly** and black tail. **Similar Species:** Larger kingbirds have yellow—not apricot—bellies. Larger American Robin has black-streaked white throat and orange chest. **Voice:** Down-slurred whistled *pdeeew*; also rising *pidireep*. **Status:** Common resident; most common in winter (Oct-mid May). **Habitat:** Open landscapes including deserts, valleys, foothills, and large mountain canyon clearings. **Behavior:** Forages low. Perched bird often dips and spreads tail. Frequently nests on buildings.

Male

Female

Juvenile

Description: 6". Compact, **boxy-headed flycatcher** with long wings and short tail. MALE: **Flaming red head** with short, erectable crest and **fiery red underparts**; dark brown back, wings, and tail. FEMALE: Big head with peaked nape and diffuse white eyebrow; neutral brown upperparts; streaked breast; "monokini" of **watermelon pink on lower belly**. JUVENILE: Streaked white underparts, becoming red in first winter male and yellow in first winter female.

Similar Species: Adult male is distinctive. Larger Say's Phoebe (p. 223) lacks female Vermilion's whitish eyebrow and streaked breast.

Voice: Sweet series of rapid-fire *ti-ti-ti-ti-tit-hee* notes.

Status: Common in summer (mid Feb-mid Sep) and uncommon in winter, especially west of San Pedro River (mid Sep-mid Feb). **Habitat:** Valley and foothill canyon pastures and weedy fields adjacent to mesquite, willow, and cottonwood groves. Also uses large grassy parks, golf courses, and sewage pond fields.

Behavior: Flycatches from low perches, usually flying low and occasionally snatching insects from ground. Dips tail like phoebes. Male performs spectacular "butterfly dance" display flight, fluttering high in the sky with chest puffed out.

Noteworthy: Vermilion Flycatcher is the symbol of the Tucson Audubon Society.

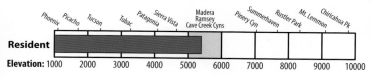

**Dusky-capped Flycatcher
Adult**

**Dusky-capped Flycatcher
Juvenile**

Brown-crested Flycatcher

DUSKY-CAPPED FLYCATCHER, *Myiarchus tuberculifer*

Description: 7.25". Medium-small flycatcher with **dusky-brown, bushy crest**; long, thin-based bill; **pewter gray chest** and yellow belly; **gray undertail**. JUVENILE: Coppery tail edges. **Similar Species:** Larger Brown-crested Flycatcher (below) has big, thick-based bill, medium-brown crest, and extensive rufous in undertail. **Voice:** Mournfully-whistled *Pierre* or *wee-earrr*. **Status:** Common in summer (Apr-Aug). **Habitat:** Foothill groves within oak woodland and mountain canyons within Sierra Madrean pine-oak woodland and adjacent slopes. Casual in winter in foothill canyon groves. **Behavior:** Hunts insects within canopy. Nests in woodpecker holes or natural cavities. **Noteworthy:** One of SE Arizona's earliest fall migrants, most Dusky-caps are gone by late August, and few remain through September.

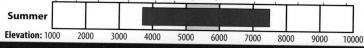

Summer									
Elevation: 1000	2000	3000	4000	5000	6000	7000	8000	9000	10000

BROWN-CRESTED FLYCATCHER, *Myiarchus tyrannulus*

Description: 8.75". Medium-large flycatcher with **medium-brown, bushy crest**; long, thick-based bill; pale gray chest and yellow belly; **rufous undertail** with parallel gray outer edges. **Similar Species:** Smaller, overall paler Ash-throated Flycatcher (p. 229) has medium-long bill, light-brown crest, whitish chest, and undertail has large dark corners. **Voice:** Sharp *hwhit* and a rolling *brit-r-bewww*. **Status:** Common in summer (late Apr-mid Aug). **Habitat:** Sonoran Desert saguaro stands, foothill cottonwood groves, and mountain canyon sycamore groves. **Behavior:** Hunts large insects within canopy. Quite rarely catches hummingbirds near feeding stations. Nests in woodpecker holes. **Noteworthy:** Saguaros and big trees with cavities large enough to accommodate Brown-crested Flycatchers apparently limit this flycatcher's distribution within the arid valleys and canyons of SE Arizona.

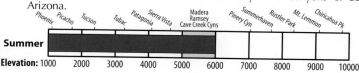

	Phoenix	Picacho	Tucson	Tubac	Patagonia	Sierra Vista	Madera Ramsey Cave Creek Cyns	Pinery Cyn	Summerhaven	Rustler Park	Mt. Lemmon	Chiricahua Pk
Summer												
Elevation: 1000	2000		3000	4000		5000	6000		7000	8000	9000	10000

Ash-throated Flycatcher

Nutting's Flycatcher

ASH-THROATED FLYCATCHER, *Myiarchus cinerascens*

Description: 8". Medium-sized flycatcher with light-brown, bushy crest; medium-long, medium-thick bill; pink interior mouth; grayish ears; **off-white chest; yellow-tinged belly; rufous undertail with dusky corners that usually merge to form bar across tip. Similar Species:** Larger Brown-crested Flycatcher (p. 227) has bigger, thicker-based bill, medium- brown crest, and tail with parallel gray outer edges. **Voice:** Sharp *pit;* also *ka-beerrr* and *ka-brick.* **Status:** Common in summer (mid Mar-mid Sep); rare in midwinter (mid Sep-mid Mar), primarily west of Sonoita Creek. **Habitat:** Deserts, valley grasslands, foothill woodlands, and lower mountain canyon sycamore groves. **Behavior:** Hunts insects from a watch-post. Also eats cactus fruits and berries. Nests in almost any available cavity, including pipes and hollow fence posts. **Noteworthy:** Ash-throated is the most common and widespread flycatcher in Arizona.

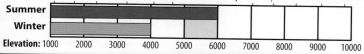

NUTTING'S FLYCATCHER, *Myiarchus nuttingi*

Description: 7.3". Medium-small flycatcher with medium-brown, **rounded crest**; relatively short, thin-based bill; **orange interior mouth**; brownish ears; pale gray chest; yellow belly; rufous **undertail with dusky blobs in the corners**. Voice useful for identification. **Similar Species:** Larger Ash-throated Flycatcher (above) has bushier crest, whitish breast, paler belly, and undertail has large dark corners that often form a bar across tip. **Voice:** Sharp *wheep!* Whining *ka-wheek whe-eek whe-eek* calls. **Status:** Accidental in winter (Dec-Mar). **Habitat:** Canyon mesquite woodland and hackberry thickets within foothill thornscrub. **Noteworthy:** Two recent records: Patagonia Lake 1997-98 and Colorado River Bill Williams Delta 2011-12.

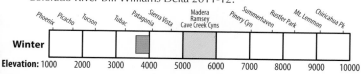

Sulphur-bellied Flycatcher

Great Kiskadee

SULPHUR-BELLIED FLYCATCHER, *Myiodynastes luteiventris*

Description: 8.5". Medium-sized flycatcher with and streaked underparts; coppery rump and tail. Larger Great Kiskadee (below; accidental in our area) has bolder, cleaner black and white facial stripes, reddish wings, unstreaked back, and unstreaked underparts. Squealing *queee-u* notes; series of emphatic *p'dee* calls; squeaky *pee-d'ree* dawn song. Fairly common in summer (mid May-mid Sep). Canyon sycamore groves within mountain pine-oak woodland. Sallies from canopy perches to catch insects; also eats some fruit. Most nests are in natural cavities or in flicker holes in sycamores, often re-used in successive years. Nest cavities are frequently limited in SE Arizona border range canyons, and this may lead to prolonged battles with earlier-arriving Elegant Trogons. In one exceptional case, these two species actually struck one another over 200 times before the trogons eventually won the nest hole.

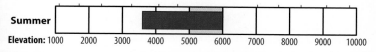

Summer									

Elevation: 1000   2000   3000   4000   5000   6000   7000   8000   9000   10000

GREAT KISKADEE, *Pitangus sulphuratus*

Description: 9.75". Large, heavy-set flycatcher with and tail; egg-yolk yellow belly. Smaller Sulphur-bellied Flycatcher (above) has brown facial stripes, streaked back and underparts. Squealing *greee* and *greea*; explosive *kis-ker-wah* similar to its name. Accidental in winter and spring (late Dec-mid May). Valley and foothill groves near water. There are several records of Great Kiskadees since 1978, including one from Sonoita Creek near Patagonia in March 2000.

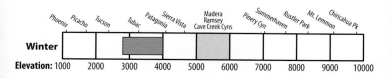

Phoenix   Picacho   Tucson   Tubac   Patagonia   Sierra Vista   Madera Ramsey Cave Creek Cyns   Pinery Cyn   Summerhaven   Rustler Park   Mt. Lemmon   Chiricahua Pk

Winter									

Elevation: 1000   2000   3000   4000   5000   6000   7000   8000   9000   10000

Tropical Kingbird

Notched tail

**Thick-billed Kingbird
Fall**

Spring

TROPICAL KINGBIRD, *Tyrannus melancholicus*

Description: 9.25″. Large, gray-headed kingbird with **long bill**; greenish back; **yellowish breast; notched brown tail**. **Similar Species:** Western Kingbird (p. 235) has short bill, pale gray breast, square-ended, jet-black tail usually showing white outer edges. **Voice:** Accelerating *pt pt prrt prrrrrrrrt* ending in a high, thin musical trill. **Status:** Uncommon in summer (May-Sep). **Habitat:** Valley cottonwood and pecan groves bordering open pastures, fields, or golf courses, usually near permanent water. **Behavior:** Hunts insects from open, often high perches. **Noteworthy:** Although its distribution is spotty, since first recorded in Arizona near Tucson in 1905, Tropical Kingbird has expanded its range to include most of the Santa Cruz and San Pedro Rivers north of the border, as well as outposts in other drainages.

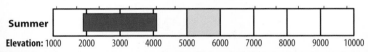

Summer

Elevation: 1000 2000 3000 4000 5000 6000 7000 8000 9000 10000

THICK-BILLED KINGBIRD, *Tyrannus crassirostris*

Description: 9.5″. Large, heavy-set kingbird with **bicolored head**, blackish above and whitish below; **big, thick bill**; dark back; whitish breast, variably yellow belly; dark tail. **Similar Species:** Smaller Eastern Kingbird (p. 237) has small bill, white belly, and white-tipped black tail. **Voice:** Loud and abrupt *purrppt* and a questioning *pureerr?* Harsh "rattlesnake" rattle. **Status:** Uncommon in summer (late Apr-early Sep). **Habitat:** Foothill sycamore and cottonwood groves, usually near permanent water; rarely in valley gallery forest with nearby bluffs. **Behavior:** Hunts insects from open, high perches. **Noteworthy:** Thick-billed Kingbird was first discovered in Guadalupe Canyon in 1958 and near Patagonia in 1961.

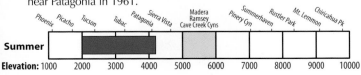

Summer

Elevation: 1000 2000 3000 4000 5000 6000 7000 8000 9000 10000

Cassin's Kingbird

Western Kingbird

CASSIN'S KINGBIRD, *Tyrannus vociferans*

Description: 9". Stocky kingbird with **blue-gray head**; medium-sized bill; **white chin**; gray back; lead-gray breast; dark **tail with translucent tip**. **Similar Species:** Pale gray Western Kingbird (below) has much paler gray breast that does not contrast with its chin, and a jet-black tail usually showing white outer edges. **Voice:** Rough, imperative *c'mere!* call; rapidly repeated *ch'keer ch'keer ch'keer*. **Status:** Common in summer (Apr-Oct); casual in winter (Nov-Mar). **Habitat:** Valley, foothill, and lower mountain canyon groves bordering open areas, primarily above 3,000'. **Behavior:** Hunts insects from exposed, often high perches. **Noteworthy:** Cassin's is the only kingbird expected to over-winter in SE Arizona, although it is not reported every winter.

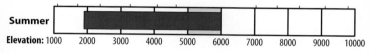

Summer									
Elevation: 1000	2000	3000	4000	5000	6000	7000	8000	9000	10000

WESTERN KINGBIRD, *Tyrannus verticalis*

Description: 8.75". Pale gray kingbird with **short bill**; gray back tinged with olive; pale gray breast; **jet-black tail with white outer edges**. **Similar Species:** Darker Cassin's Kingbird (above) has white chin contrasting with lead-gray breast, dark tail usually showing a paler, translucent tip. **Voice:** Querulous, rolling *p'dik p'dik p'dik dik dik dik dik*. **Status:** Common in summer (mid Mar-Oct); casual in early winter (Nov-Dec). **Habitat:** Open deserts, valley grasslands, and farms, up to the base of the mountains. **Behavior:** Hunts insects from open, often low perches. Nests in the highest available saguaro, tree, utility pole, or tower. **Noteworthy:** Loose flocks of hundreds may gather in September prior to fall migration.

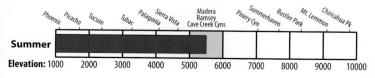

Phoenix	Picacho	Tucson	Tubac	Patagonia	Sierra Vista	Madera Ramsey Cave Creek Cyns	Pinery Cyn	Summerhaven	Rustler Park	Mt. Lemmon	Chiricahua Pk

Summer									
Elevation: 1000	2000	3000	4000	5000	6000	7000	8000	9000	10000

Eastern Kingbird

Scissor-tailed Flycatcher

EASTERN KINGBIRD, *Tyrannus tyrannus*

Description: 8.5". **Two-toned kingbird** with black head and slaty upperparts; white below; black tail with **white tail tip**. **Similar Species:** Larger Thick-billed Kingbird (p. 233) has much larger bill, yellowish wash on belly, and lacks white terminal band on tail. **Voice:** Tiny, buzzy, insect-like *bzzeer*; series of sharp, sputtering *bzeet* notes. **Status:** Rare migrant (mid May-mid Jun and mid Jul-mid Oct). **Habitat:** Open areas within valley, foothill, and lower mountain canyon groves, usually near water. **Behavior:** Hunts insects from open, often low perches. **Noteworthy:** Although it migrates and winters in flocks in South America, only single Eastern Kingbirds have been recorded in SE Arizona.

Migrant

Elevation: 1000 2000 3000 4000 5000 6000 7000 8000 9000 10000

SCISSOR-TAILED FLYCATCHER, *Tyrannus forficatus*

Description: 13". **White-headed kingbird** with salmon-pink belly; extravagant, **long black and white tail**. JUVENILE: Black tail with white outer edges is not disproportionately long. FLIGHT: Pink underwings; tail splayed like open scissor blades. **Similar Species:** Adults are unmistakable. Immature resembles Western Kingbird (p. 235) but has white head and underparts, and lacks any yellow on belly. **Voice:** Deliberate *pek pek pek pur-ree* rising in pitch and speeding up at end; loud *pip* calls. **Status:** Rare in summer (mid Apr-mid Oct), especially during the summer rainy season in August; casual in winter (mid Oct-mid Apr). **Habitat:** Open areas in deserts, valleys, and—exceptionally—in lower mountain canyons. **Behavior:** Hunts insects from open, often low perches. **Noteworthy:** Nested once, at Dudleyville, in SE Arizona.

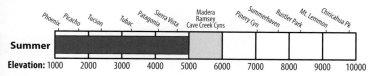

Summer

Elevation: 1000 2000 3000 4000 5000 6000 7000 8000 9000 10000

Rose-throated Becard
Male

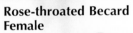

Rose-throated Becard
Female

Gray-collared Becard
Juvenile

ROSE-THROATED BECARD, *Pachyramphus aglaiae*

Description: 7". Stout, bull-headed, short-winged and short-tailed near-relative of flycatcher clan with **black hindcrown**. MALE: Smoke gray above and pale gray below with **rose-pink throat**. FEMALE: Buff hindcollar and underparts; cinnamon-brown upperparts.

Similar Species: Distinctive. Smaller (6") Gray-collared Becard (photo lower right; one record, June 2009, from South Fork Cave Creek, Chiricahua Mountains) has short white eyebrow and bold white edgings on all wing feathers.

Voice: High, squeaky *whee-chee-e*. Also whining, violin-like *fewww* notes, and thin, excited chatter abruptly dying away like a ricocheting "BB".

Status: Rare and irregular in summer (mid May-mid Sep) and casual in winter (mid Sep-mid May). Not recorded some years. **Habitat:** Canyons within foothill thornscrub with tall sycamores or cottonwoods, some permanent water, and a well-developed understory of hackberry, elderberry, mesquite, or other short trees.

Behavior: Hunts insects primarily high within the canopy, but descends into understory on occasion for prey items, as well as small fruits or berries. Huge globular nests are ordinarily suspended from the tip of a sycamore or cottonwood branch directly over a streambed, and dimensions usually range from 15-30" in length and 12-20" in width, with a single entrance located low on the structure.

Noteworthy: After the first Rose-throated Becard was discovered in the Huachuca Mountains in 1888, none were seen in Arizona again until 1947, when a small colony was located on Sonoita Creek just south of Patagonia. Has also been found irregularly California Gulch and lower Sycamore Canyon in the Atascosa Mountains and, casually in winter (mid Oct-mid Jan), along the Santa Cruz River south of Tubac.

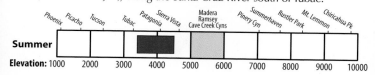

Loggerhead Shrike

Northern Shrike

LOGGERHEAD SHRIKE, *Lanius ludovicianus*

Description: 9". Compact shrike with bold black **mask joined above bill**; hooked, thick black bill. JUVENILE: Finely barred above and below. FLIGHT: Conspicuous white patches on black wings; white rump contrasts with black tail on Arizona race. Flight is low and rapid, ending with upsweeping glide to perch. **Similar Species:** Longer and slimmer Northern Mockingbird (p. 309) lacks black mask and has a small, thin bill; does not show white rump in flight. **Voice:** Thin and squeaky *squeent*; repeated gurgles; electric buzzer *bzzz*. **Status:** Uncommon in summer (Apr-Sep) and fairly common in winter (Oct-Mar) when migrants from north augment resident population. **Habitat:** Flat to gently rolling open deserts, valley grasslands, farm fields and pastures. **Behavior:** Assumes watch-posts on fence lines, utility wires, and tops of shrubs; pursues primarily large insects, but also lizards and small birds, with bursts of speed. **Noteworthy:** Impaling prey on thorns or barbed wire to store for later use earned it the colloquial name of "Butcher Bird."

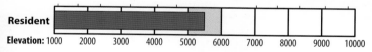

Resident

Elevation: 1000   2000   3000   4000   5000   6000   7000   8000   9000   10000

NORTHERN SHRIKE, *Lanius excubitor*

Description: 10". **Long-tailed** shrike with black stripes through eyes; **white forehead line**; hooked, long black bill; faintly barred underparts. JUVENILE: Dusky facial stripes; brownish barring below. **Similar Species:** Smaller Loggerhead Shrike (above) has black line on forehead above shorter bill and lacks faint barring on underparts. **Status:** Accidental in winter (mid Dec-late Mar) in same areas as Loggerhead Shrikes.

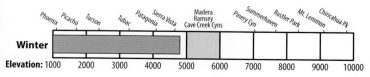

Phoenix   Picacho   Tucson   Tubac   Patagonia   Sierra Vista   Madera Ramsey Cave Creek Cyns   Pinery Cyn   Summerhaven   Rustler Park   Mt. Lemmon   Chiricahua Pk

Winter

Elevation: 1000   2000   3000   4000   5000   6000   7000   8000   9000   10000

"Arizona" Bell's Vireo

Gray Vireo

"ARIZONA" BELL'S VIREO, *Vireo bellii arizonae*

Description: 4.75". **Small vireo** with **both a pale eyebrow and a broken eye-ring**, neither sharply defined; forward wingbar weaker than rear wingbar; long tail expressively waved. **Similar Species:** Larger Gray Vireo (below) has unbroken narrow white eye-ring and lacks eyebrow. **Voice:** Song usually consists of a question, often repeated, and an answer *cheedle-cheedle-cheedle-dee? cheedle-cheedle-cheedle-der*; also nasal *cherr cherr cherr* calls. **Status:** Common in summer (mid Mar-Sep). **Habitat:** Dense thickets in desert, valley, and foothill washes up to mountain canyon outlets. **Behavior:** Hunts insects actively in dense thickets and vine tangles. Sings throughout the summer. **Noteworthy:** "Arizona" race birds are intermediate between green and yellow Eastern forms and monochromatic gray "Least" Bell's Vireos of California.

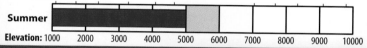

Summer									
Elevation: 1000	2000	3000	4000	5000	6000	7000	8000	9000	10000

GRAY VIREO, *Vireo vicinior*

Description: 5.5". **Gray and whitish vireo** with a narrow **white eye-ring**; usually shows only **one faint wingbar**; flicks long tail. **Similar Species:** Plumbeous Vireo (p. 247) has bold white "spectacles," two conspicuous white wingbars, shorter tail never flicked. **Voice:** Musical series of *cheup cheuu* notes delivered faster than Plumbeous Vireo song; also nasal *cheh* calls. **Status:** Uncommon and local in summer (late Mar-Sep). **Habitat:** Hillside pinyon-juniper woodlands, and chaparral with pinyon pines and junipers scattered through the brush. **Behavior:** Hunts insects actively at low levels in brush and short trees. Sings often during the breeding season. **Noteworthy:** A short-distance, although rarely-encountered migrant, Gray Vireos winter in SW Arizona and NW Mexico.

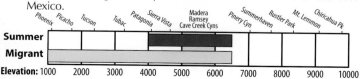

	Phoenix	Picacho	Tucson	Tubac	Patagonia	Sierra Vista / Ramsey Cave Creek Cyns	Madera Cyns	Pinery Cyn	Summerhaven	Rustler Park	Mt. Lemmon	Chiricahua Pk
Summer												
Migrant												
Elevation: 1000	2000		3000	4000	5000	6000		7000	8000	9000		10000

White-eyed Vireo

Yellow-throated Vireo

WHITE-EYED VIREO, *Vireo griseus*

Description: 5″. **Small vireo** with **yellow spectacles**; two white wingbars; yellow flanks. ADULT: Green cap; **white iris**. JUVENILE: Gray cap; brown iris. **Similar Species:** None similar. **Voice:** Song rendered *chick-for-free, you!*; also nasal *breh breh breh breh* scold. **Status:** Casual in summer (Apr-Aug). **Habitat:** Dense thickets in desert, valley, and foothill washes up to lower mountain canyons. **Behavior:** Hunts insects actively in dense thickets and vine tangles. Sings throughout the year. **Noteworthy:** Approximately one-third of a White-eyed Vireo's diet is moths, butterflies, and their larvae.

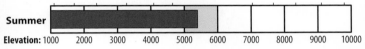

Summer									
Elevation: 1000	2000	3000	4000	5000	6000	7000	8000	9000	10000

YELLOW-THROATED VIREO, *Vireo flavifrons*

Description: 5.5″. **Yellow-headed vireo** with **bright yellow spectacles**; two bold white wingbars; short tail. **Similar Species:** Cassin's Vireo (p. 247) may have olive-gray–not yellow–head and has bold white–not yellow–spectacles. **Voice:** Loud series of *chu-wee che-uu cher-ruu* notes similar to Plumbeous Vireo song; also harsh, nasal *cheh cheh cheh* scold. **Status:** Rare in summer (May-Sep); accidental in fall (Oct). **Habitat:** Valley, foothill, and mountain canyon groves, usually with permanent water. **Behavior:** Moves deliberately through the canopy as it hunts for insects. Sings throughout the breeding season. **Noteworthy:** In SE Arizona, foothill and mountain canyon records usually come in May and June. Valley cottonwood grove records of Yellow-throated Vireos span May-September; some valley birds stay for weeks or months.

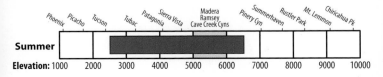

Summer									
Elevation: 1000	2000	3000	4000	5000	6000	7000	8000	9000	10000

245

Plumbeous Vireo

Cassin's Vireo

PLUMBEOUS VIREO, *Vireo plumbeus*

Description: 5.5". **Lead-gray vireo** with **bold white spectacles**; gray wing edgings; whitish underparts. SPRING: Gray flanks. FALL: Flanks often tinged yellow. **Similar Species:** Cassin's Vireo (below) has greenish back, greenish wing edgings, and yellow flanks. See Gray Vireo (p. 243). **Voice:** Slow, conversational *wheeu wheeu wheeu whe-you*; loud, harsh *jhhh jhhh jhhh* scold. **Status:** Common in summer (Apr-Sep); rare in winter, primarily from the Santa Cruz Valley west. **Habitat:** SUMMER: Mountain pine-oak woodland, canyon groves, and Ponderosa pine forest. WINTER: Sonoran Desert oases and valley groves. **Behavior:** Forages methodically for insects along branches and in leaves. Persistent singer, often heard throughout the day during summer. **Noteworthy:** Plumbeous is usually the easiest summering vireo species to observe in Arizona.

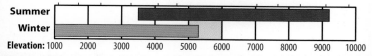

Summer									
Winter									
Elevation: 1000	2000	3000	4000	5000	6000	7000	8000	9000	10000

CASSIN'S VIREO, *Vireo cassinii*

Description: 5.25". **Greenish-backed, greenish-naped vireo** with **bold white spectacles**; greenish wing edgings; yellow flanks. **Similar Species:** Plumbeous Vireo (above) has gray back, grayish wing edgings, and usually whitish flanks. **Voice:** Similar to Plumbeous, but slightly higher and faster. **Status:** Uncommon spring (mid Mar-May) and fairly common fall (Sep-Oct) migrant; rare in winter (Nov-mid Mar). **Habitat:** MIGRATION: Wooded areas from desert oases to mountain Ponderosa pine forest. WINTER: Desert oases and valley groves. **Behavior:** Forages methodically for insects along branches and in leaves. **Noteworthy:** In SE Arizona during winter, Cassin's is more expected than Plumbeous Vireo.

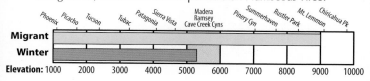

	Phoenix	Picacho	Tucson	Tubac	Patagonia	Sierra Vista	Madera Ramsey Cave Creek Cyns	Pinery Cyn	Summerhaven	Rustler Park	Mt. Lemmon	Chiricahua Pk
Migrant												
Winter												
Elevation: 1000	2000	3000	4000	5000	6000	7000	8000	9000	10000

247

Hutton's Vireo

Warbling Vireo

HUTTON'S VIREO, *Vireo huttoni*

Description: 5". **Chubby vireo with white eye-ring broken at top**; greenish wing edgings. **Similar Species:** Smaller, more energetic Ruby-crowned Kinglet (p. 291) has thin bill and black bar behind rear wingbar. **Voice:** Whiny, oft-repeated *zu-whee*; buzzy *whe-eah* scold. **Status:** Fairly common in summer (late Mar-mid Oct); uncommon in winter (mid Oct-late Mar). **Habitat:** SUMMER: Foothill groves, mountain canyon groves, pine-oak woodland, and Ponderosa pine forest mixed with Gambel's oak. WINTER: Desert oases and valley, foothill, and lower mountain canyon groves. **Behavior:** Actively hops and hovers through mid-levels of trees in search of insects. Sings monotonously throughout the summer. **Noteworthy:** Summer range of Hutton's Vireo largely mirrors the distribution of oaks in SE Arizona.

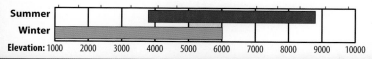

WARBLING VIREO, *Vireo gilvus*

Description: 5.2". **Slim vireo with small head and white eyebrow**; lacks wingbars. **Similar Species:** Larger, darker Red-eyed Vireo (casual; p. 251) has much sharper facial stripes, black-trimmed gray cap, and much longer bill. **Voice:** Pleasant jumbled warble, slightly slurred; harsh *whe-cheh-cheh* scold. **Status:** Fairly common in summer (Jun-Jul) and common migrant (mid Mar-May and (Aug-mid Oct). **Habitat:** SUMMER: Upper mountain canyon groves, especially near water, and coniferous forests mixed with Gambel's oak and aspen. MIGRATION: From desert oases and towns to mountain forest. **Behavior:** Avoids conifers. Forages for insects in leafy trees and shrubs. **Noteworthy:** In SE Arizona, Warbling is the only expected vireo that lacks wingbars.

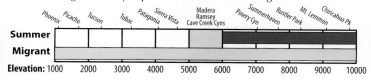

Red-eyed Vireo

Yellow-green Vireo

Yellow-green Vireo

RED-EYED VIREO, *Vireo olivaceus*

Description: 6". Large vireo with **long black bill** and **bold white eyebrow**; blue-gray crown bordered with **thin black line**; **dark loral stripe** passes through coral-red eye; drab green upperparts; mostly white below with yellowish undertail coverts. JUVENILE: Brown eye. **Similar Species:** Yellow-green Vireo (below) has larger pale bill, gray lores, lacks crisp black line above off-white eyebrow. Amount and intensity of yellow on sides is highly variable. **Voice:** Rich series of whistled deliberate robin-like *chewee cherup cherah* phrases; nasal, often descending *meyaah* scold. **Status:** Rare in summer (late Apr-mid Nov). **Habitat**: Desert oases and valley, foothill, and mountain canyon groves. **Behavior:** Searches deliberately through canopy for insects. Sings throughout the day in breeding season. **Noteworthy:** Winters in the Amazon Basin.

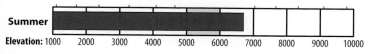

YELLOW-GREEN VIREO, *Vireo flavoviridis*

Description: 6". Large vireo with **very long pale bill** and **off-white eyebrow**; gray crown blends into olive nape; **gray loral stripe** passes through red eye; olive green upperparts; amount and intensity of yellow on sides is highly variable. **Similar Species:** Red-eyed Vireo (above) has shorter black bill, blackish lores, crisp black line above clean white eyebrow, and usually mostly white underparts, yellowish often confined to undertail coverts. **Voice:** Similar to Red-eyed Vireo but faster phrasing and higher pitched. **Status:** Casual in summer (mid Jun-late Sep). **Habitat:** Valley and foothill groves. **Behavior:** Same as Red-eyed Vireo. **Noteworthy:** Winters in the Amazon Basin.

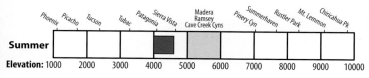

Steller's Jay

Western Scrub-Jay

Mexican Jay

Mexican Jay Juvenile

STELLER'S JAY, *Cyanocitta stelleri*

Description: 11.5". Deep-blue jay with **crested blackish head**. **Similar Species:** Western Scrub-Jay (below) and Mexican Jay (below) lack crest. **Voice:** Harsh *shreeh shreeh* and higher *whek* notes. Imitates other birds, notably Red-tailed Hawk. **Status:** Common in summer (Apr-Nov); uncommon in winter (Dec-Mar). **Habitat:** SUMMER: Upper mountain groves and coniferous forests. WINTER: Also lower canyon groves. **Behavior:** Omnivorous. Food includes seeds, nuts, eggs, and nestlings. **Noteworthy:** Irruption winters bring Steller's Jays from northern populations into Tucson or even Phoenix.

WESTERN SCRUB-JAY, *Aphelocoma californica*

Description: 11.25". Blue and gray jay with **thin white eyebrow; streaky white throat**. **Similar Species:** Larger Mexican Jay (below) lacks white eyebrow and streaked white throat. **Voice:** Squeaky upslurred *shriee* and a series of *sheelp sheelp* notes. **Status:** Fairly common resident. **Habitat:** Mountain hillside chaparral and mesquite-hackberry thickets in foothill canyons. Irruption winters bring Western Scrub-Jays from northern populations into Tucson and Phoenix. **Behavior:** Omnivorous.

MEXICAN JAY, *Aphelocoma wollweberi*

Description: 12". Blue and gray jay lacking distinctive field marks. Social, typically in family groups of 6-12 birds. JUVENILE: Mottled pink bill, unlike any other Arizona jay. **Similar Species:** Western Scrub-Jay (above) has white eyebrow and white throat. **Voice:** Only call is *wink wink wink*. **Status:** Common resident. **Habitat:** Mountain canyon groves and pine-oak woodland. **Behavior:** Omnivorous, but primary food is acorns. **Noteworthy:** Preceding generations of young help adult pairs feed nestlings.

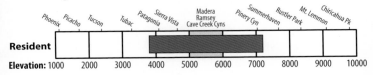

	Phoenix	Picacho	Tucson	Tubac	Patagonia	Sierra Vista	Madera Ramsey Cave Creek Cyns	Pinery Cyn	Summerhaven	Rustler Park	Mt. Lemmon	Chiricahua Pk
Resident												
Elevation:	1000	2000	3000	4000	5000	6000	7000	8000	9000	10000		

Pinyon Jay

Clark's Nutcracker

PINYON JAY, *Gymnorhinus cyanocephalus*

Description: 10.5". **Entirely dull-blue jay with long, awl-like bill;** short tail. **Similar Species:** Larger Mexican Jay (p. 253) is gray below with proportionately longer tail. **Voice:** Human-sounding *hah-ha-ha*; mewing *spii spii spii*. **Status:** Uncommon irruptive in some winters (Sep-late May), occurrences often separated by years. **Habitat:** Possible to desert foothills, but primarily arid lower mountain oaks, chaparral, and pinyon-juniper woodlands. **Behavior:** Large flocks often wander long distances in search of available mast crops, including acorns and juniper berries in SE Arizona. Flocks remain together throughout the year. **Noteworthy:** Flocks average from 100-200 birds in central Arizona, and in fall adjacent groups may gather to form a super flock numbering 1,000 or more birds.

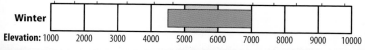

Winter									
Elevation: 1000	2000	3000	4000	5000	6000	7000	8000	9000	10000

CLARK'S NUTCRACKER, *Nucifraga columbiana*

Description: 12". Large, **gray-bodied jay with black and white wings and tail.** FLIGHT: White bars on inner wings and white outer tail feathers. **Similar Species:** Smaller, similarly-shaped Pinyon Jay (above) is dull-blue overall. **Voice:** Variably long, harsh *kraaaah* notes like electric buzzer tones. **Status:** Casual irruptive in some winters (Sep-mid Jun, accidentally through summer), occurrences often separated by years. **Habitat:** Possible to desert foothills, but primarily mountain coniferous forest. **Behavior:** Mainly feeds on pine seeds. Flocks may number up to 10, rarely more in our area. **Noteworthy:** Although Clark's Nutcrackers have exhibited nesting behavior in the Chiricahua and Santa Catalina Mountains, nests have never been documented in SE Arizona.

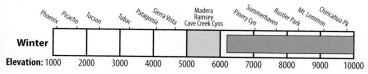

	Phoenix	Picacho	Tucson	Tubac	Patagonia	Sierra Vista	Madera Ramsey Cave Creek Cyns	Pinery Cyn	Summerhaven	Rustler Park	Mt. Lemmon	Chiricahua Pk
Winter												
Elevation: 1000		2000	3000	4000	5000	6000	7000	8000	9000	10000		

American Crow

Common Raven

Chihuahuan Raven

AMERICAN CROW, *Corvus brachyrhynchos*

Description: 17.5". Big, all-black corvid with stout bill; **short, square-tipped tail**. **Similar Species:** Larger Chihuahuan Raven (below) has longer bill, mostly feathered upper mandible, white neck visible in wind, and shaggy throat; wedge-shaped tail shows in flight. **Voice:** Usually rendered *caw caw*. **Status:** Rare irruptive in most winters (Nov-Feb), but some years none reported. **Habitat:** Valley pecan groves and farms.

COMMON RAVEN, *Corvus corax*

Description: 24". Very large, all-black corvid; long bill with **upper mandible only half-feathered**; shaggy throat. FLIGHT: Wedge-shaped tail. **Similar Species:** Smaller Chihuahuan Raven (below) shows white neck in wind, and prefers largely treeless habitats. **Voice:** Resonant *wahh wahh* croaks, deeper than Chihuahuan Raven. **Status:** Common resident. **Habitat:** Desert, woodlands, and forest. Usually absent from Chihuahuan Desert and valley grasslands. **Behavior:** Unlike crows, ravens routinely soar high like hawks. **Noteworthy:** Bold and resourceful, Common Ravens are widely considered the most intelligent of all birds.

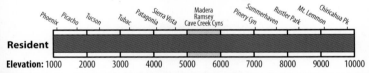

CHIHUAHUAN RAVEN, *Corvus cryptoleucus*

Description: 19.5". Large, all-black corvid; long bill with **mostly-feathered upper mandible**; shaggy throat; **neck shows white in wind**. FLIGHT: Wedge-shaped tail. **Voice:** Reverberant *wantt wantt* croaks. **Status:** Common resident. **Habitat:** Chihuahuan Desert flats and valley grasslands and farms. **Behavior:** Frequently scavenges road kills, but feeds opportunistically on fruits, eggs, lizards, etc. Nests usually have sweeping views and are located in isolated trees or on utility poles. **Noteworthy:** Forms large winter flocks that may number in the hundreds.

"Southeast Arizona" Horned Lark

"Western" Horned Lark

HORNED LARK, *Eremophila alpestris*

Description: 7". Slim pinkish-tan bird with **black horns, black mask, and black collar**; tiny bill; white underparts. MALE: Yellow throat. FEMALE: Duller overall with thinner horns. JUVENILE: Blackish crown and back both heavily spotted with white. FLIGHT: **Black tail** with narrow white edges.

Similar Species: Smaller, chubbier Chestnut-collared Longspur (p. 385) shows heavy back streaking and obvious white wingbars. Slender American Pipit (p. 317) has small head, brownish upperparts, and streaked underparts. Sprague's Pipit (p. 317) lacks the "sprinkled-with-salt" crown and back of juvenile Horned Lark.

Voice: Tinkling flight calls include *tseep, tew,* and *zip* notes. Song starts with very high, thin *terp* notes, followed by rising, tinkling flourish, often given in sustained flight.

Status: Fairly common in summer (Apr-Oct); common in winter (Nov-Mar). **Habitat:** Flat valley grasslands, ranch pastures, fallow fields, golf courses, barren pond edges, and desert openings with flat bare ground.

Behavior: Terrestrial, but will perch on low rocks and fence lines. Found in pairs in the breeding season; northern migrants join residents in fall and winter, sometimes forming large flocks.

Noteworthy: Breeding Horned Larks have seemingly evolved to match the soil colors upon which they forage. The subspecies breeding in SE Arizona, *E. a. adusta*, is the only U.S. race showing almost completely unpatterned, entirely pinkish-tan upperparts. In winter these are joined by "Western" Horned Lark, *E. a. occidentalis*, a variably reddish-backed race from northern Arizona.

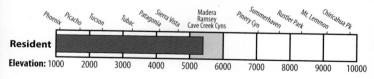

Male

Female

"SONORAN" PURPLE MARTIN, *Progne subis hesperia*

Description: 7.5". **Large swallow** with large bill. MALE: Glossy **purple-black**. FEMALE: Blue-black above with frosty forehead; whitish half-collar on sides of neck; whitish underparts with gray-streaked belly. FLIGHT: **Very broad-based wings**.

Similar Species: Much smaller Tree Swallow (p. 263) is sharply bicolored. In flight Tree Swallow's clean white underparts contrast with blackish wings. Brown-chested Martin (accidental at Patagonia Lake, Feb 2006) from South America is brown above with a diffuse but distinct brown chest band.

Voice: Rich, liquid, gurgling *w'chu cheup churrr cheup* notes. Begins to sing well before dawn.

Status: Common in summer (May-Sep); most common in September when flocks stage for migration. Casual in migration in valleys east of the Tucson area. **Habitat:** Sonoran Desert lowlands north and west of the Tucson Basin, especially near stands of saguaros.

Behavior: Spends much of the day on the wing foraging for flying insects. Perches on the tallest stems of saguaros and on utility wires. Nests in saguaro cavities created by Gila Woodpeckers and Gilded Flickers.

Noteworthy: The small SE Arizona race of Purple Martin is an ecological subspecies whose breeding range almost perfectly matches the distribution of saguaro and cardon cactus. A larger, Ponderosa pine-nesting race of Purple Martin, still present in central Arizona, disappeared from the Chiricahua Mountains about 1985 for unknown reasons.

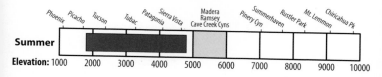

Tree Swallow
Male

Tree Swallow
Female 1st Year

Violet-green Swallow

Male

TREE SWALLOW, *Tachycineta bicolor*

Description: 5.5". Bicolored swallow; **dark cap extends below eyes**; wings reach tail tip. MALE: Glossy **deep blue** above. FEMALE: Dark brown above. JUVENILE: Brown above with diffuse gray breast-band. **Similar Species:** Smaller Violet-green Swallow (below) has white above the eyes and white patches on the sides of rump. Juvenile Tree is whiter below than Northern Rough-winged Swallow (p. 265). **Voice:** Pleasant, liquid *sidilip* or *chirrip*. **Status:** Fairly common migrant (mid Feb-mid May and Aug-Oct); casual in winter (Nov-mid Feb). **Habitat:** Valley rivers, ponds, and lakes. **Behavior:** Catches airborne insects in flight. Often perches over water. **Noteworthy:** Tree Swallows nest in central Arizona.

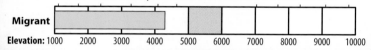

Migrant									
Elevation: 1000	2000	3000	4000	5000	6000	7000	8000	9000	10000

VIOLET-GREEN SWALLOW, *Tachycineta thalassina*

Description: 5". **Green-backed** swallow; **white on cheeks curls over eye; white-sided rump**; wings extend well beyond tail tip. MALE: Green cap; emerald-green back; violet rump. FEMALE: Tan cap; indistinct facial pattern; dull overall. **Similar Species:** Tree Swallow (above) lacks white above eye and on sides of rump; male has a deep blue back. **Voice:** Burry *chidip* calls; also paper-crackle *chip* notes. **Status:** Common in summer (mid Feb-late Oct); casual in winter (late Oct-mid Feb). **Habitat:** SUMMER: Mountain cliffs and canyons. MIGRATION: Valley rivers, ponds, and lakes. **Behavior:** Nests colonially in cliff face crevices and in woodpecker holes. **Noteworthy:** Although most common in the forested high mountains in SE Arizona, recently confirmed nesting in the desert at Organ Pipe Cactus National Monument.

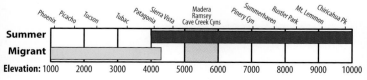

	Phoenix	Picacho	Tucson	Tubac	Patagonia	Sierra Vista	Madera Ramsey Cave Creek Cyns	Pinery Cyn	Summerhaven	Rustler Park	Mt. Lemmon	Chiricahua Pk
Summer												
Migrant												
Elevation: 1000	2000		3000		4000	5000	6000	7000	8000	9000		10000

Northern Rough-winged Swallow

Bank Swallow

NORTHERN ROUGH-WINGED SWALLOW, *Stelgidopteryx serripennis*

Description: 5.25". Brown-backed swallow with drab **buffy throat** and **dingy underparts**, darkest on breast. **Similar Species:** Smaller Bank Swallow (below) is white below with crisp brown breast band. **Voice:** Buzzy *jippt jippt*. **Status:** Fairly common in summer (Mar-Oct); rare in winter (Nov-Feb) in Santa Cruz River Valley from Tucson north. **Habitat:** Valley and foothill streams, rivers, ponds, and lakes and adjacent farm fields and pastures. **Behavior:** Nests are burrows in stream and river banks, less often in dry arroyo banks, or holes in irrigation canals and in unused pipes. Forages for insects over water or nearby fields. **Noteworthy:** Any bank-nesting swallow in Arizona belongs to this species.

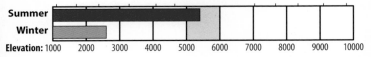

Summer
Winter
Elevation: 1000　2000　3000　4000　5000　6000　7000　8000　9000　10000

BANK SWALLOW, *Riparia riparia*

Description: 5". **Small** brown-backed swallow with **white of throat** curling up behind ears; **crisp brown breast band**; clean white belly. **Similar Species:** Northern Rough-winged Swallow (above) has dingy gray throat and breast, lacks distinct breast band. Larger juvenile Tree Swallow (p. 263) has diffuse, partial gray breast band. **Voice:** Dirty buzzing *zippur* or *chrrt*, often repeated rapidly, actual notes slightly deeper and slightly slower than Northern Rough-winged Swallow calls. **Status:** Uncommon spring (Apr-May) and fall (Aug-Sep) migrant. **Habitat:** Valley rivers, ponds, and lakes. **Behavior:** Forages over water for flying insects. **Noteworthy:** Bank Swallow is the smallest species of swallow in North America.

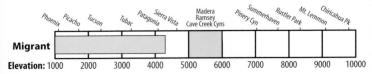

Phoenix　Picacho　Tucson　Tubac　Patagonia　Sierra Vista　Madera Ramsey Cave Creek Cyns　Pinery Cyn　Summerhaven　Rustler Park　Mt. Lemmon　Chiricahua Pk

Migrant
Elevation: 1000　2000　3000　4000　5000　6000　7000　8000　9000　10000

Cliff Swallow

Barn Swallow

CLIFF SWALLOW, *Petrochelidon pyrrhonota*

Description: 5.5". **Black-backed, black-capped swallow** with variably chestnut or whitish forehead; chestnut throat; **cinnamon rump**; square tail. **Similar Species:** Juvenile Barn Swallow (below) has solid blue back and long forked tail. Cave Swallow (casual, with a concentration of records Jul-Oct) has clear, pale orange throat. **Voice:** Creaks like a swinging rusty gate *veeehh*. **Status:** Common migrant and summer resident (mid Mar-Sep). **Habitat:** Open areas in deserts and valleys near rivers, ponds, and lakes, or buildings with expansive, irrigated lawns and fields. **Behavior:** Usually forages in flocks and nests colonially. Adobe nests are attached to cliff faces, dams, bridges, and buildings. **Noteworthy:** The "Mexican" Cliff Swallow, *P. p. melanogaster*, breeding in SE Arizona has a chestnut forehead. Migrant races of Cliff Swallow have white or pale cinnamon foreheads.

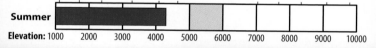

Summer									
Elevation: 1000	2000	3000	4000	5000	6000	7000	8000	9000	10000

BARN SWALLOW, *Hirundo rustica*

Description: 6.75". Large, slender, blue-backed swallow with a **long, deeply-forked tail**. **Similar Species:** Cliff Swallow (above) has cinnamon rump and square-tipped tail. **Voice:** Jumbled, squeaky *whee* or *whitt-wheal* notes alternating with low buzzes. **Status:** Common migrant and summer resident (mid Mar-Oct); casual in winter (Nov-mid Mar). **Habitat:** Lowland and foothill oases, fields, pastures, golf courses, ponds, and lakes. **Behavior:** Flies low over fields or water. Mud-based nests are on man-made structures such as bridges, barns, and verandas. **Noteworthy:** Availability of mud for nests probably determines Barn Swallow range in Arizona.

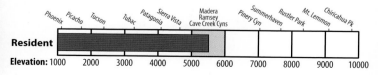

	Phoenix	Picacho	Tucson	Tubac	Patagonia	Sierra Vista	Madera Ramsey Cave Creek Cyns	Pinery Cyn	Summerhaven	Rustler Park	Mt. Lemmon	Chiricahua Pk
Resident												
Elevation:	1000	2000	3000	4000	5000	6000	7000	8000	9000	10000		

Mountain Chickadee

Mexican Chickadee

MOUNTAIN CHICKADEE, *Poecile gambeli*

Description: 5.25". Small forest acrobat with black crown and bib; **white eyebrow**; white cheek patches; pale gray flanks. **Similar Species:** Mexican Chickadee (below) lacks white eyebrow and occurs only in the Chiricahua Mountains. **Voice:** Harsh *shika-dee-dee*; whistled *fee dee dee*. **Status:** Common resident. **Habitat:** Mountain coniferous forests and upper mountain canyon groves. In SE Arizona, Mountain Chickadee is only regularly found in the Santa Catalina, Rincon, and Pinaleno Mountains. It also breeds, sporadically, in the Santa Rita Mountains. There are few recent winter records for either the Huachuca or Chiricahua Mountains. **Behavior:** Gleans insects from the surfaces of leaves and needles; forages for small seeds. Nests in tree cavities. **Noteworthy:** Caches food items for later retrieval and consumption.

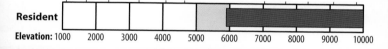

Resident									
Elevation: 1000	2000	3000	4000	5000	6000	7000	8000	9000	10000

MEXICAN CHICKADEE, *Poecile sclateri*

Description: 5". Small forest acrobat with black crown and white cheek patches; **large black bib** extending onto upper breast; smoke gray flanks. **Similar Species:** Mountain Chickadee (above, accidental in winter in the Chiricahua Mountains) has white eyebrow, less extensive black bib, and pale gray flanks. **Voice:** Querulous *zhika dee*; nasal *b-zzz b-zzz*. **Status:** Fairly common resident. **Habitat:** Mountain upper canyon groves, upper pine-oak woodland, and coniferous forests in the Chiricahua Mountains. **Behavior:** Considered a mixed flock leader in its highland habitat. Nests in tree cavities. **Noteworthy:** In the U.S., Mexican Chickadee occurs on public lands only in the Chiricahua Mountains of SE Arizona.

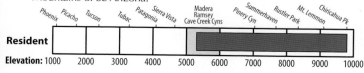

Resident									
Elevation: 1000	2000	3000	4000	5000	6000	7000	8000	9000	10000

269

Bridled Titmouse

Juniper Titmouse

BRIDLED TITMOUSE, *Baeolophus wollweberi*

Description: 5.25". Titmouse with **white cheek outlined in black. Similar Species:** Juniper Titmouse (below) lacks any pattern on gray face. **Voice:** Wren-like *che-che-che-che*; trilled *tra-la-la-la-la* notes; sputtering scold. **Status:** Common resident. **Habitat:** Primarily foothills and mountain canyon groves, and mountain oak and pine-oak woodlands. In winter some montane flocks join the small population that breeds in river valley groves. **Behavior:** Gleans insects from the surfaces of leaves and eats seeds. Nests in natural tree cavities. **Noteworthy:** A third adult Bridled Titmouse regularly joins the nucleus pair in feeding their nestlings and defending their nest.

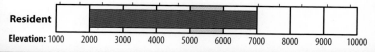

Resident

Elevation: 1000 2000 3000 4000 5000 6000 7000 8000 9000 10000

JUNIPER TITMOUSE, *Baeolophus ridgwayi*

Description: 5.25". Entirely gray titmouse lacking field marks. Blank face with black eye often gives it a vaguely puzzled expression. **Similar Species:** Bridled Titmouse (above) has boldly-patterned black and white face. Bushtit (p. 273) lacks crest. **Voice:** Speedy *che-che-che-che-che-eap*; trilled *gid-dy-up gid-dy-up gid-dy-up*. **Status:** Uncommon resident in the Chiricahua Mountains; rare in the Santa Catalina, Rincon, Dragoon, Galiuro, and Pinaleno Mountains. **Habitat:** Mountain habitats with one-seed juniper as a major component, including chaparral, oak-juniper woodland, pinyon-juniper woodland, and mountain canyon groves. **Behavior:** Gleans insects from the surfaces of leaves and eats seeds. Nests in both natural tree cavities and woodpecker holes. **Noteworthy:** SE Arizona represents the southernmost range limits of Juniper Titmouse in the U.S., although an isolated population exists just below the border in the Sierra San Luis.

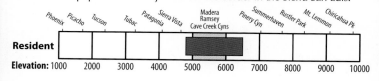

Resident

Elevation: 1000 2000 3000 4000 5000 6000 7000 8000 9000 10000

271

Verdin

Verdin
Juvenile

Bushtit
Male

Bushtit
Female

VERDIN, *Auriparus flaviceps*

Description: 4.5". Tiny gray songbird with sharp bill, dark eyes, and medium-length tail. ADULT: **Yellow head**; oft-concealed rufous shoulder patch. JUVENILE: Entirely gray with pale-based bill. **Similar Species:** Only plain gray juvenile mistakable. Bushtit (below) has fawn-brown ears and longer tail. Juniper Titmouse (p. 271) has crest; Lucy's Warbler (p. 323) has eye-ring and chestnut rump. **Voice:** High clear *chee* notes; also plaintive, sweet *tea-for-you, tea-for-you-too* song. **Status:** Common resident. **Habitat:** Desertscrub and urban areas up to foothill thornscrub. **Behavior:** Verdins are primarily insectivores, but will exploit nectar and eat fruit. Males construct large, oval twiggy nests for both roosting and nesting. **Noteworthy:** The distribution of Verdins in Arizona is almost identical to the range of Arizona's mesquite.

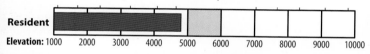

Resident

Elevation: 1000   2000   3000   4000   5000   6000   7000   8000   9000   10000

BUSHTIT, *Psaltriparus minimus*

Description: 4.5". Tiny, usually social, gray song bird with **long tail. Ears fawn brown**. MALE: Eyes dark. FEMALE: Eyes creamy white. **Similar Species:** See juvenile Verdin (above). **Voice:** Tiny, twittering *pit pit pit* notes that sound like jingling dimes in someone's pants pocket. **Status:** Fairly common resident. **Habitat:** Primarily mid-elevation woodlands, chaparral, and mountain canyons, but some also nest in valley and foothill groves. Post-breeding flocks disperse from desert mesquites to mountain coniferous forest. **Behavior:** Typical flock numbers 10-50 birds. Stocking nest is flexible enough to accommodate 7-14 birds at once. **Noteworthy:** Bushtit nests may be attended by several unmated adults, as well as nucleus pair.

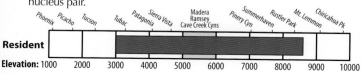

Phoenix   Picacho   Tucson   Tubac   Patagonia   Sierra Vista   Madera Ramsey Cave Creek Cyns   Pinery Cyn   Summerhaven   Rustler Park   Mt. Lemmon   Chiricahua Pk

Resident

Elevation: 1000   2000   3000   4000   5000   6000   7000   8000   9000   10000

Red-breasted Nuthatch

White-breasted Nuthatch

RED-BREASTED NUTHATCH, *Sitta canadensis*

Description: 4.5". Medium-sized nuthatch with a **white eyebrow** and **apricot underparts**. **Similar Species:** Both larger White-breasted Nuthatch (below) and smaller Pygmy Nuthatch (p. 277) lack white eyebrow and have mostly white underparts. **Voice:** Deliberate, clarion *yenk yenk yenk* notes, like a child's noisemaker. **Status:** Fairly common resident. Casual in lowlands during winter (Sep-May). **Habitat:** Mountain coniferous forest and upper canyon groves. **Behavior:** Climbs head-first down tree trunks probing for insects. Stores food for later use under bark, in holes, and in the ground. Smears pine pitch around nest entrance. **Noteworthy:** Food shortages in states farther north probably account for Red-breasted Nuthatches using the Arizona lowlands during irruption winters.

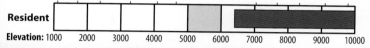

Resident									
Elevation: 1000	2000	3000	4000	5000	6000	7000	8000	9000	10000

WHITE-BREASTED NUTHATCH, *Sitta carolinensis*

Description: 5.75". Large nuthatch with **white face** and underparts; **rufous undertail**. **Similar Species:** Red-breasted Nuthatch (above) has white eyebrow. Smaller Pygmy Nuthatch (p. 277) has black eyestripe. **Voice:** Nasal *ank-ank-ank* notes in a rapid series. **Status:** Common resident. Rare in lowlands during winter (Aug-Apr). **Habitat:** SUMMER: Valley, foothill, and mountain canyon groves, pine-oak woodland, and coniferous forest. WINTER: Desert oases and urban parks to mountain Ponderosa pine forest. **Behavior:** Climbs head-first down tree trunks probing for insects. Hammers at bark and seeds with wedge-tipped bill. Often seen in pairs or family groups. Nests in cavities. **Noteworthy:** White-breasted Nuthatches "wipe" ants and beetles around their nest entrances, apparently as a chemical defense against mammalian predators.

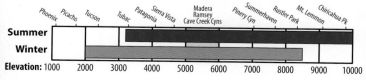

Phoenix	Picacho	Tucson	Tubac	Patagonia	Sierra Vista	Madera Ramsey Cave Creek Cyns	Pinery Cyn	Summerhaven	Rustler Park	Mt. Lemmon	Chiricahua Pk

Summer											
Winter											
Elevation: 1000	2000	3000	4000	5000	6000	7000	8000	9000	10000

Pygmy Nuthatch

Brown Creeper

PYGMY NUTHATCH, *Sitta pygmaea*

Description: 4.25″. Excitable little nuthatch with **grayish-brown crown** bordered by **black eye-line**; white lower face and throat. **Similar Species:** Larger White-breasted Nuthatch (p. 275) has white face encircling eye. Slightly bigger Red-breasted Nuthatch (p. 275) has a bold white eyebrow. **Voice:** High pleasant *peep peep* notes, rapid twittering *pip-pip-pip* calls, often given in chorus by a flock. **Status:** Common resident. **Habitat:** Mountain Ponderosa pine forests. **Behavior:** Acrobatically forages for insects or pine seeds high in Ponderosa branches and needle clusters. Usually gregarious and often joins mixed species flocks. Roosts and nests in tree cavities. Caches seeds for winter consumption. **Noteworthy:** Nesting pairs often have 1-3 helpers, usually males, that assist in feeding the young.

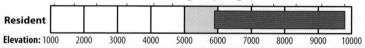

Resident									

Elevation: 1000 2000 3000 4000 5000 6000 7000 8000 9000 10000

BROWN CREEPER, *Certhia americana*

Description: 5.25″. Thin, cryptic **trunk-creeping bird** with a long, thin, **downcurved bill**. **Similar Species:** Nuthatches lack mottled-brown upperparts and downcurved bill. **Voice:** Very high, thin *tseeee* notes; rhythmic *wee-dee-seedly-see* song. **Status:** Fairly common resident. Rare and irregular in lowland groves in winter (Nov-Mar). **Habitat:** SUMMER: Mountain canyon groves and coniferous forest. WINTER: Desert oases and urban parks to mountain Ponderosa pine forest. **Behavior:** Hunts insects by flying to the base of a tree and spiraling upward around the trunk until it reaches the top. Builds nest under loose sections of tree bark. **Noteworthy:** Border range "Mexican" Brown Creepers, *C. a. albescens*, usually exhibit a gray breast and belly.

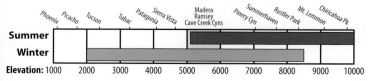

Phoenix	Picacho	Tucson	Tubac	Patagonia	Sierra Vista	Madera Ramsey Cave Creek Cyns	Pinery Cyn	Summerhaven	Rustler Park	Mt. Lemmon	Chiricahua Pk
Summer											
Winter											

Elevation: 1000 2000 3000 4000 5000 6000 7000 8000 9000 10000

CACTUS WREN, *Campylorhynchus brunneicapillus*

Description: 8.5". **Very large wren** with **scaly black throat and breast;** long white eyebrow; red eye; striped white above; streaked black below; undertail barred black and white.

Similar Species: Smaller Rock Wren (p. 281) lacks heavy black scaling on throat and breast, and lacks white stripes on back. Sage Thrasher (winter only, p. 311) has yellow eyes and lacks white stripes on back.

Voice: Chugging song, a lengthy series of *krr krr krr* notes, suggests someone cranking the motor on an older car, trying to get it started. Loud and often heard, for many the song of the Cactus Wren evokes the Arizona desert.

Status: Common resident. **Habitat:** Sonoran or Chihuahuan Desert scrub, urban areas, valley mesquite grasslands, and foothill thornscrub.

Behavior: Eats insects and cactus fruits. Obtains all the water it needs from food and does not require open water in its territory. Large, straw-colored, oven-shaped nests are woven from fine materials and usually placed in a thorny cactus or spiny tree. Males may build up to five extra "dummy" nests, which can be used as roosts, as well as to discourage would-be predators.

Noteworthy: The largest member of its family in the U.S. and one of the world's largest wren species, Cactus Wren is the Arizona State Bird.

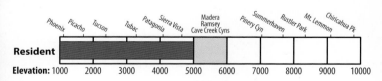

Rock Wren

Canyon Wren

ROCK WREN, *Salpinctes obsoletus*

Description: 6". **Large, pale wren** with thin eyebrow; faint breast streaks; buff belly. FLIGHT: Dull rusty rump; cinnamon tail corners. **Similar Species:** Canyon Wren (below) is rich rusty overall with white throat and breast. **Voice:** High trilled *jdeee jdeee* and *t'rreee*. **Status:** Fairly common. **Habitat:** SUMMER (mid Apr-mid Sep): Open, rocky foothills and mountain slopes. WINTER (mid Sep-mid Apr): Open deserts, valleys, and rocky foothills, especially west of the San Pedro River. **Behavior:** Bobs when perched. Forages on ground and under rocks. Paves entrance to crevice nests with pebbles. **Noteworthy:** With a summer range from 300' on the Colorado River to above 11,500' on the San Francisco Peaks, Rock Wrens nest at the widest elevational extremes of any bird in Arizona.

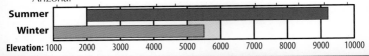

Summer									
Winter									
Elevation: 1000	2000	3000	4000	5000	6000	7000	8000	9000	10000

CANYON WREN, *Catherpes mexicanus*

Description: 5.75". **Large, rusty-red wren** with snow-white throat and breast. FLIGHT: Bright red rump and tail. **Similar Species:** Rock Wren (above) much paler overall with thin eyebrow; lacks immaculate white throat and breast. **Voice:** Downward spiraling series of pure clear whistles, often ending with sneezy *beeep* notes; hard, harsh *jeeet!* calls. **Status:** Common. **Habitat:** SUMMER (Apr-Sep): Foothill and mountain cliffs, rocky ridgelines, and rock-walled canyons. WINTER (Oct-Mar): Desert oases, valley, foothill, and mountain canyon groves, especially with nearby rocky walls. **Behavior:** Bobs when perched. Forages under rocks, and–in winter–along streambeds and in flood debris. **Noteworthy:** Canyon Wrens sing throughout the year.

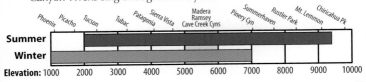

Summer									
Winter									
Elevation: 1000	2000	3000	4000	5000	6000	7000	8000	9000	10000

Bewick's Wren

Bewick's Wren

"Mexican" Carolina Wren

Sinaloa Wren

BEWICK'S WREN, *Thryomanes bewickii*

Description: 5.25". Lanky grayish-brown woodland wren with **bold white eyebrow**; largely unmarked upperparts; **long gray tail**, often expressively waved. **Similar Species:** Smaller House Wren (p. 285) is darker overall, without a bright white eyebrow, and its tail is much shorter. **Voice:** Two-note *eek-Pierre* song begins with a burry inhale and ends in an exhaled trill; calls are *clenk clenk* notes. **Status:** Fairly common resident. **Habitat:** Desert mesquite bosque and hackberry thickets; valley, foothill, and mountain canyon groves; mountain oaks, chaparral, and pine-oak woodland. **Behavior:** Actively gleans understory for insects. Nests in any suitable cavity, including woodpecker holes and nest boxes. **Noteworthy:** Grayish SE Arizona Bewick's Wrens lack reddish tones of other U.S. races and sing least complex song.

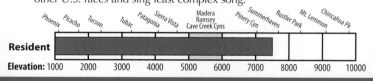

	Phoenix	Picacho	Tucson	Tubac	Patagonia	Sierra Vista	Madera Ramsey Cave Creek Cyns	Pinery Cyn	Summerhaven	Rustler Park	Mt. Lemmon	Chiricahua Pk
Resident												
Elevation:	1000	2000	3000	4000	5000	6000	7000	8000	9000	10000

SINALOA WREN, *Thryophilus sinaloa*

Description: 5.5". Brown, heavyset wren with white eyestripe; **sides of neck striped black and white; reddish rump and tail**; underparts gray without flank barring. **Similar Species:** Slimmer, longer-tailed Bewick's Wren (above) lacks rusty rump and tail. **Status:** Accidental throughout year. **Habitat:** Foothill and mountain canyon grove understory.

"MEXICAN" CAROLINA WREN, *Thryothorus ludovicianus lomitensis*

Description: 5.5". Warm-brown, heavyset wren with black-bordered white eyestripe; "wingbars" are series of white dots; **underparts cinnamon** with faint flank barring. **Similar Species:** Sinaloa Wren (above, also accidental) has striped sides of neck, rusty rump and tail, and grayish underparts. **Status:** Accidental throughout year. **Habitat:** Valley and mountain canyon grove understory.

"Western" House Wren

"Brown-throated" House Wren

Description: 4.75". Small wren with **pale bill**; jaunty, **medium-long tail**. "WESTERN": Neutral gray-brown overall with indistinct eyebrow; gray throat and breast. "BROWN-THROATED": Rich brown overall, usually with a discernible buff eyebrow and a grayish-buff throat and breast.

Similar Species: Smaller Winter and Pacific Wrens (p.287) both have short bills, distinct eyebrows and stubby tails.

Voice: Musical series of trills and tinkles, richer and slower than either species of Winter Wren; also *beeerr beeerr beeerr* calls.

Status: Fairly common in summer (Apr-Aug); common migrant (late Mar-mid May and mid Aug-Oct); fairly common in winter (Nov-late Mar). **Habitat:** SUMMER: Mountain canyon groves and mountain forests. MIGRATION: Desert thickets to mountain crest forests. WINTER: Desert thickets and valley, foothill, and lower mountain canyon grove undergrowth, especially west of the San Pedro Valley. Scarce above 6,000' in mountains.

Behavior: Actively searches for insects in the foliage of thickets, deadfall, and on the trunks of trees. Nests in natural cavities and woodpecker holes. Strongly territorial, and will destroy the eggs of other wrens or songbirds nesting nearby.

Noteworthy: The distinctive mountain-dwelling race of House Wren, *T. a. brunneicollis*, breeding close to the border in the Santa Rita, Huachuca, and Chiricahua ranges of SE Arizona was formerly considered a separate species, "Brown-throated Wren." Some breeding birds in these same mountains, however, are indistinguishable from phenotypically pure "Western" House Wrens, *T. a. parkmanii*.

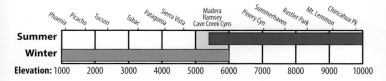

Winter Wren

Pacific Wren

WINTER WREN, *Troglodytes hiemalis*

Description: 4″. **Dark brown**, mouse-like wren with black bill, thin, but distinct buffy eyebrow; obvious, white-dotted wing coverts; **pale brown breast; short tail** usually cocked upward. **Similar Species:** Larger House Wren (p. 285) has pale bill, indistinct eyebrow, and longer tail. **Voice:** Song Sparrow-like *chimp* notes; song is a long and complex series of high, thin tinkling trills half as fast as that of Pacific Wren. **Status:** Casual in winter (late Oct–early Apr). **Habitat:** Dense undergrowth in valley, foothill, and mountain canyon groves. **Behavior:** Searches for insects in dark tangles and flood debris, usually near running water. **Noteworthy:** Call notes and–in spring–song are important for separating the Winter Wren and Pacific Wren.

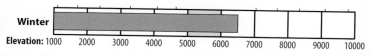

Winter

Elevation: 1000 2000 3000 4000 5000 6000 7000 8000 9000 10000

PACIFIC WREN, *Troglodytes pacificus*

Description: 4″. **Dark brown**, mouse-like wren with black bill, thin, but distinct buffy eyebrow; faintly-dotted wing coverts; **cinnamon breast; short tail** usually cocked upward. **Similar Species:** Winter Wren (above) has paler upperparts with more pronounced constellation of white dots on wing coverts; breast is much more coffee latte than cinnamon. **Voice:** Dry, Wilson's Warbler-like *tic-tic* notes; song is twice as fast as that of Winter Wren. **Status:** Rare in winter (late Oct–early Apr). **Habitat:** Dense undergrowth in valley, foothill, and mountain canyon groves. **Noteworthy:** Pacific Wren was split from Winter Wren in 2010.

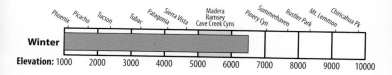

Winter

Elevation: 1000 2000 3000 4000 5000 6000 7000 8000 9000 10000

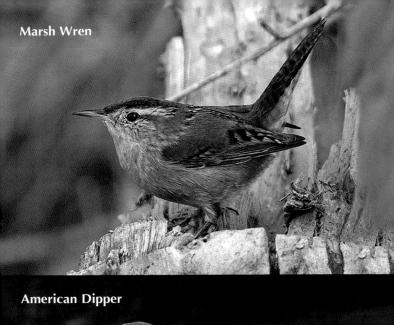

Marsh Wren

American Dipper

MARSH WREN, *Cistothorus palustris*

Description: 5″. Small **marsh denizen** with whitish eyebrow; **black and white striped back**; oft-cocked short tail. **Similar Species:** Lankier, less-patterned Bewick's Wren (p. 283) has longer tail. Smaller House Wren (p. 285) is uniform brown with a very faint eyebrow. **Voice:** Dry *kek kek* followed by an explosive, accusatory rattle. **Status:** Common in winter (Oct-Apr). **Habitat:** Emergent vegetation around valley ponds, lakes, and slow-moving rivers. **Behavior:** Gleans for insects and often calls from under cover. **Noteworthy:** In SE Arizona, the deep water marshes these wrens require for breeding are almost nonexistent.

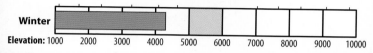

AMERICAN DIPPER, *Cinclus mexicanus*

Description: 7.5″. **Chunky**, brown-headed streamside bird with a **slate-gray body**; short tail. **Similar Species:** None. Has wren-like shape but swims and dives. **Voice:** High, buzzy *dzeet*; song is series of high whistled or trilled phrases. **Status:** Casual in summer (mid May-Oct); rare in winter (Nov-mid May). **Habitat:** SUMMER: Clear mountain streams with waterfalls. Recently nested on Ash Creek in the Pinaleno Mountains, and nested historically on Cave Creek in the Chiricahua Mountains. WINTER: Foothill and mountain streams. **Behavior:** Forages underwater for aquatic insects. Strides along stream bottoms by rowing with powerful wings. Builds domed moss nest under waterfalls. **Noteworthy:** The nictitating membranes over the eyes of an American Dipper function as goggles when the bird is submerged, and account for the flashes of white when the bird blinks on a streamside perch.

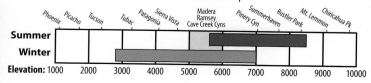

Golden-crowned Kinglet
Female

Ruby-crowned Kinglet

Ruby-crowned Kinglet
Male Displaying Crest

GOLDEN-CROWNED KINGLET, *Regulus satrapa*

Description: 4". **Tiny** songbird of boreal forest with **incandescent crown** trimmed in black; broad **white eyebrow**; white wingbars; dark flight feathers with golden edgings. MALE: Orange crown. FEMALE: Golden-yellow crown. **Similar Species:** Ruby-crowned Kinglet (below) lacks black and white head stripes. **Voice:** Hypersonic *tseee* trill; song of almost inaudibly high, thin notes accelerating into bubbly finale. **Status:** Uncommon resident; rare and irregular at lower elevations in winter (Nov-Mar). **Habitat:** SUMMER: Mountain spruce or fir forests. WINTER: Foothill and mountain groves and forests. **Behavior:** Energetically forages in conifer twig tips. **Noteworthy:** In SE Arizona only the Santa Catalina, Chiricahua, and Pinaleno Mountains furnish the extensive stands of spruce or fir forest Golden-crowned Kinglets require to breed.

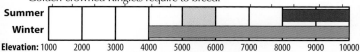

Summer									
Winter									
Elevation: 1000	2000	3000	4000	5000	6000	7000	8000	9000	10000

RUBY-CROWNED KINGLET, *Regulus calendula*

Description: 4.25". Tiny olive songbird with **broken white eye-ring; rear wingbar edged with black**. MALE: Flaming red crest often concealed. FEMALE: Lacks red crown. **Similar Species:** Golden-crowned Kinglet (above) has striped head. Hutton's Vireo (p. 249) lacks black edging behind rear wingbar. **Voice:** Dry *tsit* notes; song is high, thin *tsee* notes that build into full-throated warble. **Status:** Rare in summer (mid May-early Sep); common in winter (early Sep-mid May). **Habitat:** SUMMER: Mountain coniferous forest. WINTER: Desert oases to mountain crest. **Behavior:** Energetically hovers and gleans from shrub-level to treetops. **Noteworthy:** The Pinalenos are the only mountains in SE Arizona where Ruby-crowned Kinglets are presently known to breed.

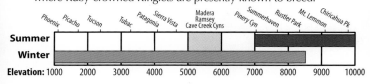

Phoenix	Picacho	Tucson	Tubac	Patagonia	Sierra Vista	Madera Ramsey Cave Creek Cyns	Pinery Cyn	Summerhaven	Rustler Park	Mt. Lemmon	Chiricahua Pk

Summer									
Winter									
Elevation: 1000	2000	3000	4000	5000	6000	7000	8000	9000	10000

Breeding Male

Non-breeding Male

Female

BLACK-TAILED GNATCATCHER, *Polioptila melanura*

Description: 4.1″. Gnatcatcher with narrow white **eye-ring broken on rear edge; short bill; mostly black undertail feathers** with small white tips. BREEDING MALE: Black cap crosses eye, accenting the narrow white upper half of eye-ring. WINTER MALE: Black eyebrow smudge. FEMALE: Brownish-tinged back and wings.

Similar Species: In foothill locations, rare Black-capped Gnatcatcher (p. 295) has much longer bill and mostly white undertail. Breeding male Black-capped's cap surrounds its eye and accents narrow white bottom half of eye-ring. Both sexes of longer-billed Blue-grays (p. 295) always show mostly white undertail. Female Blue-gray has a complete eye-ring without break on rear edge.

Voice: Deep, harsh *shesh-shesh-shesh* calls; also a childish *whee-e* note, often repeated.

Status: Common resident in Sonoran Desert; uncommon in Chihuahuan Desert. **Habitat:** Desertscrub and foothill thornscrub, as well as adjacent thickets in arroyos and canyons.

Behavior: Flicks tail while searching for insects at low levels in thickets and mesquites. Typically nests in mistletoe clumps. Remains paired throughout the year.

Noteworthy: Black-tailed Gnatcatcher is one of the first species to disappear in urban development schemes, even when desert belts are left behind for landscaping. Male shows black cap from February to July.

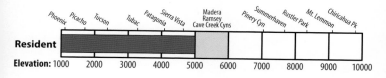

	Phoenix	Picacho	Tucson	Tubac	Patagonia	Sierra Vista	Madera Ramsey Cave Creek Cyns	Pinery Cyn	Summerhaven	Rustler Park	Mt. Lemmon	Chiricahua Pk
Resident												
Elevation:	1000	2000	3000	4000	5000	6000	7000	8000	9000	10000

Blue-gray Gnatcatcher
Breeding Male

Blue-gray Gnatcatcher
Female

Black-capped Gnatcatcher
Breeding Male

Black-capped
Gnatcatcher Female

BLUE-GRAY GNATCATCHER, *Polioptila caerulea*

Description: 4.3″. Gnatcatcher with **obvious white eye-ring**; medium-length bill; mostly white undertail. BREEDING MALE: Narrow black forehead crescent. **Similar Species:** Winter Black-capped Gnatcatcher (below) has longer bill, thinner eye-ring, and—with a good view—distinctly tiered lengths of undertail feather pairs. **Voice:** Plaintive, nasal *speew*; also a conversational-sounding, stuttering query *H'do you, you, H'do you do do?* **Status:** Uncommon in summer (mid Mar-mid Oct) and winter (mid Oct-mid Mar). **Habitat:** SUMMER: Foothill oaks; mountain chaparral and pine-oak woodland; adjacent canyon groves. WINTER: Desert washes and valley groves, primarily from Tucson basin west. **Behavior:** Flicks tail as it searches for insects, primarily in short trees and shrubs. **Noteworthy:** Blue-gray is the only migratory species of gnatcatcher.

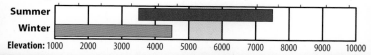

BLACK-CAPPED GNATCATCHER, *Polioptila nigriceps*

Description: 4.2″. Gnatcatcher with narrow white eye-ring; **long bill**; mostly white undertail with **short outermost feathers**. BREEDING MALE: Black cap surrounds eye. WINTER MALE: Thin black eyebrow. **Similar Species:** Black-tailed Gnatcatcher (p. 293) has short bill and mostly black undertail. Breeding male Black-tailed's cap crosses through eye and accents white upper eye-ring. **Voice:** Pleading, mewing *beeww*, fading at end of note; also an imperative, hoarse *burrr*. **Status:** Rare resident. **Habitat:** Foothill thornscrub and adjacent canyon groves. **Behavior:** Flicks tail while searching for insects, primarily in thickets and mesquites. **Noteworthy:** The first U.S. record of Black-capped Gnatcatcher came from Sonoita Creek near Patagonia in May 1971.

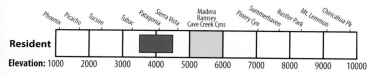

295

"Azure" Eastern Bluebird
Male

"Azure" Eastern Bluebird
Immature Male

Western Bluebird
Male

Western Bluebird
Female

"AZURE" EASTERN BLUEBIRD, *Sialia sialis fulva*

Description: 6.75". Plump blue thrush with **ear bordered orange; orange** breast; **white belly**. MALE: Blue upperparts; **orange throat and breast**. FEMALE: **White throat**. FLIGHT: Underwings uniform gray. **Similar Species:** Western Bluebird (below) has gray belly. Male has blue throat and breast and rusty sides of back; female lacks orange-bordered ear patches and throat is gray. Similarly-colored male Lazuli Bunting (p. 393) has white wingbars. **Voice:** Rich, gurgled *few-for-you* or *too-few* notes. **Status:** Uncommon in summer (mid Mar-Sep); usually slightly more common in winter (Oct-mid Mar). **Habitat:** Open foothill groves and oak savannah, and mountain pine-oak woodland. **Behavior:** Hunts ground insects from low perches. **Noteworthy:** Male "Azure Bluebirds" in SE Arizona are paler blue than the violet-blue birds of the eastern U.S.

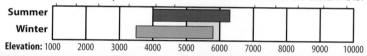

Summer									
Winter									
Elevation: 1000	2000	3000	4000	5000	6000	7000	8000	9000	10000

WESTERN BLUEBIRD, *Sialia mexicana*

Description: 6.75". Plump blue thrush with orange breast; **gray belly**. MALE: Blue upperparts with variably **rusty back; blue throat and breast**. FEMALE: **Gray throat**. FLIGHT: Dark underwing linings. **Similar Species:** See Eastern Bluebird (above). **Voice:** Breathy *phew* and *fee-phew* notes; abrupt *chut* calls. **Status:** Uncommon and local in summer (mid Mar-mid Oct); usually fairly common and widespread in winter (mid Oct-mid Mar). **Habitat:** SUMMER: Open mountain pine forest and burns. WINTER: Irregular from desert oases to mountain pine-oak woodland, especially areas with mistletoe and juniper berries. **Behavior:** Hunts ground insects from low perches. **Noteworthy:** In Arizona, Western Bluebirds compete for cavity nests with Violet-green Swallows.

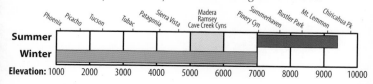

Phoenix	Picacho	Tucson	Tubac	Patagonia	Sierra Vista	Madera Ramsey Cave Creek Cyns	Pinery Cyn	Summerhaven	Rustler Park	Mt. Lemmon	Chiricahua Pk
Summer											
Winter											
Elevation: 1000	2000	3000	4000	5000	6000	7000	8000	9000	10000

Mountain Bluebird
Male

Mountain Bluebird
Female

Townsend's Solitaire

Brown-backed Solitaire

MOUNTAIN BLUEBIRD, *Sialia currucoides*

Description: 7". **Slim** blue thrush with long wings and **long tail**. MALE: **Sky blue**. FEMALE: Gray body; pale blue flight feathers and tail. **Similar Species:** Other bluebirds have short tails. **Status:** Fairly common but irregular in winter (mid Oct-mid Mar). **Habitat:** Open desert flats, valley fields and pastures, and oak and juniper savannas. **Behavior:** Sallies after insects like flycatcher, often hovers, and frequently uses ground perches. In winter consumes mistletoe, hackberry, and juniper berries. Winter flocks some years may number in the hundreds. **Noteworthy:** A pair of Mountain Bluebirds nested in grasslands near Sonoita in 1981.

TOWNSEND'S SOLITAIRE, *Myadestes townsendi*

Description: 8.25". **Slender, gray thrush** that perches upright; **white eye-ring; long tail**. FLIGHT: **Buffy wingstripe** and white-sided tail. **Similar Species:** Brown-backed Solitaire (below; accidental) has warm brown back and wings. **Voice:** Bell-timbred *eeh*; jumbled, continuous, finch-like warble. **Status:** Uncommon to irregularly fairly common in winter (mid Sep-Apr); casual in summer (May-mid Sep). **Habitat:** WINTER: Foothill and mountain juniper woodlands and canyon groves. SUMMER: Mountain coniferous forest. **Behavior:** Feeds largely on juniper and mistletoe berries in winter. **Noteworthy:** Unique among Arizona thrushes, Townsend's Solitaire defends a winter territory.

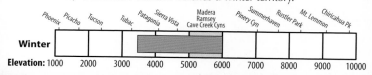

	Phoenix	Picacho	Tucson	Tubac	Patagonia	Sierra Vista	Madera Ramsey Cave Creek Cyns	Pinery Cyn	Summerhaven	Rustler Park	Mt. Lemmon	Chiricahua Pk
Winter												
Elevation:	1000	2000	3000	4000	5000	6000	7000	8000	9000	10000

BROWN-BACKED SOLITAIRE, *Myadestes occidentalis*

Description: 8.25". **Slender, brown-backed thrush** that perches upright; **broken white eye-ring**; thin, black whisker; **long tail**. FLIGHT: White outer tail feathers. **Status:** Accidental in summer and fall (mid Jul-early Aug and early Oct). **Habitat:** Canyon groves in pine-oak woodland.

"Russet-backed"
Swainson's Thrush

"Olive-backed"
Swainson's
Thrush

Hermit Thrush,
guttatus

Hermit Thrush,
auduboni

SWAINSON'S THRUSH, *Catharus ustulatus*

Description: 7". Plump, spot-breasted thrush with bold **buffy eye-ring**; ear patch edged in buff; **buff throat and breast**; flanks vary from olive-brown to tinged with rufous. **Similar Species:** Hermit Thrush (below) has white eye-ring and reddish tail. **Voice:** Liquid *whoit* call. **Status:** Uncommon spring (late Apr-early Jun) and rare fall (Sep-Oct) migrant. **Habitat:** Desert oases; foothill and mountain canyon groves. **Behavior:** Feeds on insects and fruit deep within shady woodland understory. **Noteworthy:** In SE Arizona, the "Russet-backed" race of Swainson's Thrush, *C. u. ustulatus*, from the Pacific coast is more common than the "Olive-backed" race, *C. u. swainsoni,* from the Rocky Mountains.

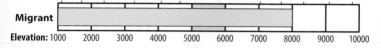

Migrant

Elevation: 1000 2000 3000 4000 5000 6000 7000 8000 9000 10000

HERMIT THRUSH, *Catharus guttatus*

Description: 6.75". Plump, spot-breasted thrush with white eye-ring; **reddish rump and tail**; grayish flanks. **Similar Species:** Swainson's Thrush (above) has buffy face pattern and lacks reddish tail. **Voice:** Call is sharp *chuk-chuk*; also whining *vreee*. Ethereal song begins with clear note, following by several quick, silvery, paired harmonics; successive songs on different pitches. **Status:** Fairly common. **Habitat:** SUMMER (Apr-Sep): Mountain canyon groves and coniferous forest. WINTER (Oct-Mar): Desert oases; valley, foothill, and mountain canyon groves. **Behavior:** Forages on the ground for insects, usually remaining in shade. **Noteworthy:** Summer breeding birds are large, pale gray *C. g. auduboni* of interior west. Most wintering birds are dark, olive-brown *C. g. guttatus* of the northwest Pacific coast.

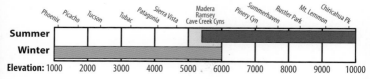

Summer

Winter

Elevation: 1000 2000 3000 4000 5000 6000 7000 8000 9000 10000

Rufous-backed Robin

American Robin
Male

American Robin
Juvenile

RUFOUS-BACKED ROBIN, *Turdus rufopalliatus*

Description: 9.5". Large, plump thrush with solid gray face; black and white striped throat; **rufous back**; brick-red breast. **Similar Species:** American Robin (below) has broken white eye crescents and gray back. **Voice:** Abrupt *chupt*. Whistled sing-song carol, notes richer and longer than American Robin's, is almost unheard in Arizona. **Status:** Casual in summer (mid Apr-Sep); rare in winter (Oct-mid Apr). **Habitat:** Desert oases and urban areas; valley, foothill, and lower mountain canyon groves. Accidental in coniferous forest. **Behavior:** Skulks in understory and thickets searching for fruits and insects. **Noteworthy:** A bird banded on the San Pedro River in June 1996 had a well-developed brood patch.

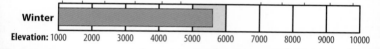

Winter									

Elevation: 1000   2000   3000   4000   5000   6000   7000   8000   9000   10000

AMERICAN ROBIN, *Turdus migratorius*

Description: 10". Large, plump thrush with **broken white eye crescents**; brick-red breast. MALE: Head blackish. FEMALE: Head concolor with back. JUVENILE: Heavily spotted. **Similar Species:** Rufous-backed Robin (above) lacks eye crescents, has bright black and white striped throat, and rufous back. **Voice:** Typically a four-part, sing-song, reedy carol; also sharp *keup* and squealing *kitty-pup* calls. **Status:** Fairly common in summer (Apr-Sep); common but irregular in winter (Oct-Mar). **Habitat:** SUMMER: Mountain canyon groves and openings within coniferous forests. WINTER: Desert oases and urban areas; foothill and mountain canyon groves and woodlands. **Behavior:** In summer, feeds on earthworms and grubs. Winter flocks seek berries and fruit. **Noteworthy:** Forms winter flocks that number from a handful to several hundred birds.

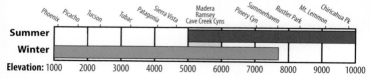

Phoenix   Picacho   Tucson   Tubac   Patagonia   Sierra Vista   Madera Ramsey Cave Creek Cyns   Pinery Cyn   Summerhaven   Rustler Park   Mt. Lemmon   Chiricahua Pk

Summer	
Winter	

Elevation: 1000   2000   3000   4000   5000   6000   7000   8000   9000   10000

Varied Thrush
Male

Varied Thrush
Female

Aztec Thrush
Male

Aztec Thrush
Female

VARIED THRUSH, *Ixoreus naevius*

Description: 9.5". **Robin-like** thrush with **orange eyebrow, throat, and complex wing pattern**. MALE: Black mask and breast-band. FEMALE: Dusky mask and breast-band. **Similar Species:** American Robin (p. 303) lacks orange eyebrow, throat, and wing pattern. **Voice:** Deep *tchupp* notes. Song, a long "policeman's whistle" note on one pitch. **Status:** Rare in winter (mid Oct-mid May). **Habitat:** Desert oases and urban areas; valley, foothill, and mountain canyon groves. Accidental to coniferous forest. **Behavior:** Forages on ground for insects, also eats seeds and berries. Shy, prefers dense understory. **Noteworthy:** Similarities in wing pattern led legendary Arizona taxonomist Allen Phillips to believe Varied Thrush is closely related to Aztec Thrush.

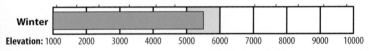

Winter									
Elevation: 1000 2000 3000 4000 5000 6000 7000 8000 9000 10000

AZTEC THRUSH, *Ridgwayia pinicola*

Description: 9.25". **Blackish, robin-like** thrush with **complex white wing pattern**. MALE: Black hood and back. FEMALE: Dark brown head and back streaked with white. JUVENILE: Brown with heavy white scaling on head and underparts. **Similar Species:** Smaller juvenile Spotted Towhee (p. 355) has shorter, thicker bill and lacks white-streaked crown. **Voice:** High *tseeer* notes; thin, hypersonic *tzeee* calls. **Status:** Accidental in spring (May); rare but irregular in late summer (mid Jul-Sep); accidental in winter (Jan-early Feb). **Habitat:** Mountain canyon groves. **Behavior:** Forages primarily for berries in SE Arizona, especially chokecherries in late summer. Inconspicuous, even when plucking berries. **Noteworthy:** The first two records of Aztec Thrush in the U.S. came in May 1978.

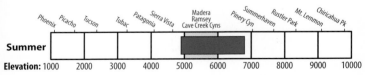

Phoenix Picacho Tucson Tubac Patagonia Sierra Vista Madera Ramsey Cave Creek Cyns Pinery Cyn Summerhaven Rustler Park Mt. Lemmon Chiricahua Pk

Summer									
Elevation: 1000 2000 3000 4000 5000 6000 7000 8000 9000 10000

Wood Thrush

Brown Thrasher

WOOD THRUSH, *Hylocichla mustelina*

Description: 7.75". Plump, spot-breasted thrush with **reddish crown and nape**, gradually becoming warm brown towards rump; white eye-ring; large black spots below; **short tail**. **Similar Species:** Other Arizona spot-breasted thrushes are smaller and lack bright red crown and nape. See larger Brown Thrasher (below). **Voice:** Call is breathy, chortled *whuh-whuh-whuh-whuh*. Evocative gurgling song begins with several swirling phrases, following by trill in a minor key. **Status:** Casual in migration (late Apr-early Jun and Oct-Nov); accidental in summer and winter. **Habitat:** Desert oases; valley, foothill, and mountain canyon groves. **Behavior:** Forages on the ground for insects and berries, usually remains low in understory. **Noteworthy:** Most spring Wood Thrush records come from mountain areas, and fall and winter records come from the lowlands.

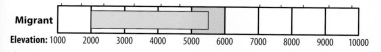

Migrant									
Elevation: 1000	2000	3000	4000	5000	6000	7000	8000	9000	10000

BROWN THRASHER, *Toxostoma rufum*

Description: 11". **Reddish-brown** mimic-thrush with **bright yellow eye**; relatively short, straight bill with pink-based lower mandible; obvious white wingbars; **crisp, reddish-brown spots in rows below**. **Similar Species:** No other Arizona thrasher has reddish-brown upperparts. **Voice:** Loud *chttt* like striking a flint. Song is rich assortment of phrases repeated several times, a pause, then a new set of repeated phrases. **Status:** Rare in winter (Oct-May); accidental in summer (Jun-Sep). **Habitat:** Desert oases; valley, foothill, and lower mountain canyon groves. **Behavior:** Forages on the ground for insects and berries, usually remains low in thickets. **Noteworthy:** Has summered at Portal.

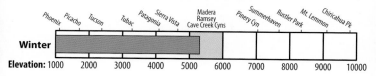

Phoenix	Picacho	Tucson	Tubac	Patagonia	Sierra Vista	Madera Ramsey Cave Creek Cyns	Pinery Cyn	Summerhaven	Rustler Park	Mt. Lemmon	Chiricahua Pk

Winter									
Elevation: 1000	2000	3000	4000	5000	6000	7000	8000	9000	10000

Gray Catbird

Northern Mockingbird

GRAY CATBIRD, *Dumetella carolinensis*

Description: 8.5". **Slate-gray** mimic-thrush with short bill, **black cap,** and rufous undertail. **Similar Species:** Larger Crissal Thrasher (p. 311) is paler gray with much longer, curved bill. **Voice:** Hoarse *mew* scolds. Song is disjointed, squeaky, scratchy, random notes. **Status:** Rare in spring (May-Jun) and casual in summer, fall, and winter (Jul-Apr). **Habitat:** Foothill and lower mountain canyon groves. Wanders to desert oases and urban plantings. **Behavior:** Forages on ground or in dense thickets for insects, seeds, and small fruits. Flight is typically low. Avoids crossing large openings. **Noteworthy:** Annual in the Portal area of the Chiricahua Mountains, where it has also summered.

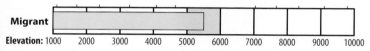

Migrant									
Elevation: 1000	2000	3000	4000	5000	6000	7000	8000	9000	10000

NORTHERN MOCKINGBIRD, *Mimus polyglottos*

Description: 10". **Pale gray** mimic-thrush with short bill and dull yellow eyes. FLIGHT: **Large white wing patches and white outer tail feathers**. **Similar Species:** Smaller Townsend's Solitaire (p. 299) has stubbier bill, white eye-ring, and buffy wing patch. **Voice:** Repeats sounds, often other bird vocalizations, an average of three times each; also *shack* notes. **Status:** Common resident in western deserts and valleys. Common in summer (Mar-mid Aug) and uncommon in winter (mid Aug-Feb) east of the San Pedro River Valley. **Habitat:** Deserts, urban areas, and open areas in valleys, foothills, and lower mountains. **Behavior:** Sings throughout the day—and often night—in spring and summer. Eats insects and berries. **Noteworthy:** Mockingbirds temporarily breed in desolate desert valleys in years of above-average precipitation.

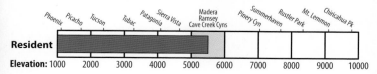

	Phoenix	Picacho	Tucson	Tubac	Patagonia	Sierra Vista	Madera Ramsey Cave Creek Cyns	Pinery Cyn	Summerhaven	Rustler Park	Mt. Lemmon	Chiricahua Pk
Resident												
Elevation: 1000		2000	3000	4000	5000	6000	7000	8000	9000	10000

Sage Thrasher

LeConte's Thrasher

Crissal Thrasher

SAGE THRASHER, *Oreoscoptes montanus*

Description: 8.5". **Small** mimic-thrush with short bill and yellow eye; two narrow white wingbars; **crisp, dark streaking below. Similar Species:** Larger Bendire's Thrasher (p. 313) has longer bill, lacks white wingbars, and has finer, lower-contrast streaking on underparts. **Voice:** Low *chup* call; song is long, clear series of warbled phrases. **Status:** Uncommon and irregular in winter (mid Sep–Mar), sometimes fairly common in migration. **Habitat:** Sparsely vegetated desert valleys and juniper stands in foothills and lower mountains. **Behavior:** Forages on the ground for insects and eats berries. **Noteworthy:** Winter abundance in SE Arizona is correlated to food availability.

LECONTE'S THRASHER, *Toxostoma lecontei*

Description: 11". **Large, light tan**, plain-breasted mimic-thrush with long, **scythe-like bill**; dark eye; **buffy undertail coverts. Status:** Rare resident. **Habitat:** Sonoran Desert saltbush and creosote flats from Picacho west.

CRISSAL THRASHER, *Toxostoma crissale*

Description: 11.5". **Large**, plain-breasted mimic-thrush with very long, **scythe-like bill**; black whisker; dull yellow eye; **russet undertail coverts. Similar Species:** Cobweb-gray LeConte's Thrasher (above) has dark eye and lacks russet undertail coverts. **Voice:** Loud *cheer-ry cheer-ry* call; song is long series of musical phrases, sometimes doubled. **Status:** Fairly common resident. **Habitat:** Desert thickets and valley mesquite grasslands, especially in dry washes, foothill thornscrub, and mountain chaparral. **Behavior:** Usually shy, but sings from tallest tree or shrub from January through March. **Noteworthy:** Near New Mexico, Crissals usually outnumber Curve-billed Thrashers on the Portal Christmas Bird Count.

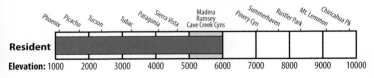

	Phoenix	Picacho	Tucson	Tubac	Patagonia	Sierra Vista	Madera Ramsey Cave Creek Cyns	Pinery Cyn	Summerhaven	Rustler Park	Mt. Lemmon	Chiricahua Pk
Resident												
Elevation:	1000	2000	3000	4000	5000	6000	7000	8000	9000	10000		

Bendire's Thrasher

Curve-billed Thrasher, *oberholseri*

Curve-billed Thrasher, *palmeri*

BENDIRE'S THRASHER, *Toxostoma bendirei*

Description: 9.75". **Medium-sized** mimic-thrush of the flatlands with straight, medium-length bill, **pale at the base**; yellow eye; **sharp, arrowhead-shaped spots below**. **Similar Species:** Larger adult Curve-billed Thrasher (below) has longer, more curved bill, lacks pale-based lower mandible, and has blurry spots below. Beware of juvenile Curve-billed Thrasher with its short bill, yellow eye, and sharp breast spots, only lacking Bendire's pale-based bill. Look for parent bird. **Voice:** Song is squeaky, unbroken, double-noted. **Status:** Fairly common resident from Sulphur Springs Valley west; fairly common in summer (late Feb-mid Sep) and rare in winter (mid Sep-early Feb) east of Chiricahua Mountains. **Habitat:** Desert flats, valley grasslands, and agricultural areas with strands of mesquite or brushy hedgerows. **Behavior:** Singing begins in mid-January, a month later than most Curve-billeds. **Noteworthy:** Although limited to Arizona and edges of adjacent states, Bendire's has the largest range within Arizona of any thrasher.

Resident

Elevation: 1000   2000   3000   4000   5000   6000   7000   8000   9000   10000

CURVE-BILLED THRASHER, *Toxostoma curvirostre*

Description: 11". **Large** mimic-thrush with long, slightly-curved bill; **bright orange eye; blurry gray spots below**. **Similar Species:** See Bendire's Thrasher (above). **Voice:** Loud *whit-wheet!* Song is rich, puppy-like mixture of barks and whines. **Status:** Common resident. **Habitat:** Desert and foothill habitats, including urban areas, especially with cholla cactus. **Behavior:** Begins singing in December and nests through early September. **Noteworthy:** Curve-bills east of the Chiricahua Mountains, *T. c. palmeri*, show thin white wingbars and more pronounced breast spots than T. c. palmeri in the remainder of Arizona.

Phoenix   Picacho   Tucson   Tubac   Patagonia   Sierra Vista   Madera Ramsey Cave Creek Cyns   Pinery Cyn   Summerhaven   Rustler Park   Mt. Lemmon   Chiricahua Pk

Resident

Elevation: 1000   2000   3000   4000   5000   6000   7000   8000   9000   10000

Description: 10". **Deep blue mimic-thrush** with straight bill; black mask; red eyes; silvery streaking on throat and breast.

Similar Species: Western Scrub-Jay (p. 253) has much stouter bill, thin white eyebrow, mostly white throat, brownish-gray back, and mostly gray underparts.

Voice: Loud, often explosive, *tchook, shiek, wheeal* and *whup* calls; variable song has five or six quick, rich, and very different phrases, followed by a brief break, before resuming.

Status: Accidental in winter and early spring (late Dec-early May); possible one-day record in late September. **Habitat:** Foothill canyons with thornscrub on adjacent slopes. Locations have been on Sonoita Creek a mile south of Patagonia, Portal at the outlet of Cave Creek Canyon in the Chiricahua Mountains, and the Slaughter Ranch 15 miles east of Douglas.

Behavior: In SE Arizona, Blue Mockingbirds use dense thickets, foraging primarily on the ground, turning over leaves for fallen hackberry fruits and insects. Once detected, usually with difficulty because this species prefers dense shady cover, Arizona birds have not been particularly wary. Individuals have stayed up to three or four months, enabling thousands of birders to add Blue Mockingbird to their U.S. life list.

Noteworthy: The first Blue Mockingbird in the U.S. was found in December 1991 on Sonoita Creek. The most recent record at the Slaughter Ranch in 2009 may have involved two birds, although this was never substantiated.

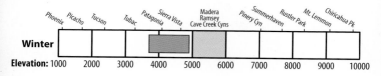

315

American Pipit

Sprague's Pipit

AMERICAN PIPIT, *Anthus rubescens*

Description: 6.25". Slender, **dark-faced** pipit with mostly **plain back**; dark legs; **long tail**. **Similar Species:** Sprague's Pipit (below) is stockier with pale face, dark-streaked back, pink legs, and short tail. **Voice:** Calls include thin *tseep* and doubled *pi-pit*. **Status:** Fairly common in winter (Sep-Apr). **Habitat:** Open desert creosote flats; valley barren pond and river edges; barren fields, golf courses, and turf farms. **Behavior:** Terrestrial, constantly pumping tail as it searches for insects. **Noteworthy:** Nesting on the San Francisco Peaks north of Flagstaff and possibly in the White Mountains above 11,000', American Pipit is the only bird that is known to breed above timberline in Arizona.

Winter									

Elevation: 1000 2000 3000 4000 5000 6000 7000 8000 9000 10000

SPRAGUE'S PIPIT, *Anthus spragueii*

Description: 6". Dumpy, **pale-faced** pipit with **large eye; heavily streaked back**; pink legs; **short tail** with white outer tail feathers. FLIGHT: Flashes white outer tail feathers when flushed. Switchbacks high into sky, then plummets until just above the ground. **Similar Species:** See American Pipit (above). Juvenile Horned Larks (p. 259) molt into adult plumage before Sprague's Pipits arrive in fall. **Voice:** High, thin *squint* note, usually repeated, delivered in flight. **Status:** Rare in winter (mid Oct-early Apr). **Habitat:** Lush valley grasslands, especially near Sonoita and in San Rafael Valley. **Behavior:** Singles lurk in grass and are usually not detected until flushed. **Noteworthy:** With experience, Sprague's distinctive flight style may be sufficient for identification.

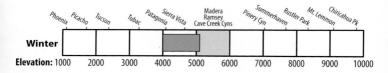

Phoenix Picacho Tucson Tubac Patagonia Sierra Vista Madera Ramsey Cave Creek Cyns Pinery Cyn Summerhaven Rustler Park Mt. Lemmon Chiricahua Pk

Winter									

Elevation: 1000 2000 3000 4000 5000 6000 7000 8000 9000 10000

317

Cedar Waxwing

Phainopepla
Male

Phainopepla
Female

CEDAR WAXWING, *Bombycilla cedrorum*

Description: 7". Plump, sleek, cinnamon, and highly sociable berry-eater with black mask and **relaxed crest; yellow-tipped tail**. **Similar Species:** Larger female Northern Cardinal (p. 387) travels singly and has stout, orange bill, mostly red wings and tail. **Voice:** Almost inaudible, high-pitched reedy *seee* calls. Large flock in chorus sounds like a steam kettle. **Status:** Fairly common but irregular in winter (mid Sep–mid May); casual in summer (mid May–mid Sep). **Habitat:** Desert oases and urban plantings; valley, foothill, and lower mountain canyon groves. **Behavior:** Gathers in flocks numbering a few to over 50. Feeds on berries of all varieties. **Noteworthy:** Nomadic; some winters none are found where common the preceding year.

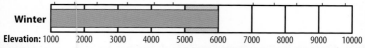

Winter

Elevation: 1000   2000   3000   4000   5000   6000   7000   8000   9000   10000

PHAINOPEPLA, *Phainopepla nitens*

Description: 7.5". Slim, silky, **long-tailed** berry-eater with **red eyes** and **spiky crest**. MALE: Black. FEMALE: Gray. FLIGHT: Shows white crescents in wings. **Similar Species:** Larger female Pyrrhuloxia (p. 387) has stubby bill, red-tinged wings and tail. **Voice:** Liquid *querp* calls; also quizzical *pretty you?* followed by affirmative *pretty you*. **Status:** Common resident with local movement from low western to higher eastern habitats as summer progresses. **Habitat:** SUMMER: Valley, foothill, and lower mountain canyon groves. WINTER: Desert oases and urban plantings; valley and foothill groves. **Behavior:** Mistletoe specialist. Nests at lower elevations in spring and higher elevations in summer. **Noteworthy:** Males construct nests alone, but females help incubate, brood, and feed the young.

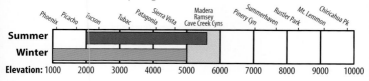

Phoenix   Picacho   Tucson   Tubac   Patagonia   Sierra Vista   Madera Ramsey Cave Creek Cyns   Pinery Cyn   Summerhaven   Rustler Park   Mt. Lemmon   Chiricahua Pk

Summer

Winter

Elevation: 1000   2000   3000   4000   5000   6000   7000   8000   9000   10000

Olive Warbler
Male

Olive Warbler
Female

Orange-crowned Warbler

OLIVE WARBLER, *Peucedramus taeniatus*

Description: 5.25". Pine-loving warbler look-alike of the mountains. **Dark ear patches form "bandito" mask.** Lacks any flank streaking. MALE: Orange head with ink-black ear patch. FEMALE: Head is yellow and ear is dull charcoal. **Similar Species:** Female Hermit Warbler (p. 333) lacks mask, usually shows faint to solid black triangle on throat. **Voice:** Calls are breathy, bluebird-like *feww* notes; song is repetitive *pita-pita-pita*. **Status:** Fairly common summer resident (Apr-Sep); rare in winter (Oct-Mar). **Habitat:** SUMMER: Mountain coniferous forest. WINTER: Primarily foothills and lower mountain canyon groves. **Behavior:** Gleans for insects among canopy pine needles; in winter usually feeds in broadleaf tree canopy. **Noteworthy:** Contrary to its name, Olive Warbler is not a true warbler species and belongs to its own family.

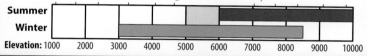

ORANGE-CROWNED WARBLER, *Oreothlypis celata*

Description: 5". Plain, variably **olive-yellow** warbler with indistinct eyebrow; dark eye-line; faint **dusky-olive breast streaking**; yellow undertail coverts; long tail. **Similar Species:** Tennessee Warbler (p. 337) has pale eyebrow, lacks breast streaks, has whitish undertail coverts and a short tail. **Voice:** Call is sharp *tik*; song is weak trill. **Status:** Rare in summer (mid May-mid Aug); fairly common migrant (mid Mar-mid May and mid Aug-Oct); uncommon in winter (Nov-mid Mar) in western lowlands. **Habitat:** SUMMER: Thickets in mountain coniferous forest. MIGRANT: Desert to mountain crests. WINTER: Valley and foothill groves. **Behavior:** Gleans and probes shrub and tree foliage for insects. **Noteworthy:** Breeds in the Santa Catalina and Pinaleno Mountains.

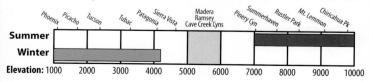

Virginia's Warbler
Male

Lucy's Warbler
Male

Lucy's Warbler
Female

VIRGINIA'S WARBLER, *Oreothlypis virginiae*

Description: 4.5". Very small, gray warbler with a **complete white eye-ring; yellow breast**; gray belly; **yellow undertail coverts**; relatively short-tailed. MALE: Rufous crown patch. FEMALE: Lacks rufous crown and shows reduced yellow on breast. **Similar Species:** Smaller Lucy's Warbler (below) lacks yellow on either chest or undertail coverts and has chestnut rump. **Voice:** Sharp *spink* call. Song is leisurely series of *cheepa* notes ending with a slow trill. **Status:** Fairly common in summer (late Mar–mid Sep). **Habitat:** Mountain chaparral, pine-oak woodland, and mixed coniferous forest. **Behavior:** Forages for insects and spiders in foliage of low shrubs and trees. Nests on the ground on steep hillsides. **Noteworthy:** Virginia's Warblers are adversely affected by prescribed burns that seek to remove understory brush.

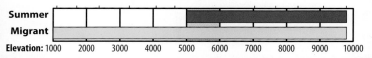

Summer									
Migrant									
Elevation: 1000	2000	3000	4000	5000	6000	7000	8000	9000	10000

LUCY'S WARBLER, *Oreothlypis luciae*

Description: 4". Very small, pearl-gray warbler with a **pale face; chestnut rump**; creamy underparts; relatively short-tailed. MALE: Rufous crown patch. FEMALE: Lacks rufous crown. **Similar Species:** Larger Virginia's Warbler (above) has bold eye-ring on darker gray face, yellow on chest and undertail coverts. **Voice:** Sharp *chink* call. Song is series of rapid, accelerating trills that end with a sputter. **Status:** Fairly common in summer (Mar–Sep). **Habitat:** Desert mesquite bosques and oases; valley, foothill, and lower mountain canyon groves. **Behavior:** Gleans leaves for insects and spiders. **Noteworthy:** Lucy's, the smallest warbler in the U.S., is the only western warbler that nests in cavities.

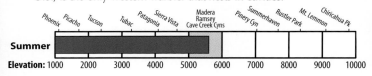

	Phoenix	Picacho	Tucson	Tubac	Patagonia	Sierra Vista	Madera Ramsey Cave Creek Cyns	Pinery Cyn	Summerhaven	Rustler Park	Mt. Lemmon	Chiricahua Pk
Summer												
Elevation: 1000	2000		3000	4000	5000		6000	7000	8000	9000	10000	

Northern Parula

Tropical Parula

Crescent-chested Warbler
Male

Crescent-chested Warbler
Female

NORTHERN PARULA, *Setophaga americana*

Description: 4.25". Small, blue-headed warbler with **split white eye-ring**; bicolored bill; green back; bold white wingbars; **white belly**. MALE: Diffuse black and chestnut breast bands. FEMALE: Diffuse chestnut breast band. **Similar Species:** Tropical Parula (below) lacks split white eye-ring, has more yellow on sides of throat and on sides of belly, and males have a black mask and tawny-orange breast. **Voice:** Sharp *tzip* call. Song is a rising buzzy trill ending with *tchup* note. **Status:** Rare year-round, but primarily in spring (Apr-May). **Habitat:** Desert oases and urban areas; valley, foothill, and lower mountain canyon groves. **Behavior:** Usually feeds deliberately in canopy of broadleaf trees.

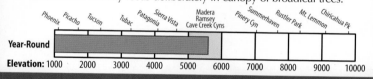

TROPICAL PARULA, *Setophaga pitiayumi*

Description: 4.25". Small, blue-headed warbler with **broad yellow throat**; bicolored bill; green back; bold white wingbars; yellow upper belly. MALE: Black mask; tawny wash on breast. **Similar Species:** Crescent-chested Warbler (below) has flaring white eyebrow and lacks white wingbars. **Voice:** Sharp *tzip* call. Accelerating *chip-chip-chip* becoming a buzzy trill ending with *ptut* note. **Status:** Accidental in summer (mid Jun-mid Sep). **Habitat:** Mountain canyon groves.

CRESCENT-CHESTED WARBLER, *Oreothlypis superciliosa*

Description: 4.2". Small, blue-headed warbler with **broad white eyebrow**; bicolored bill; green back; yellow upper belly. MALE: Chestnut crescent-shaped bar on chest. **Voice:** Hard buzz, faster and deeper than either species of parula. **Status:** Casual. **Habitat:** SUMMER (late Apr-mid Sep): Mountain canyon groves. WINTER (mid Sep-late Apr): Primarily foothill canyon groves. **Behavior:** Forages low.

Yellow Warbler
Male

Yellow Warbler
Female

Wilson's Warbler
Male

Wilson's Warbler
Female

YELLOW WARBLER, *Setophaga petechia*

Description: 5". Entirely yellow-headed warbler with **big black eye**; black wings edged bright yellow; short, **yellow undertail**. MALE: Bright yellow; **red streaks on the breast**. FEMALE: Pale yellow; thin or no red streaks on breast. **Similar Species:** Juvenile female Wilson's Warbler (below) has bright yellow eyebrow and a dusky cap; long blackish tail. **Voice:** Down-slurred *chilp*; bright song usually rendered *sweet sweet sweet I'm so sweet*. **Status:** Common in summer (mid Mar-mid Oct); casual in winter from Tucson west. **Habitat:** Desert oases; valley, foothill, and lower mountain canyon groves, especially in cottonwoods. **Behavior:** Except in spring migration, found near permanent water. Gleans insects in canopy. **Noteworthy:** The breeding race in SE Arizona, "Sonoran Yellow Warbler," is the palest and largest subspecies in the U.S.

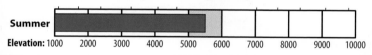

Summer									
Elevation: 1000	2000	3000	4000	5000	6000	7000	8000	9000	10000

WILSON'S WARBLER, *Cardellina pusilla*

Description: 4.75". Dainty, yellow-headed warbler with a yellow foreface, duskier behind eye; **small black cap**; olive above and bright yellow below; long black tail. ADULT: Ink black cap. JUVENILE FEMALE: May lack black cap. **Similar Species:** Yellow Warbler (above) has entirely yellow face; short tail is yellow below. **Voice:** Dry *chitt* call. **Status:** Common migrant (mid Mar-mid May and mid Aug-mid Sep); casual in winter in western lowlands. **Habitat:** Desert to mountain crest, but most common in riparian groves. **Behavior:** Actively forages for insects in understory. **Noteworthy:** During peak migration, Wilson's is the most common species of lowland warbler in Arizona.

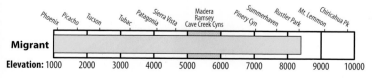

Migrant									
Elevation: 1000	2000	3000	4000	5000	6000	7000	8000	9000	10000

"Audubon's"
Male

"Myrtle"
Male

"Audubon's"
Female

"Myrtle"
Female

"AUDUBON'S" YELLOW-RUMPED WARBLER, *Setophaga coronata auduboni*

Description: 5.5". **Yellow-throated** warbler with **split white eye-ring, yellow rump, yellow sides**, and white tail spots. BREEDING MALE: Blue-gray with black chest, large white wing patch. FEMALE: Throat varies from cream to bright yellow; prominent streaking above and below. **Similar Species:** Yellow rump patch distinguishes even the dullest immatures from other regularly occurring warblers. Female "Myrtle Warbler" (below) has weak eyebrow, pale throat wraps around ear, and may appear more brownish above than "Audubon's" female. **Voice:** Dry *chipt* call; song is deliberate but ringing series of *jee jee jee jee jee juu* notes. **Status:** Fairly common in summer (May-Sep); common in winter (Oct-Apr). **Habitat:** SUMMER: Mountain coniferous forest, especially Ponderosa pine. WINTER: Desert oases and urban areas; valley, foothill, and lower mountain canyon groves. **Behavior:** Gleans insects from all levels. **Noteworthy:** Yellow-rumps are the most abundant wintering warblers in SE Arizona.

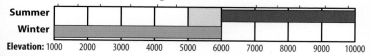

"MYRTLE" YELLOW-RUMPED WARBLER, *Setophaga coronata coronata*

Description: 5.5". **White-throated** warbler with **narrow white eyebrow**, yellow rump, yellow sides, and white tail spots. BREEDING MALE: Black face and chest; discrete white wingbars. FEMALE: Brownish upperparts. **Status:** Rare in winter (Oct-Feb); uncommon in spring (Mar-mid May). **Habitat:** Desert oases; valley, foothill, and mountain canyon groves. **Noteworthy:** Because winter-plumaged "Myrtle" race Yellow-rumped Warblers are very similar to pale-throated "Audubon's," the true status of this subspecies before they begin to acquire breeding plumage in spring is unclear.

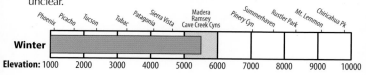

Black-throated Gray Warbler Male

Black-throated Gray Warbler Female

Black-and-white Warbler Male

Black-and-white Warbler Female

BLACK-THROATED GRAY WARBLER, *Setophaga nigrescens*

Description: 5". Warbler with **black and white face**; yellow loral spot; gray back. MALE: Black throat. FEMALE: Black on lower throat. IMMATURE: Lacks black on throat. **Similar Species:** Black-and-white Warbler (below) has striped crown and back. **Voice:** Abrupt call *tpp* like striking a match; scratchy song *buzz buzz buz zze-ze-zuu*. **Status:** Common in summer (Apr-mid Oct); rare in winter (mid Oct-Mar). **Habitat:** SUMMER: Foothill and mountain canyon groves, woodlands, and pine-Gambel's oak. WINTER: Desert oases and urban areas; valley groves, and foothill canyon groves. **Behavior:** Actively gleans insects from shrubs and trees. **Noteworthy:** Black-throated Gray Warbler is the most common mid-elevation warbler summering in the mountains of SE Arizona.

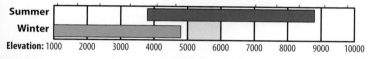

BLACK-AND-WHITE WARBLER, *Mniotilta varia*

Description: 5". **Black-and-white-striped** warbler with long, curved bill. MALE: Black ear patch; mostly black throat. FEMALE: Ear faintly streaked; white throat; unstreaked white central breast. **Similar Species:** Black-throated Gray Warbler (above) has solid crown and back and flits as it forages–does not feed by creeping on major limbs and trunks. **Voice:** Sharp, sputtering *ptt* notes; song is repetitious, lisping, very high *wee-see wee-see wee-see* phrases. **Status:** Rare in winter (Sep-May); casual in summer. **Habitat:** Desert oases and urban areas; valley, foothill, and mountain canyon groves. **Behavior:** Crawls along major limbs and the trunks of trees investigating bark for insects. **Noteworthy:** Most Black-and-white Warblers in SE Arizona are first fall immatures or females.

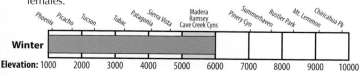

Townsend's Warbler Male

Townsend's Warbler Female

Hermit Warbler Male

Hermit Warbler Female

TOWNSEND'S WARBLER, *Setophaga townsendi*

Description: 5″. Warbler with **dark ear patch** outlined in yellow; **yellow breast; dark flank streaking**. MALE: Black throat and head pattern. FEMALE: Lacks solid black throat; head pattern dusky. **Similar Species:** Hermit Warbler (below) lacks dark ear, yellow on the breast, and obvious flank streaking. **Voice:** Call is high, lisping *tip*. **Status:** Common migrant (Apr-Jun and Aug-Oct); rare in winter (Nov-Mar). **Habitat:** MIGRANT: Mountain coniferous forest and canyon groves, infrequently to foothill canyon groves and desert oases. WINTER: Desert oases; valley, foothill, and lower mountain canyon groves. **Behavior:** Actively gleans insects in canopy. **Noteworthy:** In migration Townsend's are often in mixed flocks with Hermit Warblers.

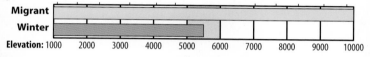

Migrant									
Winter									
Elevation: 1000	2000	3000	4000	5000	6000	7000	8000	9000	10000

HERMIT WARBLER, *Setophaga occidentalis*

Description: 5″. **Yellow-faced** warbler; **white breast** and belly; **lacks obvious flank streaks**. MALE: Yellow crown and black throat. FEMALE: Dusky throat. JUVENILE FEMALE: Yellowish forehead; brownish-olive back. **Similar Species:** Juvenile Olive Warbler (p. 321) has faint mask without yellowish eye-ring, and brownish-gray back. **Voice:** Call is high, lisping *tip*, virtually identical to Townsend's Warbler. **Status:** Common migrant (May-Jun and Aug-Oct); accidental in western lowland riparian in winter (Nov-Mar). **Habitat:** Mountain coniferous forest and canyon groves, infrequently to foothill canyon groves and desert oases. **Behavior:** Actively gleans insects in canopy. **Noteworthy:** Recent genetic studies show Hermit's are gradually being absorbed by Townsend's Warbler. Male hybrids show yellow face of Hermit with yellow breast and streaked flanks, or head pattern of Townsend's without yellow breast.

Migrant									
Elevation: 1000	2000	3000	4000	5000	6000	7000	8000	9000	10000

Grace's Warbler Male

Yellow-throated Warbler

American Redstart Male

American Redstart Female

GRACE'S WARBLER, *Setophaga graciae*

Description: 4.75". Gray warbler with **short, broad yellow eyebrow**; yellow throat and breast. **Similar Species:** Yellow-throated Warbler (below, casual) has white eyebrow, triangular black cheek, and triangular white neck mark. **Voice:** Soft *pit* note; song is an accelerating trill, higher pitched at end. **Status:** Common in summer (Apr-mid Sep); casual (Mar and Oct). **Habitat:** Mountain coniferous forest and canyon groves with tall pines. **Behavior:** Actively gleans insects in pine canopy. **Noteworthy:** In Arizona, over 90 percent of all Grace's Warblers located on the Breeding Bird Atlas project were associated with Ponderosa pine.

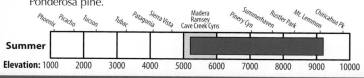

	Phoenix	Picacho	Tucson	Tubac	Patagonia	Sierra Vista	Madera Ramsey Cave Creek Cyns	Pinery Cyn	Summerhaven	Rustler Park	Mt. Lemmon	Chiricahua Pk
Summer												
Elevation:	1000	2000	3000	4000	5000	6000	7000	8000	9000	10000

YELLOW-THROATED WARBLER, *Setophaga dominica*

Description: 5". Gray warbler with **long, white eyebrow; triangular black cheek**; yellow throat and breast. **Status:** Casual (Apr-mid Sep). **Habitat:** Desert oases; valley, foothill, and mountain canyon groves. **Behavior:** Feeds in canopy.

AMERICAN REDSTART, *Setophaga ruticilla*

Description: 5". Black or gray warbler with **colorful wing and tail flash marks**. MALE: Black with orange flash marks. FEMALE: Gray head, olive-gray back, yellow flash marks. IMMATURE MALE: Like female with orange breast sides. **Similar Species:** Painted Redstart (p. 345) has white flash marks in wings and tail. **Voice:** Call is high *tsip*. **Status:** Rare migrant (May-Jun and Sep-Oct); casual in summer and winter. **Habitat:** Desert oases; valley, foothill, and–least often–mountain canyon groves. **Behavior:** Active and acrobatic, it frequently flashes wing and tail patches while foraging. **Noteworthy:** In SE Arizona, most American Redstart records pertain to females.

EASTERN WARBLERS

Tennessee Warbler
Breeding

Chestnut-sided Warbler
Non-breeding Female

Black-throated Blue Warbler
Male

Black-throated
Green Warbler
Male

TENNESSEE WARBLER, *Oreothlypis peregrina*

Description: 4.75". Warbler with pale eyebrow and dark eye-line; **white undertail coverts**; short tail. Orange-crowned Warbler (p. 321) has streaked breast and olive undertail coverts. **Status:** Rare migrant (Mar-May and Sep-Nov); casual in winter. **Habitat:** Desert oases; valley, foothill, and—least often—mountain canyon groves. **Behavior:** Actively gleans at all levels. **Voice:** Lip-smacking *tchik* of disapproval.

CHESTNUT-SIDED WARBLER, *Setophaga pensylvanica*

Description: 5". WINTER: Warbler with pale bill; white eye-ring on gray face; **lime green back**; yellowish wingbars; cocked tail. SUMMER: Yellow cap; chestnut sides. **Status:** Rare in winter (Sep-mid Mar); casual in summer. **Habitat:** Desert oases; valley, foothill, and—least often—mountain canyon groves. **Behavior:** Often forages low. **Voice:** *chilp* call.

BLACK-THROATED BLUE WARBLER, *Setophaga caerulescens*

Description: 5". Stocky warbler with **white wing patch**. MALE: Blue with black face. FEMALE: Dusky olive; thin white eyebrow and under-eye crescent; darkish ears. **Status:** Rare migrant (Apr-Jun and mid Sep-mid Dec); casual in winter. **Habitat:** Desert oases; valley, foothill, and—least often—mountain canyon groves. **Behavior:** Usually forages low, from trunk outwards onto major limbs. **Voice:** Smacking *tchuk*.

BLACK-THROATED GREEN WARLER, *Setophaga virens*

Description: 4.75". Green-backed warbler with **olive ear patch**; yellow wash across vent. MALE: Black throat and breast. FEMALE: Yellowish throat. **Status:** Casual migrant (Apr-May and Sep-Nov); accidental in winter. **Habitat:** Desert oases; valley, foothill, and mountain canyon groves. **Behavior:** Often forages high. **Voice:** Juicy *chilp* call.

EASTERN WARBLERS

Prothonotary Warbler

Hooded Warbler

Worm-eating Warbler

Ovenbird

PROTHONOTARY WARBLER, *Protonotaria citrea*

Description: 5.25". Golden warbler with **blue-gray wings**; long bill. **Status:** Rare migrant (May-Jun and Sep-Oct). **Habitat:** Desert oases; valley, foothill, and–least often–mountain canyon groves. **Behavior:** Usually forages low in trees and shrubbery near water. **Voice:** High *tseet* notes.

HOODED WARBLER, *Setophaga citrina*

Description: 5.25". **Yellow-faced** warbler with **dark lores; white outer tail.** MALE: Black cowl. Smaller female Wilson's Warbler (p. 327) has small bill, yellow lores, and smaller eye. **Status:** Rare in spring (May-Jun); casual in summer and fall. **Habitat:** Desert oases; valley, foothill, and mountain canyon groves. **Behavior:** Usually forages low in dense growth, often near water, flashing white outer tail feathers. **Voice:** Emphatic *cheat!* notes.

WORM-EATING WARBLER, *Helmitheros vermivorum*

Description: 5.25". Bob-tailed warbler with **tawny, black-striped head**; long bill. **Status:** Rare spring migrant (Apr-Jun); casual in other seasons. **Habitat:** Desert oases; valley, foothill, and mountain canyon groves. **Behavior:** Investigates lower strata dead leaf clusters and creeps up tree trunks. **Voice:** Loud *cheap* calls.

OVENBIRD, *Seiurus aurocapilla*

Description: 5.75". Plump, big-eyed warbler with white eye-ring; **orange crown** bordered by black stripes; black, thrush-like chest spotting; **cocked tail**. **Status:** Rare migrant (May and Oct-Nov); casual in summer and winter. **Habitat:** Desert oases; valley, foothill, and mountain canyon groves. **Behavior:** Forages on ground, bobbing head as it walks. **Voice:** Loud *tsuck* calls.

Northern Waterthrush

Louisiana Waterthrush

NORTHERN WATERTHRUSH, *Parkesia noveboracensis*

Description: 5.75". Brown-backed warbler with **tapering pale eyebrow; black-dotted throat**; coral red legs. Waterthrushes are best separated by full suite of field characters. **Similar Species:** Louisiana Waterthrush (below) has flaring white eyebrow, clear white throat, often rich buff-washed flanks, and pink legs. **Voice:** Metallic, loud *pink* note. **Status:** Rare migrant (mid Apr-Jun and Aug-Sep); accidental in winter. **Habitat:** Ponds and slow-moving streams at desert oases and in valley, foothill, and mountain canyon groves. **Behavior:** Forages for insects on water's edge, bobbing tail as it walks or balances on stones. **Noteworthy:** Typically more common in SE Arizona in fall than in spring.

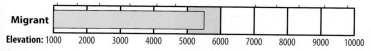

LOUISIANA WATERTHRUSH, *Parkesia motacilla*

Description: 6". Brown-backed warbler with **flaring white eyebrow; clean white throat**; often buffy flanks; pink legs. Waterthrushes are best separated by full suite of field characters. **Similar Species:** Northern Waterthrush (above) has tapering white eyebrow, black-dotted throat, lacks contrasting buffy flanks, and has duller coral legs. **Voice:** Sharp, loud *chick* note. **Status:** Casual fall migrant (mid Jul-early Sep.); rare in winter (Nov-mid Mar). **Habitat:** Primarily slow-moving rivers and streams in valley, foothill, and mountain canyon groves. **Behavior:** Forages for insects on water's edge, bobbing tail as it walks or balances on stones. **Noteworthy:** The most reliable locations for highly local wintering Louisiana Waterthrushes include the Santa Cruz River at Tubac and Sonoita Creek upstream from Patagonia Lake.

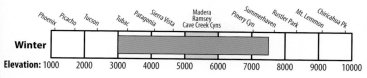

MacGillivray's Warbler
Male

MacGillivray's Warbler
Female

Nashville Warbler
Male

Nashville Warbler
Female

MacGillivray's Warbler, *Geothlypis tolmiei*

Description: 5.25". Gray-hooded warbler with pink-based bill and **split eye-ring**. MALE: Blue-gray hood, black in front of eyes and across lower breast. FEMALE: Pale gray hood. **Similar Species:** Smaller Nashville Warbler (below) has complete eye-ring and yellow throat. **Voice:** Call is hard, sharp *chik*; song abruptly changes at end *swee-swee-swee-swee chow chow*. **Status:** Rare in summer (Jun-mid Aug); fairly common migrant (Apr-May and mid Aug-mid Oct). **Habitat:** SUMMER: Meadow willow thickets, primarily in Pinaleno Mountains. MIGRATION: Thickets from desert oases to mountain crests. **Behavior:** Skulks in thickets and deep cover; nests on ground. **Noteworthy:** The Pinalenos are the southernmost breeding locality for MacGillivray's Warblers in the U.S.

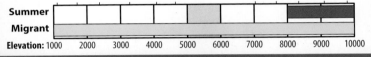

Summer									
Migrant									
Elevation: 1000	2000	3000	4000	5000	6000	7000	8000	9000	10000

Nashville Warbler, *Oreothlypis ruficapilla*

Description: 4.5". Small gray-headed warbler with **bold white eye-ring**; yellow throat; olive-green back. MALE: Inconspicuous chestnut cap. **Similar Species:** Larger MacGillivray's Warbler (above) has a gray throat and broken white eye-ring. Closely-related Virginia's Warbler (p. 323) has whitish throat and gray back. **Voice:** Dry *pitt* call. **Status:** Uncommon spring (late Mar-mid May) and fairly common fall (Aug-mid Oct) migrant; accidental in summer and winter. **Habitat:** SPRING: Desert oases; valley, foothill, and lower mountain canyon groves, primarily west of San Pedro Valley. FALL: Desert oases; valley, foothill, and mountain canyon groves throughout region. **Behavior:** Forages in understory weeds and thickets, less frequently higher in trees. **Noteworthy:** Primarily a lowland migrant in spring and a mountain migrant in fall.

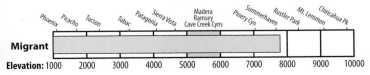

	Phoenix	Picacho	Tucson	Tubac	Patagonia	Sierra Vista	Madera Ramsey Cave Creek Cyns	Pinery Cyn	Summerhaven	Rustler Park	Mt. Lemmon	Chiricahua Pk
Migrant												
Elevation: 1000		2000	3000	4000	5000	6000	7000	8000	9000	10000		

Red-faced Warbler

Painted Redstart

RED-FACED WARBLER, *Cardellina rubrifrons*

Description: 5". Dapper gray warbler with **red face**, black head-band, and white rump. **Similar Species:** None. **Voice:** Hard, dry *chett* call; song is rollicking series of quick, piercing *zwee* notes. **Status:** Common in summer (mid Apr-mid Sep). **Habitat:** Mountain upper canyon groves and coniferous forest mixed with Gambel's oak and quaking aspen. **Behavior:** Forages from low to high levels, primarily in deciduous trees; nests on ground. **Noteworthy:** As a breeding species in the U.S., Red-faced Warbler is confined to Arizona and western New Mexico.

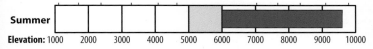

Summer									

Elevation: 1000   2000   3000   4000   5000   6000   7000   8000   9000   10000

PAINTED REDSTART, *Myioborus pictus*

Description: 5.25". **Black warbler** with white crescent below eye; **white panel in wing; red belly**; white outer tail feathers. JUVENILE: Lacks red belly. **Similar Species:** Charcoal-gray–not black–Slate-throated Redstart (p. 347) lacks white under-eye crescent, lacks white wing panel, and shows less white in the outer tail. **Voice:** Conversational *cheeu* or *chee-wee* calls; cheerful, run-on *sweeta-sweeta-sweeta-sweeta* notes. **Status:** Common in summer (mid Mar-Oct); rare in winter (Nov-mid Mar). **Habitat:** SUMMER: Mountain canyon groves with perennial water within pine-oak woodland; heavy stands of pine-oak on slopes. WINTER: Valley, foothill, and lower mountain canyon groves. **Behavior:** Usually forages in understory. Nests on banks under hummocks of grass. Migration and post-breeding wandering may take birds down into valley riparian to 2,000' or up to 9,000'. **Noteworthy:** In the major canyons of SE Arizona's larger mountains, Painted Redstarts nest at 100 yard intervals.

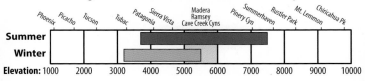

Elevation: 1000   2000   3000   4000   5000   6000   7000   8000   9000   10000

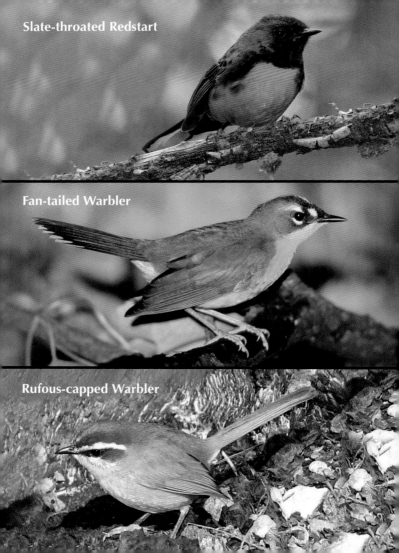

Slate-throated Redstart

Fan-tailed Warbler

Rufous-capped Warbler

SLATE-THROATED REDSTART, *Myioborus miniatus*

Description: 5.25″. **Charcoal-gray warbler** with maroon crown; orange-red chest and belly; **white tail corners. Similar Species:** Black–not slate gray–Painted Redstart (p. 345) has white under-eye crescent, large white wing panel, and shows more white in the outer tail. **Voice:** High, thin *tsip* calls; languid *twee-twee-tweea-tee* song thinner than Painted Redstart's. **Status:** Accidental in spring (mid Apr–early Jun). **Habitat:** Mountain canyon groves with perennial streams within pine-oak woodland. **Behavior:** Forages low, often fanning its tail.

FAN-TAILED WARBLER, *Basileuterus lachrymosa*

Description: 5.75″. Large gray warbler with split white eye-ring and **white accents on forehead**; narrow yellow crown; long, white-tipped tail. **Similar Species:** Larger Yellow-breasted Chat (p. 349) has complete white spectacles and lacks white-tipped tail. **Voice:** Very high *seet* calls; song is piercing *swee swee swee sweeta sweet*. **Status:** Accidental in summer (May–early Sep). **Habitat:** Foothill and mountain lower canyon groves with steep sides or cliffs. **Behavior:** Forages low, often fanning its tail.

RUFOUS-CAPPED WARBLER, *Basileuterus rufifrons*

Description: 5″. **Rufous-capped** warbler with bold white eyebrow, **rufous ears**; rich yellow throat and breast; long tail. **Voice:** Snappy *cht* and *chit* calls, sometimes in series; song is varied series of trills. **Status:** Rare resident. **Habitat:** Foothill and mountain canyon groves with steep sides or cliffs. **Behavior:** Forages low, cocks its tail and waves it like a Bewick's Wren. **Noteworthy:** First documented occurrence was in May 1977 in Cave Creek Canyon, Chiricahua Mtns. Has successfully nested in the Santa Rita and Whetstone Mountains.

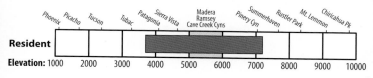

347

Common Yellowthroat
Male

Common Yellowthroat
Female

Yellow-breasted Chat

COMMON YELLOWTHROAT, *Geothlypis trichas*

Description: 5". Marsh warbler with yellow underparts brightest on throat; **cocked tail**. MALE: **Black mask** bordered by white. FEMALE: Gray face; pale yellow throat; grayish belly; yellow undertail coverts. **Similar Species:** Female MacGillivray's Warbler (p. 343) lacks yellow throat and cocked tail. **Voice:** Dry *tickk* notes; loud song is *wich-i-ty wich-i-ty wich-i-ty*. **Status:** Common in summer (Apr-Sep); fairly common in winter (Oct-Mar) west of the Chiricahua Mountains. **Habitat:** Rivers and ponds with emergent vegetation. Migrants also use dry brush. **Behavior:** Gleans insects from low marsh or water edge vegetation. **Noteworthy:** Breeding Common Yellowthroats in SE Arizona, *G. t. chryseola*, are the largest and brightest race in the U.S.

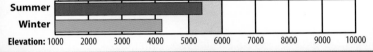

Summer									
Winter									
Elevation: 1000	2000	3000	4000	5000	6000	7000	8000	9000	10000

YELLOW-BREASTED CHAT, *Icteria virens*

Description: 7". **Large, thick-billed** warbler-like bird with **white spectacles; rich yellow throat and breast**; olive upperparts; white belly; long tail. **Similar Species:** Smaller Fan-tailed Warbler (p. 347) has white accent marks on forehead, entirely yellow underparts, and white-tipped tail. **Voice:** Loud, coughing *chuh-chuh-chuh*. Song is series of deliberate and quite different phrases, often repeated rapidly, with long pauses between each element. **Status:** Common in summer (mid Apr-Sep); casual in early fall (Oct). **Habitat:** Desert oases; valley, foothill, and lower mountain canyon groves, usually near permanent water. **Behavior:** Forages in thickets. Male's display flight is low with deep wing beats. **Noteworthy:** Recent DNA analysis suggests chats are only distantly related to typical warblers.

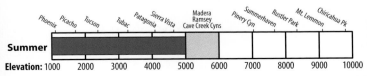

	Phoenix	Picacho	Tucson	Tubac	Patagonia	Sierra Vista	Madera Ramsey Cave Creek Cyns	Pinery Cyn	Summerhaven	Rustler Park	Mt. Lemmon	Chiricahua Pk
Summer												
Elevation: 1000	2000	3000	4000	5000	6000	7000	8000	9000	10000			

Hepatic Tanager
Male

Juvenile

Hepatic Tanager
Female

Summer Tanager
Male

Summer Tanager
Female

HEPATIC TANAGER, *Piranga flava*

Description: 7.75". Tanager with **blackish bill** and **grayish ear patch**; grayish back; gray flanks; colors brightest on forehead and throat. MALE: Orange-red. FEMALE: Mustard yellow. JUVENILE: Yellow with pin-striped breast. **Similar Species:** Summer Tanager (below) has paler bill and lacks dark ears. **Voice:** Smacking *chup* call; clear, lilting song of robin-like phrases without burry notes. **Status:** Fairly common in summer (Apr-mid Oct); rare in winter west of San Pedro Valley. **Habitat:** SUMMER: Mountain canyon groves, pine-oak woodland, and Ponderosa pine forest. WINTER: Valley and foothill canyon groves. **Behavior:** Methodically searches canopy for insects. **Noteworthy:** Recent genetic studies suggest that U.S. tanagers are more closely related to grosbeaks and buntings than to the candy-colored tanagers of the New World tropics.

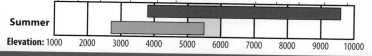

SUMMER TANAGER, *Piranga rubra*

Description: 7.25". Tanager with large **pale bill**. MALE: Red. FEMALE: Clear yellow. IMMATURE MALE: Splotchy red and green. **Similar Species:** Hepatic Tanager (above) has blackish bill and dark ear patches. **Voice:** Staccato *kid-dy-tuck-tuk* call; clear, lilting song of three-part phrases without burry notes. **Status:** Common in summer (mid Apr-Sep); casual in winter west of San Pedro Valley. **Habitat:** Desert oases; valley, foothill, and lower mountain canyon groves. **Behavior:** Methodically searches canopy for insects. **Noteworthy:** In a Bureau of Land Management study, an average of over 50 Summer Tanagers per 100 acres were noted in the San Pedro River National Conservation Area.

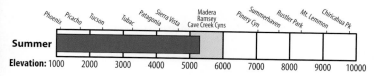

Western Tanager
Male

Western Tanager
Female

Flame-colored Tanager
Male

Flame-colored
Tanager
Female

WESTERN TANAGER, *Piranga ludoviciana*

Description: 7". Tanager with **small, olive-tinged bill and two wingbars**. BREEDING MALE: Orange face; black back; yellow forward wingbar. FEMALE: Yellow head; grayish back; belly variable from yellow to pale gray. **Similar Species:** Larger Flame-colored Tanager (below) has blackish bill, dark-bordered ear-patch, and obvious back streaks. **Voice:** Quick, almost trilled, *pret-ty-pink* call; usually seven high, slurred, sing-song phrases *I-think, you-think, we-think, you-drink*, etc. **Status:** Fairly common in summer (mid Jun-mid Jul); common in migration (mid Apr-mid Jun and mid Jul-Oct); casual in winter. **Habitat:** SUMMER: Upper mountain canyon groves and mixed coniferous forest. MIGRATION: All habitats from desert to mountain crest. **Behavior:** Methodically searches canopy for insects. **Noteworthy:** SE Arizona represents the southern limits of Western Tanager's breeding range.

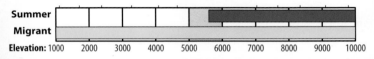

FLAME-COLORED TANAGER, *Piranga bidentata*

Description: 7.5". Tanager with large dark bill; **dark-bordered ear-patch; striped back**. MALE: Extent of reddish-orange foreparts variable. FEMALE: Yellow. FIRST SPRING MALE: Bright yellow with orange tinge on forehead. **Similar Species:** Western Tanager (above) has smaller bill, unmarked face, and lacks streaked back. Male Flame-colored x Western hybrids show lower back solid black; rump yellow. Female hybrids usually indistinguishable. **Voice:** Burry *cor-rupt!* call; deliberate, burry three- or four-part *sherree, shurroo, sherroo* song. **Status:** Rare in summer (early Apr-Aug). **Habitat:** Border mountain canyon groves. **Behavior:** Methodically searches canopy for insects. **Noteworthy:** In SE Arizona, known only from the Santa Rita, Huachuca, and Chiricahua Mountains.

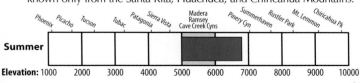

Green-tailed Towhee

Spotted Towhee

GREEN-TAILED TOWHEE, *Pipilo chlorurus*

Description: 7.25". Chestnut-capped towhee with **snow-white throat**; white whisker; **broad green edgings on wings and tail**. **Similar Species:** Smaller Five-striped Sparrow (p. 363) lacks chestnut cap, green wing and tail edgings. **Voice:** Plaintive *meww* call or very high, thin *tsip*. Song is variable trill *tip seeo see tweeeee chchchch*. **Status:** Common migrant (Apr-early May and Sep-Oct); irregular but typically uncommon in winter (Nov-Mar). **Habitat:** Desert hedgerows, arroyos, oases, and urban areas; valley, foothill, and lower mountain canyon groves. **Behavior:** Turns over leaf-litter by scratching with both feet simultaneously, often under dense cover. **Noteworthy:** Green-tailed Towhees nest less than 100 miles north of the Pinaleno Mountains.

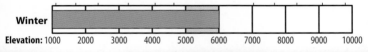

Winter									
Elevation: 1000	2000	3000	4000	5000	6000	7000	8000	9000	10000

SPOTTED TOWHEE, *Pipilo maculatus*

Description: 8.25". Large towhee with **black hood** and red eyes; **white-spotted back and wings; rufous sides**. MALE: Black head. FEMALE: Slaty head. JUVENILE: Brown head; heavily streaked back and sides. **Similar Species:** Immature Aztec Thrush (p. 305) has much longer, thinner bill and heavily streaked head. **Voice:** Harsh *wheerrr* call; song is loudly trilled *weh-weh-whit-zheeeeee*. **Status:** Fairly common resident. **Habitat:** SUMMER (Mar-Sep): Mountain canyon groves, chaparral, pine-oak woodland, and scrub thickets within Ponderosa pine forest. WINTER (Oct-Feb): Desert oases up to mountain canyon groves. **Behavior:** Turns over leaf-litter by scratching with both feet simultaneously, often under dense cover. **Noteworthy:** Spotted Towhee is the common mountain towhee in SE Arizona, nesting at 100 yard intervals in some canyons.

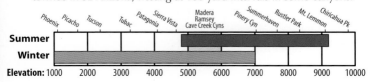

Canyon Towhee

Abert's Towhee

CANYON TOWHEE, *Melozone fuscus*

Description: 8.5". Towhee with a dull rufous cap; **buffy throat outlined by necklace of streaks**; upperparts brownish-gray; usually a central breast spot. **Similar Species:** Larger Abert's Towhee (below) has pale silvery bill accentuated by blackish foreface and is warmer brown overall. **Voice:** Hoarse *hic-cup* call; typical song is abrupt introductory note followed by a five or six dull whistles, *chop wee-wee-wee-wee-weeds*. **Status:** Common resident. **Habitat:** Dense areas of desertscrub; valley grasslands with thickets; dry foothill canyons and thornscrub; dry lower mountain canyons, chaparral, and woodlands. **Behavior:** Forages for seeds and insects on the ground. Usually found in pairs. **Noteworthy:** This is the most confiding towhee, often under cars, picnic tables, and farm machinery in rural areas.

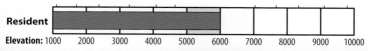

Resident

Elevation: 1000 2000 3000 4000 5000 6000 7000 8000 9000 10000

ABERT'S TOWHEE, *Melozone aberti*

Description: 9". **Silver-billed** towhee with a **black foreface**; warm brown body; ochre undertail coverts. **Similar Species:** Smaller, grayer Canyon Towhee (above) has a dull rufous cap and a buffy throat bordered by a necklace of streaks. **Voice:** Penetrating *pink* call; song is several accelerating calls followed by squealing chatter *pink-pink-pink-cheh-cheh-cheh-cheh-chech*. **Status:** Fairly common resident. **Habitat:** Flatlands with dense cover and usually nearby permanent water, such as desert oases, farms, and urban areas; valley and foothill canyon groves. **Behavior:** Forages for seeds and insects on the ground. Usually found in pairs. **Noteworthy:** Abert's Towhee is essentially confined to the lower Colorado River drainage, mostly within Arizona.

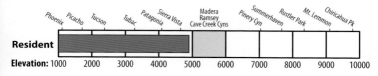

Resident

Elevation: 1000 2000 3000 4000 5000 6000 7000 8000 9000 10000

357

Cassin's Sparrow

Botteri's Sparrow

CASSIN'S SPARROW, *Peucaea cassinii*

Description: 6". Flat-headed sparrow with **black-spotted back**; gray underparts with sparse, **narrow flank streaks**; long, round-tipped tail. FLIGHT: Narrow **white tail corners**. **Similar Species:** Botteri's Sparrow (below) has short, black back-streaks and unmarked pale buff underparts. Botteri's is subtly warmer brown overall than Cassin's. Both species are best identified by their distinctive songs. **Voice:** Slow, poignant song begins with short chips segueing into trills *pi-ti-d-deeeee-deee-dee*. **Status:** Uncommon in spring (mid Mar-May) and fairly common in summer (Jul-Sep); rarely detected when silent in early summer and in winter. **Habitat:** Valley mesquite grasslands, especially in lightly grazed areas. **Behavior:** Males "skylark," rising about 20 feet, then gradually descend with head cocked and tail spread, singing all the while. **Noteworthy:** Breeding is strongly correlated to the summer monsoon rains; also sing in springs following winters of above average precipitation.

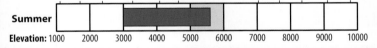

Summer										
Elevation:	1000	2000	3000	4000	5000	6000	7000	8000	9000	10000

BOTTERI'S SPARROW, *Peucaea botterii*

Description: 6". Flat-headed sparrow with short **black streaks on back**; unmarked underparts; buffy flanks. FLIGHT: Narrow gray tail corners. **Similar Species:** See Cassin's Sparrow (above). Best identified by song. **Voice:** Several hesitant notes on different pitches accelerating into one or more trills. **Status:** Uncommon in spring (May-late Jun) and fairly common in summer (late Jun-Sep). **Habitat:** Valley mesquite grasslands, especially sacaton grass, within 60 miles of Mexico. **Behavior:** Does not skylark like Cassin's Sparrow. **Noteworthy:** Breeding coincides with the summer monsoon rains.

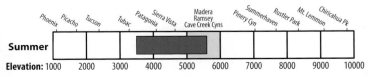

	Phoenix	Picacho	Tucson	Tubac	Patagonia	Sierra Vista	Madera Ramsey Cave Creek Cyns	Pinery Cyn	Summerhaven	Rustler Park	Mt. Lemmon	Chiricahua Pk
Summer												
Elevation:	1000	2000	3000	4000	5000	6000	7000	8000	9000	10000		

359

Rufous-winged Sparrow

Rufous-crowned Sparrow

RUFOUS-WINGED SPARROW, *Peucaea carpalis*

Description: 5.75". Flat-headed sparrow with **double black whiskers**; divided rufous crown; **rufous shoulder patch** helpful if visible; long, round-tipped tail. **Similar Species:** Smaller Chipping Sparrow (p. 365) lacks double black whisker stripes and has notched tail. **Voice:** One or two introductory notes followed by hard, extended trill *pit-pit-deeeeeee*. **Status:** Fairly common resident. **Habitat:** Level or gently sloping grassy Sonoran desertscrub and valley mesquite grassland. **Behavior:** Feeds on seeds and insects in pairs or family groups on the ground; breeding is timed to take advantage of additional food available during the summer rainy season. **Noteworthy:** One of the last North American birds described to science when discovered near Tucson in 1872, its entire U.S. range is limited to south-central Arizona.

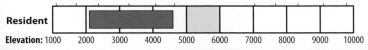

Resident

Elevation: 1000 | 2000 | 3000 | 4000 | 5000 | 6000 | 7000 | 8000 | 9000 | 10000

RUFOUS-CROWNED SPARROW, *Aimophila ruficeps*

Description: 6". Flat-headed sparrow with obvious **short white eyebrow and eye-ring** on dark face; single **heavy black whisker**; rufous crown; long, round-tipped tail. **Similar Species:** Smaller Chipping Sparrow (p. 365) lacks heavy black whisker stripe framing white throat and has a notched tail. No other solidly "rufous-crowned" sparrow likely in its habitat. **Voice:** Excited *dear dear* calls, often doubled. Song is fast, jumbled chatter notes. **Status:** Fairly common resident. **Habitat:** Foothill and mountain rocky or brushy slopes within desertscrub, thornscrub, chaparral, and woodland vegetation. **Behavior:** Forages on the ground for seeds and insects, usually in pairs. **Noteworthy:** Nests in spring, as well as during the summer monsoon season.

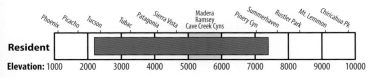

Resident

Elevation: 1000 | 2000 | 3000 | 4000 | 5000 | 6000 | 7000 | 8000 | 9000 | 10000

361

Five-striped Sparrow

Black-throated Sparrow

Juvenile

FIVE-STRIPED SPARROW, *Amphispiza quinquestriata*

Description: 6″. Gray-headed sparrow with **five white head stripes**: eyebrows, whiskers, and throat; brown back; gray breast with black spot; white belly. **Similar Species:** Smaller Black-throated Sparrow (below) has four white head stripes and big black bib. **Voice:** Raspy *chept* calls. Squeaky song with deliberate *whee-whee* and *chept* notes and chattered *fa-la-la* figures combined tunelessly. **Status:** Rare in summer (late Apr-Sep); casual in winter. **Habitat:** Hillside foothill thornscrub, usually near permanent water, usually within 10 miles of Mexico. **Behavior:** Although pairs begin to sing in May, frequency of song increases as the summer progresses, and reaches its peak after the onset of the rainy season. **Noteworthy:** The first U.S. record of a Five-striped Sparrow was in 1957 in the Santa Rita Mountain foothills.

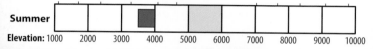

Summer

Elevation: 1000   2000   3000   4000   5000   6000   7000   8000   9000   10000

BLACK-THROATED SPARROW, *Amphispiza bilineata*

Description: 5.5″. **Black-and-white-headed** sparrow with **big black bib**. JUVENILE: Gray head with bold white eyebrows and white throat; heavily streaked breast. FLIGHT: Black tail with white corners. **Similar Species:** See Five-striped Sparrow (above). Wintering Sage Sparrow (p. 371) lacks long white eyebrow and black bib. **Voice:** Lisping *pizz* and tinkling calls. Song is pleasant, musical *je-je-jeeeeeee* ending with trill. **Status:** Common resident. **Habitat:** Desertscrub, valley mesquite grassland, foothill thornscrub, and lower mountain chaparral. **Behavior:** Forages on the ground for seeds and insects, usually in pairs and family groups. **Noteworthy:** Black-throated is Arizona's most widespread and numerous breeding sparrow.

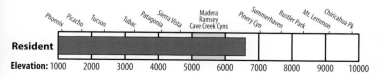

Resident

Elevation: 1000   2000   3000   4000   5000   6000   7000   8000   9000   10000

**Chipping Sparrow
Breeding**

**Chipping Sparrow
Non-breeding**

Clay-colored Sparrow

CHIPPING SPARROW, *Spizella passerina*

Description: 5.5". Small-billed, slender sparrow with **dark lores**; gray breast; **gray rump**; long, cleft tail. BREEDING: Chestnut cap; white eyebrow. NON-BREEDING: Pink bill; pale gray crown stripe. **Similar Species:** Non-breeding Clay-colored Sparrow (below) has creamy white crown stripe, pale buff lores, sandy eyebrows, well-defined dark whisker, buffy breast, and buffy rump. **Voice:** Call is soft *tik* note. Song is long, dry trill. **Status:** Uncommon in summer (mid May-mid Aug); common in winter (mid Aug-mid May). **Habitat:** SUMMER: Grassy mountain pine-oak woodlands and Ponderosa pine forest. WINTER: Openings within deserts, valleys, foothills, and lower mountain canyon groves. **Behavior:** Forages on the ground. Forms large flocks in winter. **Noteworthy:** In SE Arizona, Chipping Sparrows breed regularly only in the Chiricahua Mountains.

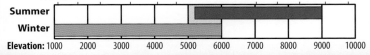

| Elevation: | 1000 | 2000 | 3000 | 4000 | 5000 | 6000 | 7000 | 8000 | 9000 | 10000 |

CLAY-COLORED SPARROW, *Spizella pallida*

Description: 5.5". Small-billed, slender sparrow with creamy crown stripe; **pale buff lores**; pale cream to sandy eyebrows; **bold whisker**; buffy breast; **buff rump**; long, cleft tail. NON-BREEDING: Pink bill; pale gray crown stripe. **Similar Species:** Non-breeding Chipping Sparrow (above) has pale gray crown stripe, dark lores, gray eyebrows, gray breast, and gray rump. **Voice:** Call is soft *tik* note. Song is four short, cicada-like buzzes. **Status:** Rare in winter (Sep-May). **Habitat:** Open areas within deserts, valleys, and lower mountain canyons. **Behavior:** Forages on the ground. **Noteworthy:** In SE Arizona, Clay-colored is usually a lone bird in a flock of Chipping Sparrows.

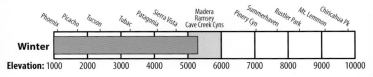

| Elevation: | 1000 | 2000 | 3000 | 4000 | 5000 | 6000 | 7000 | 8000 | 9000 | 10000 |

365

Brewer's Sparrow

Black-chinned Sparrow
Male

Black-chinned Sparrow
Female

BREWER'S SPARROW, *Spizella breweri*

Description: 5.25". Small-billed, slender sparrow with **finely-streaked crown** lacking distinct central stripe; **complete white eye-ring**; dull grayish-brown breast; **gray-brown rump** concolor with back; long, cleft tail. **Similar Species:** Non-breeding Clay-colored Sparrow (p. 365) has creamy white crown stripe, pale buff lores, sandy eyebrows, well-defined dark whiskers, buffy breast, and buffy rump. **Voice:** Call is thin *tik* note. Song is varied series of long, dry trills and buzzes. **Status:** Common in winter (late Aug-early May). **Habitat:** Open, gentle terrain within deserts, valleys, foothills, and lower mountain canyon groves. **Behavior:** Forms large flocks in winter. **Noteworthy:** In SE Arizona, numbers of Brewer's Sparrows and the areas they use for wintering may change dramatically from year to year.

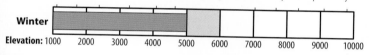

Winter									
Elevation: 1000	2000	3000	4000	5000	6000	7000	8000	9000	10000

BLACK-CHINNED SPARROW, *Spizella atrogularis*

Description: 5.75". Small-billed, slender sparrow with pink bill; **dark-streaked rusty back**; unmarked gray head and underparts; long, cleft tail. MALE BREEDING: **Black foreface and throat**. **Similar Species:** "Gray-headed" race of Dark-eyed Junco (p. 381) has solid rusty back and white outer tail feathers. **Voice:** Weak, thin *seet* calls. Song is several short whistles accelerating into trill, like a bouncing ball-bearing coming to rest. **Status:** Uncommon resident. **Habitat:** SUMMER (May-Sep): Lower mountain chaparral and pinyon-juniper woodlands. WINTER (Oct-Apr): Desert, foothill, and lower mountain canyon thickets. **Behavior:** May join other sparrows in winter flocks. **Noteworthy:** In SE Arizona, some Black-chins are altitudinal migrants wintering near breeding territories.

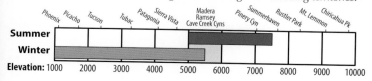

GRASSLAND SPARROWS

Vesper Sparrow

Savannah Sparrow

Grasshopper Sparrow

Baird's Sparrow

VESPER SPARROW, *Pooecetes gramineus*

Description: 6.25". Large grassland sparrow with long pink bill, dusky on top; **white eye-ring**; finely-streaked crown; usually concealed rufous shoulder patch; long tail with **white outer tail feathers**. **Status:** Common in winter (mid Sep-late Apr). **Habitat:** Desert and valley savanna, fields, and openings next to ponds and rivers. **Behavior:** Not shy; usually in small flocks. **Voice:** Chipping *tipt* notes.

SAVANNAH SPARROW, *Passerculus sandwichensis*

Description: 5.5". Small grassland sparrow with **small bill**; well-defined **eyebrow, often yellow between eye and bill**; finely-streaked crown; densely-streaked breast; short, notched tail. **Status:** Common in winter (Sep-Apr). **Habitat:** Desert and valley grasslands, fields, and openings next to ponds and rivers. **Behavior:** Not shy; uses conspicuous perches. **Voice:** Chipping *sipt* notes.

GRASSHOPPER SPARROW, *Ammodramus savannarum*

Description: 5". Small grassland sparrow with large flat head; large bill; **yellow-orange between eye and bill; creamy crown stripe**; unstreaked breast; short tail. **Status:** Fairly common in summer (Apr-Sep); uncommon in winter (Oct-Mar). **Habitat:** SUMMER: Tall valley grasslands. WINTER: Desert and valley grasslands. **Behavior:** Solitary, shy, and usually deep in grass. Monsoon nester. **Voice:** Insect-like buzz.

BAIRD'S SPARROW, *Ammodramus bairdii*

Description: 5.5". Small grassland sparrow with large flat head; large bill; **ochre face; orange crown stripe**; contrasting back streaking; **narrow band of breast streaks**; short tail. **Status:** Uncommon in winter (Oct-mid Apr). **Habitat:** Tall valley grasslands. **Behavior:** Solitary, shy, and usually deep in grass. **Voice:** High, dry *pit*.

Lark Sparrow

Sage Sparrow

Lark Bunting
Non-breeding

Breeding Male

LARK SPARROW, *Chondestes grammacus*

Description: 6.25". **Chestnut-and-white-headed** sparrow. FLIGHT: Large white tail corners. **Similar Species:** Distinctive. **Voice:** Weak *pink* calls. Fast "rock-and-rattle" song like mockingbird on caffeine. **Status:** Fairly common; rare east of Sulphur Springs Valley in winter. **Habitat:** SUMMER (Apr-Jul): Valley mesquite grasslands and rolling foothill oak savanna. WINTER (Aug-Mar): Open desert oases, valley groves, and foothill groves. **Behavior:** Late summer, post-breeding wandering takes small flocks down into desert oases and up into mountain meadows.

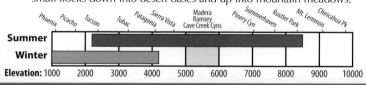

SAGE SPARROW, *Artemisiospiza belli*

Description: 6". Gray-headed sparrow with white eye-ring and **white accents on forehead**; white moustache curves under ear patch; dark-streaked, **dusty-brown back**. **Similar Species:** Darker Five-striped Sparrow (p. 363, foothill thornscrub only) has gray chest, unstreaked back. **Voice:** Tinkling *sip* calls. Evocative and reedy *twee dweedle-dee dweedle-dee* song. **Status:** Uncommon in winter (late Sep-Mar). **Habitat:** Level or gently-sloping, treeless deserts and valleys with even-sized and somewhat evenly-spaced shrubs, e.g., saltbush flats. **Behavior:** Cocks tail as it forages on ground.

LARK BUNTING, *Calamospiza melanocorys*

Description: 6.5". **Big sparrow** with **big blue bill; white wing crescents**. BREEDING MALE: Black with white wings. FLIGHT: White inner-wing patches; white tail corners. **Voice:** Sweet *heww* calls. **Status:** Irregular but usually common in winter (Aug-mid May). **Habitat:** Desert and valley openings, grasslands, farm fields, and pastures. **Behavior:** Usually in flocks as it forages. **Noteworthy:** Some years absent from areas where it was abundant the previous winter.

FOX SPARROW

"Slate-colored"

"Red"

"Sooty"

Description: 7". Large, stocky sparrow with big **yellow-based bill; reddish wings and tail**; white breast with arrowhead-shaped spots. Other markings depend on subspecies.

SLATE-COLORED: Gray head and back; red rump; dark spots on underparts.

SOOTY: Brownish head and back; brown rump; dark spots densely-packed on breast.

RED: Red crown and facial pattern; red back streaks; gray rump; red spots on underparts.

Similar Species: Smaller Song Sparrow (p. 375) is similar to "Red" race of Fox Sparrow, but lacks yellow on bill, red rump, and extensive, arrowhead-shaped spots below.

Voice: Call for Slate-colored and Red races is a smacking *chep* note; Sooty Fox Sparrow has a higher *chip* note. Does not sing in our area.

Status: Rare in winter (mid Oct-mid Apr). **Habitat:** Desert oases; valley, foothill, and lower mountain canyon groves.

Behavior: Towhee-like, uses both feet simultaneously to scratch the ground for seeds and insects.

Noteworthy: There are four field recognizable subspecies groups of Fox Sparrows, regarded by some taxonomists as separate species. "Slate-colored," *P. i. schistacea*, is the most common race wintering in SE Arizona. "Red" Fox Sparrows, *P. i. zaboria* and *P. i. altivagans* are rare in our region. "Sooty," *P. i. townsendi*, from the Pacific coast is accidental. Thus far, the aptly-named "Thick-billed" Fox Sparrow, *P. i. stephensi*, from California, is unrecorded in our area, although there are two records from SW Arizona.

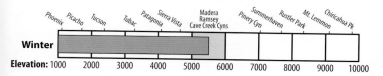

	Phoenix	Picacho	Tucson	Tubac	Patagonia	Sierra Vista	Madera Ramsey Cave Creek Cyns	Pinery Cyn	Summerhaven	Rustler Park	Mt. Lemmon	Chiricahua Pk
Winter												
Elevation:	1000	2000	3000	4000	5000	6000	7000	8000	9000	10000

"Desert" Song Sparrow

Lincoln's Sparrow

Swamp Sparrow

"DESERT" SONG SPARROW, *Melospiza melodia fallax*

Description: 6". Gray-faced sparrow with midsized bill; **rusty-red eyestripes**; whitish whiskers; **rusty-red stripes on back and breast**; central red breast spot; reddish wings; long red tail. **Similar Species:** Larger "Red" Fox Sparrow (p. 373, casual in winter) has thicker yellow-based bill, red rump, and extensive, arrowhead-shaped spots on underparts. **Voice:** Husky *chimp* calls. Midway through every song a harsh buzz introduces final notes. **Status:** Common resident. **Habitat:** Reedy edges of desert, valley, and foothill ponds and streams with permanent water. **Noteworthy:** During winter (Sep-Apr) larger, darker "Mountain" Song Sparrow, *M. m. montana*, is rare and uses brushy areas away from water.

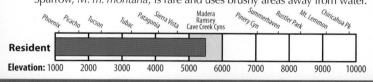

	Phoenix	Picacho	Tucson	Tubac	Patagonia	Sierra Vista	Madera Ramsey Cave Creek Cyns	Pinery Cyn	Summerhaven	Rustler Park	Mt. Lemmon	Chiricahua Pk
Resident												
Elevation:	1000	2000	3000	4000	5000	6000	7000	8000	9000	10000

LINCOLN'S SPARROW, *Melospiza lincolnii*

Description: 5.5". Gray-faced sparrow with small bill; **buffy moustache; buffy wash on black-streaked chest**; short tail. **Similar Species:** Larger "Desert" Song Sparrow (above) has white moustache; rusty-red stripes on breast and back. **Voice:** Smacking *tchep* and thin *zeet* calls. **Status:** Irregular but usually common in winter (mid Sep-early May). **Habitat:** Desert oases; valley, foothill, and lower mountain canyon underbrush.

SWAMP SPARROW, *Melospiza georgiana*

Description: 5.75". Gray-faced sparrow with small bill; white moustache; **white throat**; faintly-streaked gray chest; **wine-red wings**; short red tail. **Similar Species:** Larger "Desert" Song Sparrow (above) has rusty-red facial stripes; reddish streaks on white chest. **Voice:** Snappy *pick* and very thin *zeet* calls. **Status:** Rare in winter (Nov-mid Apr). **Habitat:** Reedy edges of desert, valley, and foothill ponds and streams with permanent water.

White-throated Sparrow Tan-striped Adult

White-throated Sparrow White-striped Adult

White-crowned Sparrow Immature

"Mountain" Adult

White-crowned Sparrow "Gambel's" Adult

WHITE-THROATED SPARROW, *Zonotrichia albicollis*

Description: 6.25". Stocky, stripe-crowned sparrow with **gray bill; yellow lores; white throat**; rich rufous wings; dark gray breast; long tail. WHITE-STRIPED ADULT: Immaculate white eyebrows behind yellow lores; black head stripes. TAN-STRIPED ADULT: Soft beige eyebrows behind yellow lores; brown head stripes. **Similar Species:** White-crowned Sparrow (below) has orange bill; lacks yellow lores and white throat. **Voice:** Ringing *pink* note. Poignant, slowly whistled *sweet dream-free sleep sleep sleep*. **Status:** Uncommon in winter (Nov-mid Apr). **Habitat:** Desert oases; valley, foothill, and lower mountain canyon underbrush. **Behavior:** White-striped morph adults sing more than tan-striped morph adults. **Noteworthy:** In SE Arizona, usually found within flocks of White-crowned Sparrows.

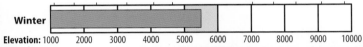

Winter

Elevation: 1000   2000   3000   4000   5000   6000   7000   8000   9000   10000

WHITE-CROWNED SPARROW, *Zonotrichia leucophrys*

Description: 6.5". Stocky, stripe-crowned sparrow with **orange bill; white eyebrow; white crown**; long tail. GAMBEL'S ADULT: Gray lores. MOUNTAIN ADULT: Tar-black lores. IMMATURE: Buff crown stripe; brown head stripes. **Similar Species:** "Tan-striped" color morph White-throated Sparrow (above) resembles immature White-crown, but has gray bill and yellow lores. **Voice:** Bleated *pinch* note. Reedy whistled song ending with trills and buzzes. **Status:** Common in winter (Oct-mid May). **Habitat:** Desert, valley, foothill, and lower mountain canyon openings, grasslands, weedy fields, brushy edges, and urban areas. **Behavior:** Forms winter flocks. **Noteworthy:** In SE Arizona, "Gambel's," *Z. l. gambelii*, is the common wintering race of White-crowned Sparrow. "Mountain" White-crown, *Z. l. oriantha*, with black lores is only regular in fall and spring, sporadic in winter.

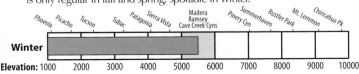

Winter

Elevation: 1000   2000   3000   4000   5000   6000   7000   8000   9000   10000

Harris's Sparrow
Breeding

Harris's Sparrow
Non-breeding

Golden-crowned Sparrow
Non-breeding

Golden-crowned Sparrow
Breeding

HARRIS'S SPARROW, *Zonotrichia querula*

Description: 7.25". Large, stocky, **black-crowned** sparrow with **flesh bill; black bib**; white belly; long tail. SUMMER ADULT: Gray cheeks. WINTER ADULT: Tawny cheeks. IMMATURE: Tawny head with black-tinged crown; white throat; "necklace" of short, black streaks on breast. **Similar Species:** Male House Sparrow (p. 421) has gray crown and large whitish cheeks. **Voice:** Imperious *peak* note. Quavering, slowly-whistled *fee bee be*. **Status:** Casual in winter (Nov-mid May). **Habitat:** Desert oases; valley, foothill, and lower mountain canyon underbrush. **Behavior:** Hop-and-scratch foraging style. Primarily terrestrial; uses low perches. **Noteworthy:** In SE Arizona, usually found within flocks of White-crowned Sparrows, often when it appears with them at a feeding station.

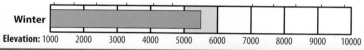

Winter

Elevation: 1000   2000   3000   4000   5000   6000   7000   8000   9000   10000

GOLDEN-CROWNED SPARROW, *Zonotrichia atricapilla*

Description: 6.75". Large, stocky, **yellow-crowned** sparrow with **dark bill**; brownish flanks; long tail. SUMMER ADULT: Yellow forecrown bordered by broad black stripes. WINTER ADULT: Muted crown pattern. IMMATURE: Yellow forehead; bicolored bill blackish above and pink below. **Similar Species:** Immature White-crowned Sparrow (p. 377) has bill entirely orange and shows well-defined eyebrow. **Voice:** Breathy *chep* notes. Very clear, slowly-whistled *oh dear me*, deeper pitched than Harris's Sparrow. **Status:** Rare in winter (late Oct-early May). **Habitat:** Desert oases; valley, foothill, and lower mountain canyon underbrush. **Behavior:** Hop-and-scratch foraging style. Primarily terrestrial; uses low perches. **Noteworthy:** In SE Arizona, usually found within flocks of White-crowned Sparrows, often when it appears with them at a feeding station.

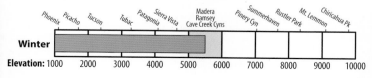

Winter

Elevation: 1000   2000   3000   4000   5000   6000   7000   8000   9000   10000

DARK-EYED JUNCO

"Slate-colored"

"Oregon"

"Pink-sided"

"Gray-headed"

"SLATE-COLORED" DARK-EYED JUNCO, *Junco hyemalis hyemalis*

Description: 5.75". Pink bill; white central belly; white outer tail feathers. MALE: **Slate-gray upperparts**. FEMALE: **Uniform brownish upperparts**. **Status:** Rare in winter (Oct-Apr). **Habitat:** Desert oases and urban areas to mountain canyons. **Behavior:** Usually a solitary bird joining a flock of other junco races. **Voice:** Snapping *pit* note.

"OREGON" DARK-EYED JUNCO, *Junco hyemalis montanus and others*

Description: 5.75". Pink bill; **dark hood**; reddish-brown back; rufous flanks; white central belly; white outer tail feathers. MALE: Black or slaty hood. FEMALE: Gray hood. **Status:** Common in winter (Oct-early May). **Habitat:** Desert oases and urban areas to mountain tops. **Behavior:** Flocks with other junco races; most common race of desert and valley junco. **Voice:** Snapping *pit* note.

"PINK-SIDED" DARK-EYED JUNCO, *Junco hyemalis mearnsi*

Description: 6". Pink bill; dark lores; **blue-gray hood** with paler gray throat; brownish back; **pinkish-cinnamon flanks**; white central belly; white outer tail feathers. **Status:** Common in winter (Oct-Apr). **Habitat:** Desert oases and urban areas to mountain tops. **Behavior:** Flocks with other junco races; forages for seeds on ground. **Voice:** Snapping *pit* note.

"GRAY-HEADED" DARK-EYED JUNCO, *Junco hyemalis caniceps*

Description: 6". Pink bill; dark lores; **gray head**; reddish back; gray flanks; white central belly; white outer tail feathers. **Status:** Common in winter (Oct-May). **Habitat:** Desert oases and urban areas to mountain tops. **Behavior:** Flocks with other junco races; most common form of Dark-eyed Junco in mountains. **Voice:** Snapping *pit* note.

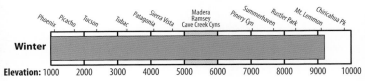

381

"Red-backed" Dark-eyed Junco

Yellow-eyed Junco

Yellow-eyed Junco Juvenile

"RED-BACKED" DARK-EYED JUNCO, *Junco hyemalis dorsalis*

Description: 6″. **Bicolored bill** with black upper mandible and **silvery lower mandible**; dark lores; gray head with **pale gray throat**; red back, red occasionally extending onto the wings; white outer tail feathers. **Similar Species:** "Gray-headed" Dark-eyed Junco (p. 381) has a smaller, all-pink bill and lacks contrastingly paler gray throat. **Voice:** Snapping *pit* note. **Status:** Casual in winter (mid Oct–early Apr). **Habitat:** Desert oases and urban areas to upper mountain canyons. **Behavior:** Flocks with other junco races; forages for seeds on ground. **Noteworthy:** This essentially non-migratory race of Dark-eyed Junco is common in central Arizona.

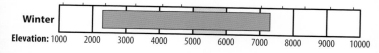

Winter

Elevation: 1000   2000   3000   4000   5000   6000   7000   8000   9000   10000

YELLOW-EYED JUNCO, *Junco phaeonotus*

Description: 6.25″. **Bicolored bill** with black upper mandible and **yellow lower mandible**; dark lores; **yellow eyes**; gray head with pale gray throat; red back, red often extending onto the wings; white outer tail feathers. JUVENILE: Heavily streaked with pale gray iris. **Similar Species:** "Red-backed" Dark-eyed Junco (above) has a dark eye and silver lower mandible. **Voice:** Snapping *pit* note. Song begins with a series of rich introductory notes on one pitch, followed by variegated trills. **Status:** Common resident. **Habitat:** Mountain canyon groves, pine-oak woodland, and coniferous forests. **Behavior:** Does not flock with other junco races and does not form flocks larger than family group. Forages for seeds on ground with unique shuffling gait. **Noteworthy:** In the U.S. found exclusively in southeastern Arizona and–rarely–adjacent New Mexico, primarily in mountains with summits above 8,000′.

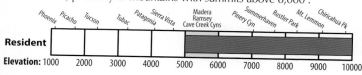

Resident

Elevation: 1000   2000   3000   4000   5000   6000   7000   8000   9000   10000

**McCown's Longspur
Non-breeding**

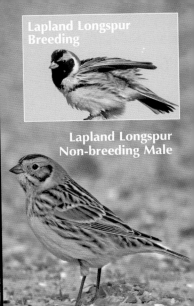

**Lapland Longspur
Breeding**

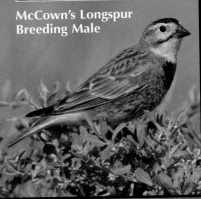

**McCown's Longspur
Breeding Male**

**Lapland Longspur
Non-breeding Male**

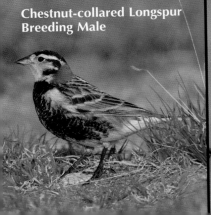

**Chestnut-collared Longspur
Breeding Male**

**Chestnut-collared Longspur
Non-breeding**

MCCOWN'S LONGSPUR, *Rhynchophanes mccownii*

Description: 6". Stout longspur with **large bill; dull ear-patch pattern;** sometimes-concealed chestnut "shoulder bar" on upper wing. BREEDING MALE: Black bill; black breast-band. NON-BREEDING: Pale bill; unstreaked dusky breast. FLIGHT: **Inverted black "T" on white tail.** **Similar Species:** Non-breeding Chestnut-collared Longspur (below) has small dark bill, dark rear margin of ear-patch, mottled black underparts, yellowish cheeks and throat. **Status:** Rare in winter (mid Oct-Mar). **Habitat:** Valley savanna with bare patches and barren pastures. **Noteworthy:** Usually found mixed in flocks of Horned Larks.

LAPLAND LONGSPUR, *Calcarius lapponicus*

Description: 6.25". Slender longspur with **sharp bill;** heavy rear ear-patch outline; **rusty panel on mid-wing.** BREEDING MALE: Yellow bill; black foreface and chestnut hindcollar. NON-BREEDING: Dusky coral bill; orange rear eyebrow; black-streaked chest and flanks. FLIGHT: **White outer tail feathers.** **Status:** Casual in winter (late Oct-late Apr). **Noteworthy:** Usually with other longspurs.

CHESTNUT-COLLARED LONGSPUR, *Calcarius ornatus*

Description: 5.75". Small longspur with **small bill; white eye-ring;** dark rear margin of ear-patch; white shoulder patch diagnostic, if visible; short tail. BREEDING MALE: Black bill; yellow foreface; chestnut hindcollar. NON-BREEDING: Grayish bill; mottled black underparts. FLIGHT: **Black triangle on white tail.** **Similar Species:** Larger non-breeding Lapland Longspur (above) lacks eye-ring; has streaking on breast and flanks; in flight shows white outer tail feathers. **Voice:** Repeated rattling *chiddle* calls. **Status:** Common in winter (Oct-mid Apr). **Noteworthy:** Flocks often seen at stock tanks.

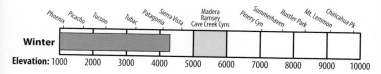

	Phoenix	Picacho	Tucson	Tubac	Patagonia	Sierra Vista	Madera Ramsey Cave Creek Cyns	Pinery Cyn	Summerhaven	Rustler Park	Mt. Lemmon	Chiricahua Pk
Winter												
Elevation:	1000	2000	3000	4000	5000	6000	7000	8000	9000	10000

Northern Cardinal
Male

Northern Cardinal
Female

Pyrrhuloxia
Non-breeding Male

Pyrrhuloxia
Breeding Female

NORTHERN CARDINAL, *Cardinalis cardinalis*

Description: 8.5". **Bushy-crested cardinal** with **black foreface** and **triangular, orange-red bill**. MALE: Entirely red. FEMALE: Warm cinnamon overall with reddish crest, wings, and tail. JUVENILE: Black bill. **Similar Species:** Female Pyrrhuloxia (below) has slimmer crest; stubby, rounded, yellowish bill; red eye-ring. **Voice:** High *pink* note, as if from a smaller bird. Loud *whoit whoit whoit, cheer-ry cheer-ry, too too too* song in changing sequences. **Status:** Common resident. **Habitat:** Desert thickets, oases, and urban areas; valley, foothill, and lower mountain canyon groves. **Behavior:** Forages for seeds, fruits, and insects. Male feeds female during courtship. **Noteworthy:** Northern Cardinals apparently colonized southern Arizona from Sonora via the Santa Cruz River Valley in the mid-1800s.

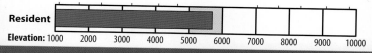

Resident									
Elevation: 1000	2000	3000	4000	5000	6000	7000	8000	9000	10000

PYRRHULOXIA, *Cardinalis sinuatus*

Description: 8". **Taper-crested cardinal** with **red foreface** and **rounded, straw-yellow bill**; red crest, wings, and tail. MALE: Lipstick smear down breast. FEMALE: Red eye-ring; neutral gray-brown breast. NON-BREEDING ADULT: Gray or horn-colored bill. JUVENILE: Black bill. **Similar Species:** Female Northern Cardinal (above) has bigger, bushier crest; larger, triangular, orange-red bill; black smudge between eyes and bill. **Voice:** Thin *tchik* note. Thin *tuwheet tuwhee tuwheet tuwheet, chew-y chew-y chew-y, chew-chow!-chow!-chow!* reedier than Northern Cardinal song. **Status:** Common resident. **Habitat:** Desertscrub and urban areas; valley thickets; open foothill canyon groves with underbrush. **Behavior:** Forages for seeds, fruits, and insects. **Noteworthy:** In winter, some Pyrrhuloxias form small flocks and some range into lower mountain canyons.

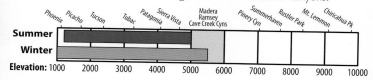

	Phoenix	Picacho	Tucson	Tubac	Patagonia	Sierra Vista	Madera Ramsey Cave Creek Cyns	Pinery Cyn	Summerhaven	Rustler Park	Mt. Lemmon	Chiricahua Pk
Summer												
Winter												
Elevation: 1000	2000	3000	4000	5000	6000	7000	8000	9000	10000			

387

Rose-breasted Grosbeak Male

Rose-breasted Grosbeak Female

Black-headed Grosbeak Male

Black-headed Grosbeak Female

ROSE-BREASTED GROSBEAK, *Pheucticus ludovicianus*

Description: 7.35". Grosbeak with **pink bill**. MALE: Black head and back; **rose breast**. FEMALE: Brown head with white stripes; pin-striped breast and flanks. FLIGHT: **Red underwing linings**. **Similar Species:** Female Black-headed Grosbeak (below) has dark upper mandible, unstreaked center of breast, and center of belly washed yellow. **Voice:** Call is squeaking *peak*; song is rollicking series of rich, whistled notes. **Status:** Rare in summer (mid Apr-mid Nov); casual in winter (mid Nov-mid Apr). **Habitat:** Desert oases and urban areas; valley, foothill, and mountain canyon groves; mountain pine-oak woodland. **Behavior:** Searches for fruits and insects in canopy; also eats seeds. **Noteworthy:** In SE Arizona, Rose-breasted Grosbeaks seldom remain at a location for over a week.

BLACK-HEADED GROSBEAK, *Pheucticus melanocephalus*

Description: 7.5". Grosbeak with **bicolored bill, upper mandible blackish**. MALE: Mostly black head; **orange breast**. FEMALE: Brown head with white stripes; unstreaked center of breast; center of belly washed yellow. FLIGHT: **Yellow underwing linings**. **Similar Species:** Female Rose-breasted Grosbeak (above) has pin-striped center of breast and whitish center of belly. **Voice:** Call is smacking *whick*; song is rollicking series of rich, whistled notes. **Status:** Common in summer (Jun-Jul) and in migration (late Mar-May and Aug-mid Oct). **Habitat:** SUMMER: Mountain canyon groves, pine-oak woodland, coniferous forest. MIGRATION: Desert washes to mountain tops. **Behavior:** Both sexes sing from nest. **Noteworthy:** Although widespread in migration, they remain most common in the mountains.

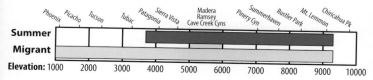

Yellow Grosbeak
Male

Blue Grosbeak
Male

Blue Grosbeak
Female

YELLOW GROSBEAK, *Pheucticus chrysopeplus*

Description: 9″. Grosbeak with **massive, lead-gray bill; entirely yellow underparts**. MALE: Yellow head and back. FEMALE: Finely-striped crown; dusky ear-patch. **Similar Species:** Female Flame-colored Tanager (p. 353) lacks massive bill. Evening Grosbeaks (p. 415) have green bills and gray heads. **Voice:** Squeaking *peep* call; song is hurried series of three or four rich, whistled phrases, followed by a pause before resuming. **Status:** Casual in summer (May-mid Aug). **Habitat:** Desert oases; valley, foothill, and lower mountain canyon groves. **Behavior:** Searches for fruits and insects in canopy; also eats seeds. **Noteworthy:** Most Yellow Grosbeak records are in June and July.

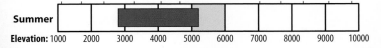

Summer									
Elevation: 1000	2000	3000	4000	5000	6000	7000	8000	9000	10000

BLUE GROSBEAK, *Passerina caerulea*

Description: 6.75″. Grosbeak with **silver-blue bill; broad, chestnut wingbars**. MALE: Deep blue body. FEMALE: Warm cinnamon-brown. **Similar Species:** Smaller Indigo Bunting (p. 393) lacks large, thick bill and broad, chestnut wingbars. **Voice:** Explosive *spink!* call; song is reedy warbling whistles. **Status:** Common in summer (early May-mid Oct); casual in winter in western lowland riparian groves. **Habitat:** Desert oases; valley mesquite grasslands, foothill and lower mountain canyon groves. In SE Arizona usually associated with mesquite. **Behavior:** Usually forages on ground or in thickets for seeds, fruits, and insects. Male singing reaches its peak in August. **Noteworthy:** Blue Grosbeaks arrive comparatively late in spring and seem to time their breeding to the summer monsoon.

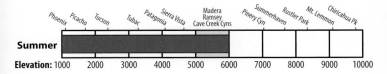

Summer									
Elevation: 1000	2000	3000	4000	5000	6000	7000	8000	9000	10000

Lazuli Bunting
Male

Lazuli Bunting
Female

Indigo Bunting
Male

Indigo Bunting
Female

LAZULI BUNTING, *Passerina amoena*

Description: 5.25". Bunting with **obvious wingbars; sky-blue rump**. MALE: Sky-blue head; thick white forward wingbar; solid cinnamon chest. FEMALE: Brownish above with grayish throat; cinnamon wash across breast; whitish belly. **Similar Species:** Female Indigo Bunting (below) has whitish throat, faint streaking on breast, and lacks blue rump. **Voice:** Dry *ptt* call and high frequency *ink* notes. Song is reedy whistled notes and trills, usually twice repeated. **Status:** Fairly common migrant (Apr-May and mid Jul-late Oct); rare breeder in summer and rare in winter in western lowland riparian groves. **Habitat:** Tall grasses and weeds in desert oases; valley, foothill, and mountain canyon groves. **Behavior:** Males seldom breed until their second summer. Forms flocks in migration. **Noteworthy:** SE Arizona harbors the southernmost known breeding populations in North America.

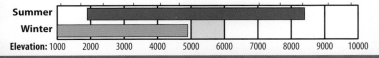

Summer									
Winter									
Elevation: 1000	2000	3000	4000	5000	6000	7000	8000	9000	10000

INDIGO BUNTING, *Passerina cyanea*

Description: 5.25". Bunting with blue tail edgings. MALE: Entirely **deep blue**. FEMALE: Brownish above with **whitish throat; fine streaking on breast; narrow brownish wingbars**. **Similar Species:** See female Lazuli Bunting (above). **Voice:** Dry *ptt* call and high frequency *ink* notes. Song is reedy whistled notes and trills, usually twice repeated, slower than song of Lazuli Bunting. **Status:** Uncommon in summer (late Apr-Sep); casual in winter in western lowland riparian groves. **Habitat:** Tall grasses in valley, foothill, and lower mountain canyon groves. **Behavior:** Often forages near woodland edges. **Noteworthy:** Probably most common on the upper Santa Cruz River.

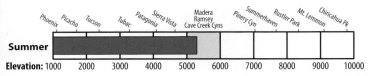

Phoenix	Picacho	Tucson	Tubac	Patagonia	Sierra Vista	Madera Ramsey Cave Creek Cyns	Pinery Cyn	Summerhaven	Rustler Park	Mt. Lemmon	Chiricahua Pk

Summer									
Elevation: 1000	2000	3000	4000	5000	6000	7000	8000	9000	10000

Varied Bunting Male

Varied Bunting Female

Painted Bunting Male

Painted Bunting Female

VARIED BUNTING, *Passerina versicolor*

Description: 5.25". Bunting with **curved upper mandible.** MALE: **Blue, red, and purple above**; mostly rich burgundy below. FEMALE: **Uniform warm brown above**; entirely pale brown below. **Similar Species:** Female Indigo Bunting (p. 393) lacks curved upper bill; has whitish throat, faint streaking on breast, and thin brown wingbars. **Voice:** Dry *ptt* call. Song is reedy warbled phrases with pauses, phrases not repeated, deeper than other buntings. **Status:** Fairly common in summer (mid May-Sep); casual in spring and fall. **Habitat:** Prefers foothill thornscrub and mesquite thickets. Also desert oases; valley, foothill, and lower mountain canyon thickets. **Behavior:** Often forages in dense brush. Breeding seems timed to coincide with the summer monsoon. **Noteworthy:** SE Arizona harbors the northernmost known breeding populations of Varied Buntings.

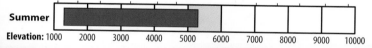

Summer									
Elevation: 1000	2000	3000	4000	5000	6000	7000	8000	9000	10000

PAINTED BUNTING, *Passerina ciris*

Description: 5.25". Bunting with **narrow eye-ring; green back.** MALE: Blue head with red eye-ring; olive-green back; red rump; entirely red below. FEMALE: Green head with pale eye-ring; grass-green upperparts; yellowish-green underparts. **Similar Species:** Distinctive. **Voice:** Dry *ptt* call. Song is sweet, high-pitched reedy phrases without pauses, notes not repeated. **Status:** Uncommon in summer (Jul-Sep); casual in winter in western lowland riparian groves. **Habitat:** Overgrown fields and rank growth in valley, foothill, and lower mountain canyon groves. **Behavior:** Often forages in tall grasses. **Noteworthy:** In SE Arizona most Painted Bunting records pertain to female-plumaged birds.

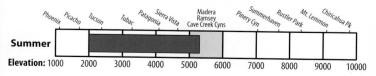

	Phoenix	Picacho	Tucson	Tubac	Patagonia	Sierra Vista	Madera Ramsey Cave Creek Cyns	Pinery Cyn	Summerhaven	Rustler Park	Mt. Lemmon	Chiricahua Pk
Summer												
Elevation: 1000	2000	3000	4000	5000	6000	7000	8000	9000	10000

Dickcissel
Non-breeding

Bobolink
Breeding Male

Bobolink
Non-breeding Adult

DICKCISSEL, *Spiza americana*

Description: 6.25". Triangular-billed grassland bird with **yellow foreface**; long eyebrow, and broad lower eye-ring; **rufous shoulder patch; yellow wash on chest**. BREEDING MALE: Black triangle on throat. NON-BREEDING ADULT: Lacks black throat. **Similar Species:** Larger non-breeding Bobolink (below) has obvious crown stripes, lacks rufous on shoulder, and is entirely yellow below. **Voice:** Electric buzzer *bzzzt* call. Song is burry *dic-chee-chee* or *dic-chee-chee-cheh*, like name. **Status:** Rare fall migrant (Sep-mid Oct); accidental in other seasons. **Habitat:** Desert oases; valley fields and openings. **Behavior:** Forages on the ground but often perches in mesquite and other short trees. **Noteworthy:** Dickcissels in SE Arizona usually occur singly.

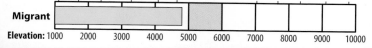

Migrant									
Elevation: 1000	2000	3000	4000	5000	6000	7000	8000	9000	10000

BOBOLINK, *Dolichonyx oryzivorus*

Description: 7". Triangular-billed grassland bird with **spiny-tipped tail**. BREEDING MALE: Black with buffy hindhead; white slashes in wings; white rump. NON-BREEDING: Pink bill; blank yellowish face with brown stripes; yellow below with pin-striped flanks. **Similar Species:** Non-breeding Dickcissel (above) has yellow on face confined to eyebrow and moustache areas, and shows a rufous shoulder patch. **Voice:** Rough *tech* calls and *quink* notes. Song is cascading, jingling series of notes that accelerates at end. **Status:** Casual in fall (mid Aug-mid Oct); accidental in other seasons. **Habitat:** Desert oases; valley fields and reed beds adjacent to ponds. **Behavior:** Often forages in tall grasses or weeds; male sings in flight. **Noteworthy:** In SE Arizona most Bobolink records pertain to non-breeding plumaged birds.

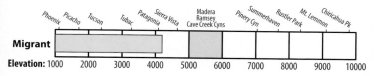

Phoenix Picacho Tucson Tubac Patagonia Sierra Vista Madera Ramsey Cave Creek Cyns Pinery Cyn Summerhaven Rustler Park Mt. Lemmon Chiricahua Pk

Migrant									
Elevation: 1000	2000	3000	4000	5000	6000	7000	8000	9000	10000

"Lilian's" Eastern Meadowlark

"Lilian's" Eastern Meadowlark

Western Meadowlark

Western Meadowlark

"LILIAN'S" EASTERN MEADOWLARK, *Sturnella magna lilianae*

Description: 9". **Clear-cheeked** meadowlark with contrasting **dark head stripes**. BREEDING: White moustache stripe. FLIGHT: Four completely white outer tail feathers. **Similar Species:** Western Meadowlark (below) shows brown head stripes, darker cheeks that do not contrast with eye stripes, and less white in tail. **Voice:** Burry *drrrt* calls. High, piercing *for-fear, fear-oh-dear* song. Meadowlarks best separated by voice. **Status:** Common resident south and east of Tucson; uncommon in lower western deserts in winter (Oct-Mar). **Habitat:** Valley grasslands, farm fields, and pastures. **Behavior:** Males sing from elevated perches and usually have two mates. **Noteworthy:** Some authorities consider "Lilian's" Meadowlark, the breeding form in SE Arizona, a full species.

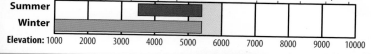

Summer									
Winter									
Elevation: 1000	2000	3000	4000	5000	6000	7000	8000	9000	10000

WESTERN MEADOWLARK, *Sturnella neglecta*

Description: 9". **Dirty-cheeked** meadowlark with low-contrast **brownish head stripes**. BREEDING: Yellow moustache stripe blends with throat. FLIGHT: Three white outer tail feathers with dark outer edges. **Similar Species:** "Lilian's" Eastern Meadowlark (above) shows darker head stripes, paler cheeks that contrast with eye stripes, and whiter tail. **Voice:** Loud *cluck* calls. Rich, musical song of flute-like notes. Meadowlarks best separated by voice. **Status:** Rare and irregular in summer (mid May-mid Sep) in western valleys; fairly common in winter (mid Sep-mid May). **Habitat:** Open desert and valley grasslands, farm fields, and pastures. **Behavior:** Probes earth for seeds and insects with long bill. Forms winter flocks after breeding. **Noteworthy:** Known to breed east of Tucson only after exceptionally wet winters.

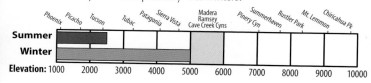

Phoenix	Picacho	Tucson	Tubac	Patagonia	Sierra Vista	Madera Ramsey Cave Creek Cyns	Pinery Cyn	Summerhaven	Rustler Park	Mt. Lemmon	Chiricahua Pk
Summer											
Winter											
Elevation: 1000	2000	3000	4000	5000	6000	7000	8000	9000	10000		

Red-winged Blackbird Male

Red-winged Blackbird Female

Yellow-headed Blackbird Male

Yellow-headed Blackbird Female

Yellow-headed Blackbird Male

RED-WINGED BLACKBIRD, *Agelaius phoeniceus*

Description: 8″. Sharp-billed marsh blackbird. MALE: **Black; red epaulets** with yellow rear edge. FEMALE: **Obvious eyebrow; heavily streaked** above and below. **Similar Species:** Non-breeding European Starling (p. 421) has slender bill, white spots above and below, and short tail. **Voice:** Dry *chek* call. Song often transcribed as *Uncle Lee-e-e-e*. **Status:** Common resident; northern migrants swell population in winter. **Habitat:** Desert and valley rivers, ponds and lakes; irrigated fields and pastures; feedlots. **Behavior:** Forages on seeds and insects in reeds, rank weed growth, farms, and on waste grain. Colonial nester. Males often have harems of five or more females. **Noteworthy:** Thousands of Red-winged Blackbirds may gather on a single winter roost.

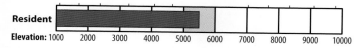

Resident

Elevation: 1000　2000　3000　4000　5000　6000　7000　8000　9000　10000

YELLOW-HEADED BLACKBIRD, *Xanthocephalus xanthocephalus*

Description: 9.5″. Sharp-billed marsh blackbird with **yellow head**. MALE: Bright yellow head and chest. FEMALE: Dull yellow face; dusky brown body. MALE IN FLIGHT: **White crescents on upperwing**. **Similar Species:** Smaller female Brewer's Blackbird (p. 403) lacks yellow face and is very gray—not brownish. **Voice:** Loud *kuck* notes. Rasping *ye-ow ow-ow* song seems forced. **Status:** Uncommon in summer (mid Apr-Aug); common in winter (Sep-mid Apr). **Habitat:** Desert and valley ponds and lakes; irrigated fields and pastures; feedlots. **Behavior:** Forages in reeds, farms, and feed lots. Colonial nester. Males usually have harems of two to five females. **Noteworthy:** SE Arizona winter roosts of Yellow-headed Blackbirds are primarily composed of males.

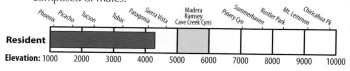

Resident

Elevation: 1000　2000　3000　4000　5000　6000　7000　8000　9000　10000

401

**Brewer's Blackbird
Male**

**Brewer's Blackbird
Female**

**Rusty Blackbird
Female Non-breeding**

BREWER'S BLACKBIRD, *Euphagus cyanocephalus*

Description: 9". Slender, medium-sized blackbird. MALE: Glossy purple head with **pale yellow eye**; greenish gloss on body. FEMALE: **Dark eye**; sooty gray. **Similar Species:** Brownish non-breeding Rusty Blackbird (below) has very slender bill, pale yellow eye, pale eyebrow, rusty edges on wing feathers, and contrasting sooty gray rump. **Voice:** Dry *chep* call. Also other nasal notes and noisemaker vocalizations. **Status:** Common in winter (mid Sep-early May). **Habitat:** Open desert and valley grasslands, farm fields, pastures, and feedlots. Also urban parks, golf courses, and cemeteries. **Behavior:** Forages on ground for seeds and insects in open areas. Forms flocks in winter. **Noteworthy:** In SE Arizona, Brewer's Blackbird frequently occurs in mixed flocks which include Red-winged and Yellow-headed Blackbirds, Brown-headed Cowbirds, and European Starlings.

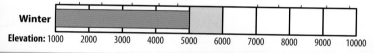

Winter
Elevation: 1000   2000   3000   4000   5000   6000   7000   8000   9000   10000

RUSTY BLACKBIRD, *Euphagus carolinus*

Description: 9". Slender, medium-sized blackbird with **very slender bill**. NON-BREEDING ADULT: Warm brown head, back, and underparts; pale yellow eye; **pale eyebrow; rusty edges on wing feathers; contrasting sooty gray rump**. **Similar Species:** Female Brewer's Blackbird (above) has dark eyes and is sooty gray overall. Larger female grackles (p. 405) lack contrasting gray rumps. **Voice:** Soft *tchek* notes. **Status:** Casual in winter (mid Oct-Mar). **Habitat:** Open desert oases; valley pastures and sewage ponds. **Behavior:** Occurs with Brewer's Blackbirds. **Noteworthy:** Probably because breeding males are difficult to distinguish from male Brewer's, usually only female Rusty Blackbirds are reported from Arizona.

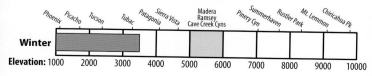

Phoenix	Picacho	Tucson	Tubac	Patagonia	Sierra Vista	Madera Ramsey Cave Creek Cyns	Pinery Cyn	Summerhaven	Rustler Park	Mt. Lemmon	Chiricahua Pk

Winter
Elevation: 1000   2000   3000   4000   5000   6000   7000   8000   9000   10000

Great-tailed Grackle Female

Great-tailed Grackle Male

Common Grackle Male

Common Grackle Female

GREAT-TAILED GRACKLE, *Quiscalus mexicanus*

Description: Male: 16″; female: 11.5″. **Very large blackbird** with large bill and pale yellow eyes; **very long, keeled tail.** MALE: Glossy purple-black head gradually changes to green-black body. FEMALE: **Dull brown** with paler eyebrow and throat. **Similar Species:** Much smaller Common Grackle (below) shows abrupt contrast between purple foreparts and bronzy-green body. **Voice:** Squeaky *wi-wi-wi-wi-wheep!* and other creaky calls—as if its voice box needs oiling. **Status:** Common resident. **Habitat:** Open deserts and valleys with some trees and water, especially urban areas and farms. **Behavior:** Forages opportunistically. Nests colonially. Males are polygamous. Forms flocks in winter. **Noteworthy:** Great-tailed Grackles apparently followed agricultural development from Mexico into SE Arizona in 1935, when they were first reported from Safford.

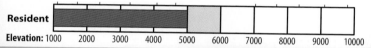

Resident

Elevation: 1000 2000 3000 4000 5000 6000 7000 8000 9000 10000

COMMON GRACKLE, *Quiscalus quiscula*

Description: 12.5″. **Large blackbird** with stout bill and pale yellow eyes; **glossy purplish-blue head contrasts with bronzy-green body**; long, keeled tail. **Similar Species:** Much larger male Great-tailed Grackle (above) not as colorful and lacks abrupt contrast between purple-black foreparts and blue-black body. Smaller male Brewer's Blackbird (p. 403) has thin bill and lacks keeled tail. **Voice:** Emphatic *bzeeet!* and other creaky calls—like a child playing horn instrument first time. **Status:** Casual in winter (Nov-mid May). **Habitat:** Desert oases; valley and foothill woodlands, especially urban areas and farms. **Behavior:** Forages opportunistically. **Noteworthy:** Common Grackles apparently followed agricultural development from New Mexico into NE Arizona in 1980.

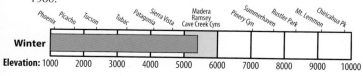

Winter

Elevation: 1000 2000 3000 4000 5000 6000 7000 8000 9000 10000

Bronzed Cowbird
Male

Bronzed Cowbird
Juvenile

Brown-headed Cowbird
Male

Brown-headed Cowbird
Juvenile

Female

BRONZED COWBIRD, *Molothrus aeneus*

Description: 8″. Stocky cowbird with **long, thick bill; red eyes**. MALE: Glossy; expandable ruff. FEMALE: Sooty gray. JUVENILE: Brownish; dark eyes; streaked below. **Similar Species:** Smaller Brown-headed Cowbird (below) has shorter bill and brown eyes. Females are streaked below; juveniles typically more yellowish than juvenile Bronzed. **Voice:** Dry rattles and strained *wheeer* sounds. Hypersonic whistles like escaping steam. **Status:** Fairly common in summer (Mar-Aug); rare in winter in Tucson area (Sep-Feb). **Habitat:** Desert oases and urban areas to mountain canyon groves. **Behavior:** Forages primarily in grassy areas. Male inflates neck feathers as it performs helicopter display flight several feet above one or two females. **Noteworthy:** Arizona range of Bronzed Cowbird mirrors range of Hooded Oriole, its primary nest host.

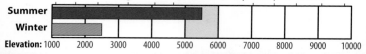

Elevation:	1000	2000	3000	4000	5000	6000	7000	8000	9000	10000

BROWN-HEADED COWBIRD, *Molothrus ater*

Description: 7″. Slim cowbird with conical bill; **dark eyes**. MALE: Brown head and neck. FEMALE: Neutral brown with vague streaking below. JUVENILE: Paler than female, usually tinged yellowish; obvious streaking below. **Similar Species:** See Bronzed Cowbird (above). **Voice:** Dry rattles. Pleasant, liquid song is high *glu-glu-glu-gleee*, piercing at end. **Status:** Fairly common in summer (Apr-Jul); common in winter in deserts and valleys (Sep-Mar). **Habitat:** Desert oases and urban areas to mountain canyon groves. **Behavior:** Forages opportunistically. Forms large flocks in fall. **Noteworthy:** In SE Arizona, Brown-headed Cowbird eggs are laid principally in the nests of Black-tailed Gnatcatcher, Yellow Warbler, and Bell's Vireo.

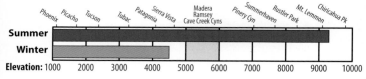

Elevation:	1000	2000	3000	4000	5000	6000	7000	8000	9000	10000

Hooded Oriole
Male

Hooded Oriole
Female

Orchard Oriole
Male

Orchard Oriole
Female

Streak-backed Oriole
Male

Streak-backed
Oriole
Female

HOODED ORIOLE, *Icterus cucullatus*

Description: 7.5″. Slender oriole with **long, curved bill**; long tail. MALE: Golden with black back, scaly in winter. YEARLING MALE: Reduced black foreface. FEMALE: Yellow below; olive back. **Similar Species:** Female/yearling male Orchard Oriole (below) has short, straight bill, contrasting wingbars, relatively short tail, and is lemon-yellow below. **Voice:** *Check-check* scolds; *wink* calls; fast, rollicking song of scolds, calls, and whistles. **Status:** Fairly common in summer (late Mar–mid Sep); casual in winter. **Habitat:** Desert oases and urban areas; valley, foothill, and lower mountain canyon groves.

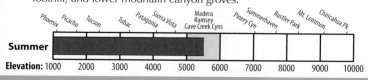

ORCHARD ORIOLE, *Icterus spurius*

Description: 6.75″. Compact oriole with **short, straight bill**; white wingbars on blackish wing. BREEDING MALE: Black and chestnut. YEARLING MALE: Lemon-yellow below; black lores and throat. FEMALE: Lemon-yellow below; grayish-olive back. **Status:** Casual migrant (late Apr–mid Jun and Sep–mid Oct); accidental otherwise. **Habitat:** Desert oases and urban areas; valley, foothill, and lower mountain canyon groves.

STREAK-BACKED ORIOLE, *Icterus pustulatus*

Description: 8.25″. Large oriole with **thick-based, straight bill**; black lores and narrow black throat; **streaked back**. MALE: Orange crown, cheeks, and breast. FEMALE: Tinged orange. **Similar Species:** Smaller Hooded Oriole (above) has thinner, more curved bill, and male's back is solid black or, in winter, scaly black–never streaked. **Voice:** Chattering scolds; whistled *wheap* call. Song is *tu-wheap-sweet-pea tu-wheap tu-wheap*. **Status:** Casual in summer (Apr–mid Oct); rare in winter (mid Oct–Mar). **Habitat:** Desert oases and urban areas; valley and foothill groves.

Bullock's Oriole
Male

Bullock's Oriole
Female

Baltimore Oriole
Male

Baltimore Oriole
Female

Scott's Oriole
Male

Scott's Oriole
Female

BULLOCK'S ORIOLE, *Icterus bullockii*

Description: 7.75". Stocky oriole with **straight bill** and distinct eyebrow; **bright orange cheeks**. MALE: Orange with white wing panel. YEARLING MALE: Black lores and throat. FEMALE: Whitish belly. **Similar Species:** Female/yearling male Baltimore Orioles (below) lack eyebrows and have drab cheeks; usually not as white-bellied as Bullock's. **Voice:** Husky *chek* scolds, sometimes in series. Song is whistled variant of *witchy-gee-goo-goo*. **Status:** Fairly common in summer (Apr-mid Sep); casual in winter. **Habitat:** Desert oases; valley, foothill, and lower mountain canyon groves.

BALTIMORE ORIOLE, *Icterus galbula*

Description: 7.75". Stocky oriole with **straight bill; bright orange breast.** MALE: Black hood and orange underparts. YEARLING MALE: Drab cheeks; black lores and throat. FEMALE: Drab brownish cheeks; pale belly. **Status:** Casual migrant (mid Apr-Jun and late Aug-mid Oct); accidental otherwise. **Habitat:** Desert oases; valley, foothill, and lower mountain canyon groves. Found once in mountain coniferous forest.

SCOTT'S ORIOLE, *Icterus parisorum*

Description: 8". **Yellow** oriole with **long, straight, and sharp bill**. MALE: Black hood and breast. YEARLING MALE: Blackish face and bib. FEMALE: Dusky streaking on back; blackish breast. **Similar Species:** Smaller female Hooded Oriole (p. 409) has thinner, more curved bill and lacks back streaks. **Voice:** Harsh *chack* note; whistled *perp?* call. Song is musical whistle that includes word *Albuquerque*. **Status:** Fairly common in summer (Apr-Sep); casual in winter. **Habitat:** Desertscrub; valley grassland; foothill oak savanna; mountain chaparral and pine-oak woodland.

Cassin's Finch
Male

Cassin's Finch
Female

"Pacific" Purple Finch
Male

"Pacific" Purple Finch
Female

House Finch
Male

House Finch
Female

CASSIN'S FINCH, *Haemorhous cassinii*

Description: 6.25″. Stocky red finch with **long, straight bill** and distinct facial stripes; **pale eye-ring; crisp, contrasting back streaks**; short tail. MALE: Reddest on erectable cap. FEMALE: Underparts white with crisp, dark streaks. **Similar Species:** Purple Finch (below) has slightly curved bill, lacks eye-ring, and lacks crisp, contrasting back streaking. Male Purples have darker red spread more evenly across head. Female Purples have blurry, low-contrast streaking below. **Voice:** Rich *chid-r-rew* calls. Song is rich, slightly reedy caroling, like virtuoso House Finch. **Status:** Irregular and uncommon in winter (Oct-May); accidental in summer. **Habitat:** Desert oases to mountain tops.

"PACIFIC" PURPLE FINCH, *Haemorhous purpureus californicus*

Description: 6″. Stocky red finch with **slightly curved bill** and distinct facial stripes; **low-contrast back streaks**; undertail coverts typically lack streaks; short tail. MALE: Uniform red on cap and throat. FEMALE: Underparts off-white with blurry streaks. **Status:** Casual in winter (Oct-Apr). **Habitat:** Desert oases; valley, foothill, and lower mountain canyon groves.

HOUSE FINCH, *Haemorhous mexicanus*

Description: 5.75″. **Slim** red finch with **stubby, curved bill** and indistinct eyebrow; **long tail**. MALE: Red with heavily streaked flanks. FEMALE: Unpatterned face; underparts off-white with blurry streaks. **Similar Species:** Cassin's and Purple Finches (above) have larger bills, bigger heads, striped facial patterns, and short, notched tails. **Voice:** Call is upslurred query *beerr? beerr?* Song is cheerful warble that includes burry notes. **Status:** Common resident. **Habitat:** Desertscrub to mountain canyon groves.

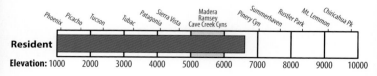

	Phoenix	Picacho	Tucson	Tubac	Patagonia	Sierra Vista	Madera Ramsey Cave Creek Cyns	Pinery Cyn	Summerhaven	Rustler Park	Mt. Lemmon	Chiricahua Pk
Resident												
Elevation:	1000	2000	3000	4000	5000	6000	7000	8000	9000	10000

Red Crossbill Male

Red Crossbill Female

Evening Grosbeak Male

Evening Grosbeak Female

RED CROSSBILL, *Loxia curvirostra*

Description: 6.25". Stocky, big-headed finch with **crossed mandible tips**; long, dark wings; short, notched tail. MALE: Red or orange. FEMALE: Grayish-olive; yellow highlights on crown, breast, and rump. JUVENILE: Streaked brown; short bill. **Similar Species:** Female Cassin's Finch (p. 413) lacks crossed mandibles. **Voice:** Smacking *kip kip kip* calls. **Status:** Irregularly uncommon resident; rare in Tucson in winter (Nov-Mar). **Habitat:** Pines from desert oases and urban areas to mountain tops. **Behavior:** Uses strong, crossed bill to extract seeds from cones. Nests in early winter. **Noteworthy:** Breeding mountain residents are "Strickland's," the largest subspecies; irruptive wintering lowland birds are primarily pale "Bendire's" race.

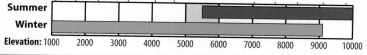

| Elevation: | 1000 | 2000 | 3000 | 4000 | 5000 | 6000 | 7000 | 8000 | 9000 | 10000 |

EVENING GROSBEAK, *Coccothraustes vespertinus*

Description: 7". Chunky finch with **massive pale bill; black wings with white patches**; short tail. MALE: Brown head and neck with yellow crescent on forehead. FEMALE: Gray head and yellow nape. **Similar Species:** Larger Yellow Grosbeak (p. 391) has dark bill and yellow head. **Voice:** Pleasant whistled *puip*. **Status:** Rare in summer (mid May-mid Oct); irregular and uncommon in winter (mid Oct-mid May). **Habitat:** SUMMER: Mountain mixed coniferous forest. WINTER: Mountain canyons and lower coniferous forest; casual in desert oases and foothill groves. **Behavior:** Primarily searches for seeds in canopy. Usually in flocks; during some winter irruptions flocks may number in the hundreds. **Noteworthy:** Populations seem to be declining in SE Arizona, with few recent records from Rincon, Santa Rita, or Pinaleno Mountains.

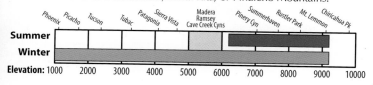

| Elevation: | 1000 | 2000 | 3000 | 4000 | 5000 | 6000 | 7000 | 8000 | 9000 | 10000 |

Pine Siskin

Lawrence's Goldfinch
Non-breeding Male

Lawrence's Goldfinch
Female

PINE SISKIN, *Spinus pinus*

Description: 4.75". Small, **streaky finch** with **sharp, straight bill**; yellow wing edges. FLIGHT: **Yellow stripes on underwings**; yellow patches at base of tail. **Similar Species:** Larger female House Finch (p. 413) has bigger, blunt bill and lacks yellow in the wing. **Voice:** Burry questioning *bzzzeee?* rising at end. Song is stuttering *What d'ya what d'ya see see.* **Status:** Uncommon in summer (Jun-Oct); fairly common in winter (Aug-May). **Habitat:** SUMMER: Mountain coniferous forest. WINTER: Desert oases; valley, foothill, and mountain canyon groves; mountain coniferous forest. **Behavior:** Eat seeds. Forms flocks after breeding. **Noteworthy:** Breeds in the Santa Catalina, Chiricahua, and Pinaleno Mountains.

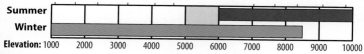

Summer

Winter

Elevation: 1000 2000 3000 4000 5000 6000 7000 8000 9000 10000

LAWRENCE'S GOLDFINCH, *Spinus lawrencei*

Description: 4.5". Small **gray finch** with **stubby gray bill; yellow accents in wings**; yellow blush on chest. MALE: Black foreface. FEMALE: Gray head. **Similar Species:** Larger non-breeding female American Goldfinch (p. 419) has yellow surrounding eye and brownish back. **Voice:** Violin-string *tooeee.* Jumbled tinkling imitations of other bird calls, each repeated several times. **Status:** Irregularly rare to fairly common in winter (Oct-Apr); casual in summer. **Habitat:** Weed patches in desert oases, and valley, foothill, and lower mountain canyons, usually near water. **Behavior:** Forages for seeds in weeds and shrubs. **Noteworthy:** Limited numbers are present in the Santa Cruz Valley almost every winter, but every 5-10 years a major irruption sweeps Lawrence's Goldfinches east to the New Mexico state line.

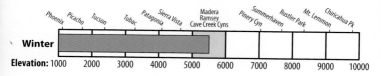

Winter

Elevation: 1000 2000 3000 4000 5000 6000 7000 8000 9000 10000

417

Lesser Goldfinch
Male

Lesser Goldfinch
Female

American Goldfinch
Non-breeding Male

American Goldfinch
Non-breeding Female

LESSER GOLDFINCH, *Spinus psaltria*

Description: 4.5″. Small, yellow finch with **sharp, dark bill;** white flash marks in wings. MALE: Black cap. **Similar Species:** Larger non-breeding American Goldfinch (below) has thicker bill, limited yellow on face and throat, brownish back, and white undertail coverts. **Voice:** Plaintive *tleeee?* or *wheer?* rising at end. Song is complex, rapid repetitions of local bird calls delivered in minor key. **Status:** Common resident. **Habitat:** Usually near water. SUMMER (May-Oct): Desert oases and urban areas to mountain coniferous forest. WINTER (Nov-Apr): Desert oases to lower mountain canyon groves. **Behavior:** Forages for seeds in weeds, shrubs, and trees. In flocks throughout year. **Noteworthy:** Almost all male Lesser Goldfinches in Arizona are "Green-backed" color morph; "Black-backed" color morph is quite rare.

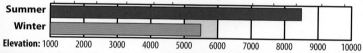

AMERICAN GOLDFINCH, *Spinus tristis*

Description: 5″. Small yellow finch with **thick bill; solid dark wings with one broad white wingbar;** white undertail coverts. BREEDING: Pink bill; yellow underparts. NON-BREEDING: Black bill; yellow on face and throat; brownish back. **Similar Species:** Smaller Lawrence's Goldfinch (p. 417) has gray back and yellow in wing. **Voice:** Violin-string *toe'o'weee.* Short collection of high, sweet, run-on phrases, oft-repeated. **Status:** Irregularly rare to uncommon in winter (mid Oct-early May); casual in summer. **Habitat:** Desert oases; valley, foothill, and lower mountain canyon groves, usually near water. **Behavior:** Forages for seeds in weeds, shrubs, and trees. **Noteworthy:** In SE Arizona, seen in full breeding plumage only after mid-April.

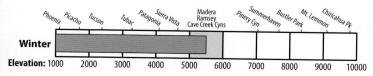

INTRODUCED SPECIES

European Starling Breeding

European Starling Non-breeding

House Sparrow Male

House Sparrow Female

EUROPEAN STARLING, *Sturnus vulgaris*

Description: 8.5". Stocky, **blackish** bird with **straight, sharp bill; short, squared tail**. BREEDING: **Yellow bill**; lustrous purple head and greenish back. WINTER: Bill black; body spangled white. JUVENILE: Gray-brown. FLIGHT: Broad-based, triangular wing silhouette. **Similar Species:** Female Red-winged Blackbird (p. 401) is striped–not spotted. **Voice:** Buzzy *dzrrrr* call. Varied mechanical song of buzzes, clicks, rattles, and squeals. **Status:** Common resident. **Habitat:** Urban areas, farms, and ranches, and nearby riparian groves. **Behavior:** Waddles on ground and probes for food. Also consumes fruit, grain, and insects. Will usurp saguaro cavities from native birds. Large post-breeding flocks may number in the thousands. **Noteworthy:** White winter spotting wears away to reveal darker breeding plumage. Introduced to New York in 1890, European Starlings arrived in Arizona in 1946.

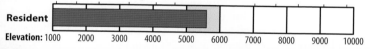

Resident

Elevation: 1000   2000   3000   4000   5000   6000   7000   8000   9000   10000

HOUSE SPARROW, *Passer domesticus*

Description: 6.25". **Chunky, sparrow-like bird** from Eurasia with a stout bill; **one white wingbar**. MALE: **Black bib, gray crown**; whitish cheeks; striped brown back. FEMALE: Dull yellowish bill; broad, creamy eyebrow; tan and brown back stripes. **Similar Species:** Male Harris's Sparrow (p. 379) lacks gray crown. **Voice:** Cheerful *chirp* or *cheep* notes; song is monotonous series of call notes. **Status:** Common resident. **Habitat:** Urban areas, towns, farms, and ranches. **Behavior:** Forages for waste foods on ground. Forms small nesting colonies. **Noteworthy:** In 1851 House Sparrows were introduced in New York City, and they arrived in Tucson in 1903.

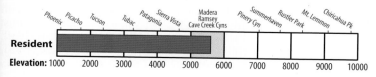

Resident

Elevation: 1000   2000   3000   4000   5000   6000   7000   8000   9000   10000

Acknowledgments, Photographer Credits

This book owes much to many. Writing **Birds of Southeastern Arizona** was made possible by the collective experience and knowledge of Southeastern Arizona's energetic community of birders. Thousands of hours of observations by skilled observers provided the foundation for every bird account. Special thanks, however, go to Moez Ali, Mark Stevenson, and Rick Wright for reviewing the manuscript for accuracy. I also wish to acknowledge the considerable talents of my editor Barbara Bickel, who brought a birder's perspective into the process. Eric Taylor transformed my concept of an elevation graph into reality and supervised the creation of the maps. Thanks to Gina Calle for the design and layout of the book and Nicholas Hausman for the revisions. Many photographers rose to the dual challenge of producing beautiful images that nonetheless convey crucial field marks. Each and every one materially improved the utility and appearance of this book, but particular thanks is owed to Jim Burns for his stunning cover photograph of an Elegant Trogon. Special thanks to local photographers Jim Burns, Dick Dionne, Richard Fray, Laurens Halsey, C. Allan Morgan, Tom Ryan, Alan Schmierer, Robert Shantz, and Bryan J. Smith, who contributed the visual foundation for this book. Finally, Bob and Christina Morse married the disparate elements of words, graphics, and photos into a cohesive field guide.

- Richard Cachor Taylor

The letters following the page numbers refer to the position of the photograph on that page; T = top, M = middle, MT = middle top, MB = middle bottom, B = bottom, L = left, R = right, N = inset.

Moez Ali: 92B. **Lee Barnes:** 34TL, TR, 76T, 104T, B, 146T, BL, 206TL, 266T, 334BL, 338TR, 388TR. **Tony Beck/VIREO:** 178T. **Bob Behrstock:** 186TL, 190TR. **Rick and Nora Bowers:** 150TN, 250T. **Keith Brady:** 20T, 142MR, 254B, 262TR, 412ML, MR, 414BL, BR. **Jim Burns:** 56B, 112TR, 118BR, 132BR, 180BR, 190BR, 238BL, 286T, 294B, 296TL, TR, 304BR, 330BR, 332BR, 336TL, 352BL, 392BR, 398T, 408ML, MR, BL. **Dick Cannings:** 302BR. **Cliff Cathers:** 170B, 180BL,

232T, 362B. **Herb Clarke:** 20B, BN, 72BL, 124TN, 354T, 410BR, 416BR. **Paul Cozza:** 344B. **Dick Dionne:** 30B, 42BL, 52B, 136B, 154T, 168T, 188BL, 198TR, 208BL, BR, 224B, 242T, 282T, 290BR, 294TN, 302T, 310T, 314T, 326BL, 348B, 350TR, BL, 354B, 386TR, BL, 404TN. **Mike Donahue:** 96BN, 144BL, BR. **Mike Dossett:** 22B, 26B, TN, 32B, 34ML, 38TR, 54TR, 152BR, 236T, 246B, 302BL, 330TL, 332BL. **Richard Fray:** 44B, 56T, 64, 120TR, 166T, 180BN, 182BR, 258B, 270T, 296BL, BR, 304TL, 306T, 364M, 368BL, 370TL, 374BL, 380TR. **Don Graham:** 38BR. **Denny Granstrand:** 22T, 162T. **Pete Grube:** 90BR, 162B, 184BL, 186BN, 392TL. **Laurens Halsey:** 42M, 182TR, 184N, 186TR, 194B, 284T, 346B, 408TL, TR. **Ed Harper:** 298BR, 304BL, 324BR, 346T. **Joe Higbee:** 56TN, 218T. **Ralph Hocken:** 32MB, 34BL, 40BL, BR, 60BR, 84TR, 100BR, 112BR, 120TL, 122TL, 144TR, 172BL, 300TR, 316T, 342TR, 400TL. **Jillian Johnston:** 238BR. **Lip Kee:** 324TN. **Dave Kutilek:** 94M, 114T, 132TL, 234B, 260TN, 274T, 310BN, 332TL, 420BL. **Greg Lavaty:** 250B. **Jerry Liguori:** 102TR, 148TL, 298BL. **Mark Lockwood:** 214TN. **Stuart MacKay:** 134BR, 138BR. **Dick McNeely:** 174BN, 240B, 256TL, 372BR. **Bob McKay:** 84TL. **Narca Moore-Craig:** 182TL. **C. Allan Morgan:** 38TL, 48B, BN, 108, 184TL, BR, 188TL, 192B, 200BL, BR, 202TR, 230B, 234T, 236B, 312BL, 388BL, 408BR. **Pete Moulton:** 68TR, 70T. **Tom Munson:** 222B. **Oliver Niehuis:** 402B. **Ollie Oliver:** 182BL. **James Ownby:** 324BL. **Suzette Paduano:** 28B. **Jim Pruske:** 38BL, 62, 70TN, 106TR, 150B, 400TR. **David Quanrud:** 320B, 398BN. **Ian Routley:** 176T, 276T. **Bob Royse:** 22TN, 30M, 32MT, 42BR, 56BN, 68TL, BR, 106B, 110B, 112TL, BL, 116BR, 122BL, 124B, 126T, 128TR, BL, 130T, 132BL, 138BL, 140TR, 142TL, TR, BL, BR, 144TL, 148TR, 152M, 172BR, 206TR, 212T, 222TN, 242B, 244T, B, 246T, 268T, 276B, 278, 282BN, 292T, 306B, 310B, 312T, BR, 320TL, TR, 322T, BL, 328TN, BN, 330BL, 334T, TN, 336B, BR, 338TL, BL, 340T, 342TL, BL, 344T, 358B, 360T, 362T, 364B, 366B, 368BR, 370TR, BN, 372BL, 374BR, 376TL, TR, 380TL, 384TL, TR, BL, 386BR, 388TL, 392BL, 394TL, TR, 410ML, 412TR, 416T. **Bart Rulon:** 24BR, 304TR. **Tom Ryan:** 34MR, 42TL, 46B, BN, 58B, 60TL, 78T, 84BR, 88TTN, 90TL, BL, 96TTN, 100TL, TR, 122TR, 128BR, 152BL, 180TL, 206BL, 222T, 224T, 226B, 240T, 260T, B, 272TL, 288T, 290BL, 318BR, 330TR, 332T, 368TL, 374T, 416BL, 418TL, TR. **Larry Sansone:** 70BN, 102BR, 120BR, 124T, 140BR, 210T, 228B, 262BN, 266TN, 292B, 316B, 356B, 378BR, 404BL.

Alan Schmierer: 88BBN, 180TR, 224BN, 226TL, 340BN, 362TN, 376BN, 384BR, 390BR. **Robert Shantz:** 34BR, 40TR, 46T, 48T, 52BN, 54BL, BR, 66BL, BR, 74T, B, TN, BN, 76TN, 78B, 80TL, TR, BL, 82TN, 88B, BN, 90TR, 92TL, TR, TN, 94BR, 96T, 98, 102TL, BL, 106TN, 116T, BL, 126B, 132TR, 136T, 138TL, TR, 142ML, 146BR, 160, TN, 164B, 172TL, TR, 174T, 178B, 184TR, 186BL, BR, 190BL, 204TR, 210B, 212B, 216T, 228T, 252TL, 256TR, B, 258T, 260BN, 266B, BN, 272BL, BR, 274B, 280T, B, 282TN, 284B, 294BN, 298TR, 322BR, 326TL, TR, BR, 328T, B, 348TL, 350BR, 352TL, TR, 360B, 362BN, 366T, 368TR, 370B, 376BL, BR, 380BR, 382T, B, BN, 384BN, 388BR, 396T, 398B, TN, 400BR, BN, 402TL, TR, 406TR, BL, BN, 412TL, BL, BR, 414TR, 418BL, BR. **Brian Small:** 18RTN, 30TR, 42TR, 48TN, 54TL, 66T, 70B, 78TN, BN, 84BL, 120BL, 122BR, 130B, 134TL, TR, BL, 140TL, BL, 148BR, BL, 154BL, 156T, 176B, 190TL, 196B, 198BR, 204TL, 216B, 218B, 226TR, 230TR, 232B, 238T, 248B, 270B, 272TR, 294T, 300BR, 334BR, 336TR, 340B, 342BL, 348TR, 378TL, 380BL, 390B, 392TR, 404BR, 410TR, MR, BL, 420TL. **Bryan J. Smith:** 26T, 36T, B, TN, 50T, 72T, 114B, 118T, 158, 166B, 194T, 202BL, BR, 214, 230TN, 308B, 314B, 356T, 364T, 386T. **Margaret St Clair:** 30TL, 40TL, 50B, 262TL, 286B. **Rick Taylor:** 18LTN, 20N, 44T, 52T, 58T, 60TN, TR, BL, 62TN, 88T, TN, 90TN, BN, 96TN, 98TN, 108TN, 118BL, 136BN, 150T, 152T, 154BR, 164T, 170T, 174TN, 176M, 188TR, 196T, 202TL, 206BR, 220T, BR, 232BN, 252TR, BN, 284T, 300BL, 308T, 318BL, 350TL, TN, 352BR, 358T, 366BN, 372T, 378BL, 384TRN, 404TL, 406BR. **Glen Tepke:** 282B. **Khanh Tran:** 24TL. **Hank Tseng:** 24TR, BL, 28TL, 82T, B, 110T, 128TL, 174B, 192TR, 198TL, 288B, 298TL, 318T, 384TLN, 400BL, 420BR. **George Vlahakis:** 58BN, 68BL, 72BR, 96B, 106TL, 188BR, 200T, 204BL, BR, 208TL, TR, 220BL, 252B, 254T, 264T, B, 378TR, 414TL. **Barry Wahl:** 28TR, 262B, 290T, 420TR. **Brian Wheeler:** 80BR, 86T, B, 94TL, TR, BL, 100BL, 156B. **John Williams:** 32T. **Cathy Wise:** 410TL. **Joe Woodley:** 390T. **Michael Woodruff:** 396BR. **Lee Zieger:** 250BN. **Jim Zipp:** 18, 168B, 198BL, 268B, 292TN, 300TL, 324TL, 338BR, 346M, 394BL, BR, 396BL, 406TL. **William Zittrich:** 192TL. **Tim Zurowski:** 36BN.

The success of this guide is the success of all those who contributed to it. Their participation is sincerely appreciated.

Index/Checklist of Birds of Southeastern Arizona

Use this checklist to keep a record of the birds you have seen. Bold numbers are for the main Species Account page. Common local bird denoted by 'clb'.

426

Other Species Seen

_____

_____

_____

_____

_____

_____

About the Author

Lynne Taylor

RICHARD CACHOR TAYLOR

A lifelong resident of Southeastern Arizona, he conducted an eight-year-long study of the Elegant Trogon that led to the publication of *Trogons of the Arizona Borderlands* in 1994. During the course of his research he reported the first Eared Quetzal seen in the U.S. In 1980 he founded Borderland Tours, a birding travel company dedicated to responsible ecotourism as a means of providing an economic platform for the preservation of the world's wildlife communities. In 1995 the American Birding Association published his *A Birder's Guide to Southeastern Arizona*, which he revised in 2005. He is also the author of location bird checklists for both the Huachuca and the Chiricahua Mountains.